THE DECEITFUL CULT OF A FAKE NARAYAN

STORY OF THE SWAMINARAYAN INVASION ON SANATAN DHARMA AND THE RESPONSE GIVEN BY THE HINDU SOCIETY

DR KAUSHIK CHAUDHARY

Dedicated to:

Every Sanatani in history who, abandoning the fleeting gains and losses of life, fought a battle to protect Sanatan Dharma and its revered deities.

Contents

Recognize the Signs of Corruption

In the Hindu Sanatan tradition, the word "Swami" holds various meanings, but at its core, it is always associated with the concept of lordship or mastery. Most commonly, God is referred to as the Lord of the universe or the ruler of the three worlds, earning the title "Swami of Trilok." Another significant meaning is "master of the senses," where one who has complete control over the senses is recognized as a realized yogi. These two meanings form the primary foundation, followed by other, more worldly applications. For instance, the head of a spiritual institution or monastery is addressed as "Swami," indicating his role as the leader of that institution. Even in a household, a wife traditionally refers to her husband as "Swami," symbolizing his position as the head or ruler of the family. Thus, the word "Swami" encompasses these four key meanings, all implying some form of authority or control.

In this book, however, we will delve into a different kind of "Swami." These are individuals who adopt the attire of Hindu monks, wear tilak on their foreheads, and keep a shikha (tuft of hair), but whose mindset and actions resemble those of Muslim clerics or Christian priests. Within Hinduism's inclusive tradition, these Swamis introduce an Islamic-style model of worship, claiming the superiority of one god while disparaging others through fabricated stories. These Swamis are not masters of their senses; rather, they have mastered the art of indulging in sensory desires. They are frequently accused of engaging in activities such as money laundering, converting black money into white, seizing land under the pretext of temple construction, committing fraud, and even exploiting women and young boys. Such allegations have become so common that they no longer shock anyone. Just as scandals involving Christian priests have surfaced globally for centuries, scandals involving these Swamis emerge not annually, but monthly. Similar to Christian missionaries, who establish schools, hospitals, and charities to promote their religion, these Swamis run Gurukuls, hospitals, and charity programs with a similar hidden agenda. Their ultimate goal is to convert Hindus into believing in one supreme god, severing their connection to the gods of the Vedas, Upanishads, and

Puranas. Whether it's the Swamis elevated to divine status like Mother Teresa or the young, business-like Swamis who appear more like shopkeepers, none are exempt from this agenda.

It can be signified by examples such as seeing numerous foreigners in ISKCON chanting 'Hare Rama Hare Krishna' and taking up monastic lives. ISKCON was established less than seventy years ago. You may have also seen many foreigners as true devotees of Neem Karoli Baba reciting the Hanuman Chalisa and living as ascetics, and it has only been around eighty years since then. Over a hundred and thirty years ago, many foreigners became monks, identifying with Indian and Hindu traditions after following Swami Vivekananda, and even today, you see numerous foreign monks in the Ramakrishna Mission. But in the sect that has existed for two hundred years, and that, within twenty years of Vivekananda's success in the West, went abroad to build temples—today, even after a hundred years, you will not find a single Westerner in that sect who has embraced Hinduism!

Other Hindu organizations go to the West, integrating local foreigners into various aspects of Hinduism, establishing them in Sanatan Dharma. In contrast, for the last hundred years, this sect has been building temples in various countries, trying to bind the resident Hindus to a fake 'Narayana,' a singular supreme god similar to the Christian Jesus or the Islamic Allah. This god is taught as the only one worth worshiping, rejecting all other Sanatan deities worshiped by Hindus until now. All those temples built abroad have actually been used to convert resident Hindus into a religion akin to Christianity, centering around a new god like Jesus. This book will reveal the truth of this deceptive sect of the fake Narayana.

The term "Narayan" appears in the Vedas as one of the names of Lord Vishnu. In the Rig Veda, the oldest scripture of Sanatan Dharma and of humanity, Vishnu is the most widespread deity among the thirty-three koti (categories) of gods and is referred to as the highest god among them in the very first verse of the Aitareya Brahmana of the Rig Veda. In the Yajur Veda, written after the Rig Veda, it is said that from Vishnu emanates "Nira" (water), and because of this, He is called "Narayan." Additionally, because He resides in all places, He is also called "Vasudev." In the Vedas, Vishnu is invoked approximately twenty-five times in the Vishnu Gayatri mantra:

> "*Om Narayanaya Vidmahe Vasudevaya Dhimahi*
> *Tanno Vishnuh Prachodayat.*"

Meaning:
We meditate on Narayan, who is the same as Vasudev, and also
Vishnu. May that Vishnu inspire us."

We are all familiar with this Bhagwan Vishnu-Narayan, and we will explore this topic further in Volume 2, with proper scriptural understanding. However, we have to discuss another individual who emerged by stealing the name "Narayan"—a figure marked by strange peculiarities. First, followers of this sect abducted the name "Narayan" from Lord Vishnu to set up this new Fake-Narayan, and later went as far as claiming that Vishnu was his servant. Moreover, they belittled the incarnations of Vishnu, such as Ram and Krishna, stating that the combined radiance of millions of Rams and Krishnas would not compare to that of this fake Narayan's disciples or young followers. As a result, when a boy from his sect visits a Krishna temple, it is not to seek the darshan of Krishna, but rather to give darshan to Krishna! These absurd stories do not stop with Vishnu; this sect spreads narratives that demean every deity of Sanatan Dharma to set up their new god as superior to everyone. Perhaps that is why this fake Narayan blesses with his left hand as if to differentiate himself from all other gods. He instructs his followers not to look at women, claiming that he himself never does.

According to the books of this sect, the fake Narayan once saw a wedding procession, which sparked in him a desire to marry. His devotees, thinking "Let's get the god married," arranged for a beautiful woman to be his bride. The woman joyfully adorned herself and approached the fake Narayan. But upon seeing her, this false Narayan began vomiting and exclaimed, "Remove this pile of excrement from my sight." The humiliated woman was taken away, but his vomiting and diarrhea continued unabated. Finally, someone suggested, "Feed Maharaj food cooked by a man who has never touched a woman, and his vomiting and diarrhea will stop." The devotees followed this advice, and the false Narayan's condition improved. From that day, his disciples avoid even looking at women.

In another instance, the fake Narayan needed to relieve himself urgently but could not untie the drawstring of his loincloth. A devoted follower approached and untied the string using his mouth. This string has since been preserved and displayed in a museum. However, when the time of this false Narayan's death came, his sect's books once again mentioned vomiting and excrement. During a stomach illness, he defecated in his bed and thrashed about, spreading feces everywhere. His devotees, witnessing this, pleaded, "If even God behaves like this, where will devotees find the strength?" At this, the fake Narayan momentarily calmed down, basking in the praises of his divinity.

In this book, we will explore the rise of this fake Narayan, the actions of his deceitful Swamis, and the damage they have done to the Sanatan Dharma.

Well, all this is found in the books of that sect itself. But let's see what Swami Dayanand Saraswati, the founder of Arya Samaj, who was born in the same region of Gujarat five or six years before the death of that fake Narayana, writes about him in his book Satyarth Prakash written in the 1880s. Below is the portion from the eleventh chapter (Samulyaas) of Satyarth Prakash presented as it is:

"*Question: What is the opinion about 'Swaminarayan'?*

Answer (Swami Dayanand Saraswati): Swaminarayan is as involved in the expropriation of wealth as Gosais.

The 'Sahajanand' who was born in a village near Ayodhya, wandered as a celibate in Gujarat, Kathiawad, Kutch, Bhuj, etc. He observed that the people of this land are ignorant and innocent and that he could easily convert them to his belief. He made two or three disciples. They conspired together and spread the word that Sahajanand was an incarnation of Narayana, extremely accomplished, and would reveal himself in the form of four arms.

In Kathiawad, there was a 'Kathi', a man named 'Dadakhachar', who was a landowner (Bhoomiyo) in Gadhada. Sahajanand's disciples said to him, "If you wish to see the four-armed Narayana, we can request Sahajanandji for it." Dadakhachar, being an innocent man, agreed. In a room, Sahajanand wore a crown, holding a conch and discus in two hands, and behind him stood another man holding a mace and lotus, extending his arms from the sides of Sahajanand to give the appearance of four arms. His disciples told Dadakhachar, "Look up once, then close your eyes and look again briefly, or else Narayana will become angry." Their intention was that he wouldn't scrutinize their trick too closely. They lit a lamp suddenly, and Dadakhachar, upon seeing the four-armed figure, was convinced. He bowed down, did namaskar, and then was led away, thinking that he had seen Narayana. Meanwhile, Sahajanand changed his clothes and sat on a cushion. His disciples said, "See! Now he is sitting here in another form." Dadakhachar was trapped in their scheme, and from there, the roots of their sect began to grow, as Dadakhachar was a large landowner. From there, Sahajanand spread his influence, wandered here and there, giving teachings, converting many into saints, and sometimes manipulating his followers into believing in his mystical abilities. The simple people of Kathiawad fell into these schemes. When Sahajanand died, his disciples spread even more deceit and manipulation."

The reference to Swami Dayanand Saraswati's statements about this sect is necessary because he was born in the same region where this sect flourished, and in the same time period when the sect was in its early stages of expansion.

Now, for the context of this book's topic, let's look at the history of the sect as described in their own words. According to the writings of the sect, the accepted popular descriptions, and the various pages found about the sect on the internet, their history is presented as follows:

According to the writings of the Swaminarayan sect, in 1781, a boy named Ghanshyam Pandey was born in the village of Chhapaiya in Uttar Pradesh. At the age of eleven, he took sannyas (renunciation) and adopted the name 'Neelkanth Varni'. He traveled across India as a sannyasi and became proficient in Ashtanga Yoga. In 1799, at the age of 18, he arrived in Gujarat, where he met Ramanand Swami, the original guru of a Vaishnava sect called Uddhav Sampraday in Gadhada. Ramanand Swami initiated the 18-year-old Neelkanth Varni (Ghanshyam Pandey) and gave him the name 'Sahajanand Swami'. Three years later, in 1802, Ramanand Swami passed away, and the Uddhav Sampraday came under the leadership of Sahajanand Swami. It is said that Sahajanand's elder gurubhai, Raghunathdas, objected, claiming that the leadership of the sect should go to him. A legal case ensued between the two in Mangrol State, where the verdict declared that Raghunathdas would continue to worship Lord Ram, while Sahajanand Swami would continue to worship Krishna. Thus, the claim of Sahajanand Swami over Uddhav Sampraday remained intact.

The day after Swami Ramanand's death, Sahajanand Swami gathered a large assembly of the sect's followers and gave them the 'Swaminarayan' mantra, instructing them to immerse themselves in Krishna bhakti (devotion to Krishna). However, according to the sect's own early writings, Sahajanand Swami said that three things were essential for this devotion: first, knowledge (Jnana) of the scriptures to prevent superstition and deceit; second, the observance of dharma (righteousness); and third, renunciation (Vairagya). Thus, Krishna bhakti with the Swaminarayan mantra, combined with knowledge, dharma, and renunciation, became the main path prescribed by Sahajanand Swami. From here, Sahajanand Swami himself began to be called 'Swaminarayan', and his Uddhav Sampraday became known as the 'Swaminarayan Sampraday'. In the Shikshapatri written by Swaminarayan in 1824, he declared Lord Krishna as his deity and built six Krishna temples during his lifetime. And here comes the point about his association with British rulers and Christian missionaries.

In 1818, during Sahajanand's time, after the Peshwas were defeated by the British, Gujarat came under British rule, and from that point onwards, Sahajanand Swami had close connections with British officials like John Malcolm and Christian missionaries. Before British rule, the king of Ahmedabad had banned Sahajanand Swami from entering Ahmedabad. However, in November 1817, Ahmedabad came under British East India Company control, and in February 1818, John Andrew Dunlop was appointed as the first collector of Ahmedabad. In 1818, a British officer named Iron Saahib, working under Dunlop, invited Sahajanand Swami to meet and offered him land in Ahmedabad. Iron Saahib is the name mentioned in the sect's books for Edward Ironside, the British official working under collector Dunlop. Ironside also contacted the followers of Sahajanand Swami and offered to build a large hall as a residence for Sahajanand Swami and his monks. In 1819, he met Sahajanand Swami and promised to provide a plot of land in Kalupur for the construction of a temple. Collector Andrew Dunlop obtained permission from Britain to grant the land for building a temple in Kalupur. In 1822-23, the Kalupur temple was completed, and Sahajanand Swami inaugurated it in the presence of 50,000 people.

Regarding this entire sequence of events, historian Raymond Brady Williams writes in his book An Introduction to Swaminarayan Hinduism, "In 1820, the collector of Ahmedabad granted land to Sahajanand Swami to build a temple, and the first temple of Swaminarayan sect was constructed there. Thus, the British were involved in the construction of the first temple of the sect, which was a perfect symbol of the fact that 'Pax Britannica' and 'Pax Sahajananda' were parallel movements working towards a common goal. In 1823, when the Nar-Narayan temple was inaugurated, Sahajanand

Swami was accompanied by 50,000 people. Therefore, the years before the British arrival were years of opposition and persecution for Sahajanand, but the last ten years after the British arrival were years of great success, high esteem, and major social reforms."

Thus, with the support of the British authorities, Sahajanand Swami's influence continued to expand in Gujarat, and in the following ten years, he established five more temples. Among these was the Lakshmi-Narayan temple in Vadtal, where he installed his own idol, naming it Harikrishna Maharaj. According to the discourses of Vadtal Swamis, his intention behind this was that when people visited the temple and worshipped Lakshmi-Narayan, their faith in Sahajanand Swami as the supreme god (Sarvopari Ishwar) would gradually solidify through the Harikrishna Maharaj form. In Raymond Williams' book, the term "Pax Britannica" is mentioned, referring to a movement carried out by the British government between 1815 and 1914. The phrase means "British peace." Wherever the British established colonial rule around the world, they sought to maintain peace with the local society and ensure their long-term presence by fostering harmony. In Gujarat, this movement became known as "Pax Britannica - Pax Sahajananda," meaning fostering harmony with Sahajanand Swami to establish British-Hindu peace. This is referenced in the diary of William Hodge, the principal of Bishop College in Calcutta. His diary mentions several meetings between Sahajanand Swami, Christian clergy, and British officials, detailing how Swaminarayan redefined Hindu scriptures under their influence.

In summary, it states, "The Swaminarayan Hindu documents from the 1820s help reconstruct the relationship between the British and the Swaminarayan movement. Hindu relations with colonial officers, as well as early Christian-Hindu dialogues, significantly advanced during this time. Swaminarayan revived and purified aspects of Hindu scriptural thought and practice, leading British officials and Christian clergy to interpret him as a religious and social reformer whose reforms contributed to societal order and welfare."

Sahajanand Swami died in 1830 due to illness. But before his death, he had arranged for the governance of the sect. He divided the management of the Swaminarayan sect in Gujarat into two parts: the Kalupur (Ahmedabad) seat in the north and the Vadtal seat in the south.

According to the sect's accounts, Sahajanand Swami did not want ascetics to be involved in the sect's administration, as they might become entangled in materialism and lose their spirituality. Hence, he summoned some of his close brothers from Uttar Pradesh and adopted two of them as sons. One of these sons was made the Acharya of the Kalupur seat in Ahmedabad, and the other was made the Acharya of the Vadtal seat. He entrusted the administration of the temples and the sect to these Acharyas, instructing them to live a household life. Rules were also established for the Acharyas' household lives, and it was decreed that future Acharyas should be chosen from among their descendants through hereditary succession.

BAPS (Bochasanwasi Akshar Purushottam Sanstha):

After Sahajanand Swami's death in 1830, the administration of the sect was handed over to the household Acharyas, and the spiritual work was given to the ascetics. However, as hereditary Acharyas emerged, corruption and conflicts between ascetics and Acharyas over control of the sect became frequent. While Sahajanand Swami had established Krishna as the deity in temples, over time, the idols of Krishna were rebranded as those of Swaminarayan, and the worship of Sahajanand Swami began. By the late 19th century, one of Sahajanand's ascetic disciples, Bhagat Maharaj, told his close disciple Shastriji Maharaj, "Bhagwan Swaminarayan once said that to understand and worship Purushottam Ishwara, one must first become 'Akshar.' And in another instance, Sahajanand called Gunatitanand Swami his 'Akshar.' Thus, essentially, both Akshar and Purushottam should be worshiped together." This meant that the Acharyas were of no significance. Only Purushottam Bhagwan, Sahajanand Swami, and the chief ascetic of the sect, representing Akshar, were worthy of worship and were supreme. Both should be worshiped together. After Bhagatji Maharaj's death, Shastriji Maharaj developed this argument further and was eventually expelled from the sect in 1905 for his insistence. He formed a separate institution dedicated to the joint worship of Akshar and Purushottam, which attracted many ascetics from the Swaminarayan sect. However, after losing a legal battle, this institution was forbidden from using the name Swaminarayan, and it became known as the "Bochasanwasi Akshar Purushottam Sanstha" (BAPS).

However, it is important to note that Shastriji Maharaj was a Patel by caste, both before and after becoming an ascetic, which increased the Patel community's inclination towards BAPS. Even Sardar Vallabhbhai Patel was persuaded by his father to fight the court case against the main seat. Initially, Sardar Patel refused his father's request, advising him not to get involved in the case of deceitful ascetics claiming to be gods, but he later relented due to his father's insistence. Today, the book "Bochasan Revolt's History" is still available in Gujarati as 'Bochasan Band no Itihas', detailing the many instances of false gods and deception within the sect, including cases of ascetics claiming to be supreme deities.

This was the start of the 20th century. After Swami Vivekananda gained global recognition for Hindu spirituality during his travels abroad, people from various Hindu sects began traveling abroad as well. Shastriji Maharaj also traveled abroad and, under the banner of Hinduism, began raising funds to build grand temples both in India and abroad. Gradually, collecting funds and constructing large temples became the main goal, and devotion to Krishna faded away. Every subsequent leader of BAPS continued this work. It is also true that after Shastriji Maharaj, the next leaders—Yogiji Maharaj, Pramukh Swami, and the current leader Mahant Swami—were all from the Patel community. The devotion that had replaced Krishna worship with Swaminarayan now shifted to the worship of the sect's leader, known as Akshar.

With money and grand temples as the primary focus, multimillionaire merchants and industrialists became the main targets. As a result, spiritual discussions and teachings vanished from the ascetics' discourses, and instead, business-minded merchants began receiving motivational talks on family counseling and business expansion. The discourses of the saffron-clad ascetics shifted from spiritual teachings to stories of how Bill Gates, Warren Buffet, Steve Jobs, and Jack Ma amassed their fortunes. Scandals involving sexual exploitation of women and boys, financial fraud, land scams, abductions, and even murders of ascetics have emerged from most branches of the Swaminarayan sect, including BAPS. In 2013, P.D. Swami, who had been Pramukh Swami's chief disciple for decades, filed an FIR in Ahmedabad, accusing Pramukh Swami of sexually exploiting him on numerous occasions at different locations. Since then, P.D. Swami has not been heard from.

Thus, a shift in purpose naturally changes the path, which is evident in the Swaminarayan Gadi and BAPS. The Uddhav sect, which began with devotion to Krishna, has now completely disappeared, replaced by the Swaminarayan sect, which has reached an extreme of idolizing a person and distorting and disrespecting the deities of Sanatan Dharma. From BAPS, a separate faction has emerged called Haridham Sokhda, which itself has further split into two groups. Numerous divisions have also arisen from the original two Gaadis.

Today, this sect expands its influence among Hindus in new locations by converting them through a three-tiered strategy. First, they establish Lord Krishna as God and present Sahajanand Swami as a Krishna-devotee guru. Once a temple is established in a new location and gains acceptance, within a couple of years, they claim that Swaminarayan and Lord Krishna are one. In the Bhagavad Gita, where Lord Krishna describes himself as Purushottam, this Purushottam is separated from Krishna and it is stated that Purushottam first came as Krishna and has now returned in modern times as Swaminarayan. Once certain followers are firmly committed, they introduce the third level, claiming that this Purushottam is indeed their Swaminarayan, and that deities like Ram, Krishna, etc., are actually incarnations of this Purushottam Swaminarayan. Eventually, distorted stories are introduced that depict all the deities of Sanatan Dharma—Brahma, Vishnu, Shiva, Mother Shakti, and Lord Ganesha—as mere servants of this new god. Followers are led to believe, as in Islam with Allah, that no god other than Swaminarayan is worthy of worship, thus erasing Sanatan deities from their households. This fourth layer in society is foundational for this sect and is now visible in Gujarat.

☙

From here, this narrative abandons its lighter tone and sarcasm, adopting a more serious approach to explain a grave threat faced by the Sanatan civilization. The sect that established its foundation in Gujarat with the help of British officials and Christian clergy has now taken on a new form, posing a significant threat to Sanatan Hindu society. Through this book, we will learn about the challenges this sect has created. It will start by sharing how I became acquainted with this sect, and the circumstances under which I joined the fight of awakened Sanatanis against it. And then, we will walk through my journey in this battle by exploring the current context in Gujarat related to this sect.

– Dr. Kaushik Chaudhary
Date: September 30, 2024

Fake Narayana Deceitful Sect

I
Entering the Scene

As the COVID-19 pandemic gradually came to an end, we emerged from the devastation of the second wave—a crisis avoided during the first wave due to stringent lockdowns. The mild third wave from April to July 2022 signaled that the worst was finally over, marking a turning point. Life was ready to resume, and people returned with a renewed sense of clarity, purpose, and resilience. I, too, became focused on institutionalizing the work I had begun with my first book. In 2015, I published "It's not a Creation, It's a Projection through Expression", a book that introduced a new model of the multiverse, rooted in the fundamental principles of Sanatan Dharma's scriptures and integrated with the foundations of physics. This work attracted the attention of prominent scientists worldwide. Later, I translated it into Gujarati and Hindi, but I realized that the work extended beyond a single book. It marked the start of a sustained effort—a venture that would require an institution to pave the way for future scientific discoveries inspired by Vedanta to be shared with the world, starting from India. With a blueprint in hand for this research society, I began visiting various places, primarily seeking support from friends within the Rashtriya Swayamsevak Sangh.

At the same time, my attention was drawn back to the Swaminarayan sect, after nearly three years, due to the open statements made by certain Swamis against the deities of Sanatan Dharma. Weekly broadcasts on local Gujarati channels and social media showed various Swamis from this sect making statements that were unsettling. This resurgence of focus reminded me of my first encounter with the sect, which had occurred three years earlier.

My initial experience with the sect was in March-April 2019, when BAPS organized a five-day sermon series in Palanpur's Patel area. This event marked the sect's first significant attempt to establish a presence in Banaskantha district, where it had been previously absent. Though names like Pramukh, Akshar, and Akshardham—typical of BAPS—had already begun appearing in residential society names, they were merely precursors. The sermon series aimed to introduce the Patel community in Banaskantha to the sect, encouraging them to adopt traditional markers like wearing beads and applying forehead marks, although these efforts hadn't yet gained traction. The Patels of Banaskantha held deep reverence for Lord Shiva, remained staunchly dedicated to Sanatan Dharma, and upheld strong spiritual and religious values. Sectarian hypocrisy and superficial practices had not penetrated this community. Nevertheless, when an invitation for the sermon series reached my clinic, all the attendees were local Patel shopkeepers.

The city was covered in large billboards, and even rickshaws and cars displayed the event posters. Contact numbers were collected while handing out invitations, and attendees received daily reminders to attend. Like most others, I assumed that "Swaminarayan" referred to either Lord Vishnu or Lord Krishna or perhaps their founder, Sahajanand Swami, as an incarnation of Lord Krishna. Influenced by relatives, my parents attended one session but left within half an hour. Their reaction was lukewarm: "It was fine, but nothing special—just everyday matters, like mother-in-law and daughter-in-law conflicts. Some came to discipline their family members, while others seemed interested only in the Khichadi and Ice-cream Candies."

Our home nurtured a deeply spiritual atmosphere, initially shaped by my father's readings of Vivekananda's works and later reinforced by my own spiritual pursuits. Books by experienced yogis regularly filled our discussions.

The next evening, as I walked on my rooftop, I could hear the Swami's voice projecting from half a kilometer away. The speaker, Swami Apoorvamuni, said, "Does any Muslim need to be told to go to the mosque? Does any Christian need to be reminded to go to church? If you fail to bring two others to tomorrow's sermon, I'll consider you to be like Aurangzeb's descendants." This statement felt abrasive, and I withdrew to my room. The following day, respectable locals criticized the Swami's words, and some Patel community members confronted him, although he deflected by saying,

"I am a Patel, just like you."

Months after this event, another video featuring the same Swami went viral. This time, he spoke at a program in Surat, saying, "In government offices, you hear things like 'Parmar Saheb is coming,' 'Chauhan Saheb is coming.' Should the son of a Patel wait for Parmar Saheb (Dalit Caste)? Our people should be in these offices."

On the final day of the sermon, some Patel friends urged me to attend and present my book to the Swami. I briefly met him, gifting him the Gujarati translation of my multiverse theory. However, the sermon left me with an unsettling impression. The sect's religious opulence, underpinned by wealth, seemed to mirror a Christian model, albeit in Hindu garb. On May 5, 2019, I penned an article on Facebook, suggesting that a religious institution and ascetic should offer spiritual awakening, not commercial and political entrapment. If the sect continued to charge its followers as churches do, these temples would become centers of sin, detached from the Hindu ethos.

Driven to understand why the sect deviated so significantly, I researched its history, eventually writing another article on May 13, 2019, titled "The History of the Swaminarayan Sect: From Devotion to Krishna to Worship of an Individual." This article, which you read in the book's prologue, highlighted their connections with British administrators and Christian missionaries. Afterward, I dismissed the sect as merely another group misusing religion for profit, devoid of genuine spirituality.

Then, in 2020, the coronavirus pandemic struck, subsiding by 2022, and I returned to my work. But as normalcy returned, the sect's Swamis resumed making offensive statements about Sanatan Dharma's deities. These comments were promptly met with public outcry, yet each Swami offered a familiar apology: "My tongue slipped; I apologize." Yet similar statements continued. Although I had distanced myself from these controversies, one day I stumbled across a Facebook post featuring an outburst from Swami Anand Sagar, who described a dream where Lord Shiva (The Sect only says 'Shivji', not God or Lord) met a member of their sect at a gate and declined entry to meet their guru, Hariprabodh Swami, deeming himself unworthy. (Video link: https://www.youtube.com/watch?v=10TZqJCSOL0)

Disturbed, I commented on the video: "How can you utter such nonsense? The only reason I'm not reacting further is the respect for your saffron robes." The reaction caught the attention of others, and I began receiving messages from Sanatani individuals urging me to act against this sect, describing it as a threat to Hinduism.

For some time, I did not grasp the importance of their pleas, as I remained focused on advancing my own work. I was engaged with the Prime Minister's scientific advisory team and connected with institutions like RFRF, discussing ideas with members from the BJP and RSS, hoping my thoughts would reach Prime Minister Modi. I advised the concerned individuals to document the sect's statements, in case a legal action became necessary.

In September or October 2022, a group of concerned citizens from Rajkot traveled to meet me. They spoke of an imminent threat, claiming the sect was gaining influence over Hindu temple trusts and local politics. At first, I thought they were referring to Islamization concerns, but they clarified that this was about the Swaminarayan sect. Despite their urgency, I remained focused on my work, reassured them, and dismissed the sect as mere opportunists.

Yet, every week, I continued to receive messages on social media, urging me to intervene. These messages came from regular Hindus, some running small businesses, others affiliated with the RSS, all sharing a sense of desperation. Although they mostly used pseudonyms, they were actively opposing the sect through a Facebook group called "Beware of the Swaminarayan Sect," which had amassed around eleven thousand members.

Observing their mounting despair, I began paying more attention to their posts. Then came December, and with it, the Pramukh Swami Janma Shatabdi Mahotsav—a grand celebration meticulously marketed across the state. Prime Minister Narendra Modi himself inaugurated the event. Social media and WhatsApp groups echoed with praises for BAPS and Pramukh Swami, and for the first time, I felt compelled to act.

At 10 PM one night, I messaged one of the concerned accounts, asking, "What information have you gathered about this sect? Send me everything." Within minutes, I received a reply, brimming with relief and urgency. They provided newspaper clippings, video links, and screenshots, which I have included in the following chapter for you to see the full picture. This journey is one I wish to share with you so that you, too, can feel the same shock, anger, and hope that fueled my resolve. Prepare to uncover the hidden deception in the next chapter.

II

Deception

In the historical account of this sect presented in the prologue, you encountered unsettling details. However, the upcoming revelations will reveal even more shocking insights, offering a clearer view of how Sahajanand Swami's exchanges with Christian missionaries and subsequent Hindu-Christian dialogue led the British to see him as a reformer who reinterpreted Hindu scriptures. What you are about to witness is an unprecedented level of malice and distortion—something previously unimaginable in the 15,000-year history of Sanatan civilization. This journey will evoke memories of demonic figures like Hiranyakashipu, Ravana, and Paundraka, who proclaimed themselves as the Supreme God, demanded worship, and labeled Lord Vishnu as their subordinate. Here, you will uncover efforts aimed at erasing the deities of Sanatan Dharma by appropriating words, names, and descriptions from their scriptures and attributing them to a new deity.

Take a moment to steady yourself, temper your anger, and prepare to journey into the depths of deception that await.

Videos Full of Insult to Sanatan Dharma Gods:

Let us start with the videos. While they cannot be directly displayed in this book, their words will be described, and the identities of the speakers will be provided, along with links to access the videos online. In this age of AI, I trust you can navigate to these web links by capturing their text, even if you're reading from a physical book. For ebook readers, a simple click should suffice. We included such a link in the previous chapter, showcasing one of these distorted statements. Now, here are additional statements that reveal the true nature of this sect.

- In one video, Rugnathcharan Swami from Rajkot Gurukul claims that one day, Lord Shiva (whom these Swamis simply call 'Shivji') came to have darshan of Sahajanand Swami, also known as Swaminarayan. At the entrance to his chamber, another disciple, Sachchidanand Swami, stopped Lord Shiva and said that not just anyone could meet God. Only true devotees are granted his darshan. When Lord Shiva asked how he could prove himself, the Swami replied, "You must wrestle with me. If you win, we will accept you as a true devotee." A wrestling match ensued, in which the Swami lifted Shiva onto his shoulder and was about to throw him when Lord Shiva raised his hands and said, "Yes, yes. I concede that you are a greater devotee of God than I am." This story is also written on page 75 of the book Shri Haricharitra Chintamani, screenshots of which have gone viral. (Video link: https://www.youtube.com/watch?v=I7PTcAWBk3c)

- Another video that caused controversy shows a Swami named Gnyandip from Vadtal referring to Jagat Janani Maa Ambika as an apsara (Beutiful dancers of heaven) and making obscene comments about her body. This Swami was later slapped by Sanatanis in a Surat mall. (Video link: https://www.youtube.com/watch?v=n3g3I9jUk4Y)

- Hariprakash Swami, in yet another video, speaks about Goddess Durga, saying, "Millions of goddesses became powerful by singing the praises of Swaminarayan. You can keep a photo of the goddess, but to the side. The main seat on the throne should always be occupied by Lord Swaminarayan. You may worship your deities, but always remember that I am the chanter of the name who grants power to them. The power of our Maharaj flows through all these deities." (Video link: https://drive.google.com/file/d/1TljHO8bBy3xxjdYArPqzb1dQGqlz7jxV/view?usp=sharing)

- In a video from Bhuj Temple, a Swami recounts a conversation between a disciple and his guru. The disciple asked, "Guruji, why were you laughing while urinating today?" The guru responded, "Yes, I knew you would ask that. While I was urinating, Brahma was swept away in my urine. A bug was floating by, but when I looked closer, I realized it was Brahma. In his previous life, he had been Indra." (Video link: https://www.youtube.com/watch?v=fk5ZNKT7-Mo)

- Dharmavallabh Swami from Surat Gurukul, in one video, says, "Rama and Krishna were murderers. So what if the varnshankar (hybrid) Pandavas worshiped them? Does that make them gods? Was Krishna really God? Call Shishupal; he knew who Krishna was—a mere cowherd." (Video link: https://www.youtube.com/watch?v=EvaGM84U1_g)

- In another video, a Swami from Sokhada Temple narrates a story where a devotee asked Yogiji Maharaj (a former leader of BAPS), "Should I go for darshan to Dakor?" Yogiji Maharaj responded, "What are you saying? Don't you know who we are? Don't you know our status? Go and give darshan." (Video link: https://www.facebook.com/kinner.aacharya.5/videos/473167711349376/)

- Harishwarupdas Swami from SGVP takes a particularly extreme approach with his brainwashing tactics. In numerous sermons, I have heard him say things like, "When Lord Swaminarayan walks through the court of Akshardham, Brahma, Vishnu, Mahesh, and all other gods and goddesses fall at his feet, folding their hands in obeisance." In another video, this Swami explains the creation of the universe according to Shrimad Bhagavad, describing multiple Brahmandas, only to conclude that the supreme creator of them all, including Mahavishnu's is none other than Lord Swaminarayan. In yet another video, he declares, "Anyone who has ever smoked or consumed alcohol cannot enter Lord Swaminarayan's Akshardham. They can only go to Shiva's Kailash, where all the drug addicts and weed smokers gather. Such people have no place in Akshardham." (Video link: https://drive.google.com/file/d/19EKiYW01cjwUBiTozveOCorPppCBz0jn/view?usp=drive_link)

- In another video from Sokhada Temple, a Swami named Shreeji Saurabh narrates a story about a female devotee who was a great worshiper of Shiva. She would constantly pray and ask Shiva for a son who would become a devotee of the sect. Shiva, pleased with her devotion, told her, "The guru you serve is someone even I have not had the fortune of having darshan of. To serve him, I will be born through your womb." (Video link:

https://www.facebook.com/1285774587/videos/609220480748416/)

- Additionally, in another video, a Swami from Kalupur Temple claims that Lord Swaminarayan once said, "Had Brahma, Vishnu, and Mahesh known my glory, they would have also attained Akshardham." This video has since been removed. In yet another video, a Swami tells a story where, while bathing, water flowed off Lord Swaminarayan's body into the drain, where it touched three frogs. These frogs then turned into Brahma, Vishnu, and Shiva. (Video link: https://rumble.com/v2gq3pu-nityaswarupdas-swami-of-sardhar-swminarayan-temple-insulting-sanatan-dharma.html)

- In Vadtal, a Swami named Brahmaswaroopdas speaks about Khodiyar Mata and says: "(Some of our satsangis) cannot let go of their family deities; they feel that these deities might get upset. But they shouldn't worry about that. When the family deity realizes that a member of their lineage has become a devotee of the supreme Purushottam Narayan, they feel blessed. Swaminarayan Bhagwan once went to Joban Pagi's farm and, noticing something, asked, 'Who is this?' Joban Pagi replied, 'This is my family deity, Khodiyar Mata.' Then Maharaj sprinkled water on Khodiyar Mata and said, 'From today, Khodiyar Mata has also become one of our satsangis.' After this, did Khodiyar Mata get angry with Joban Pagi? No, she didn't. This is how it is." (Video link: https://drive.google.com/file/d/15gEo_DLRb9oMvp3GkpKiCSw915MQ8xyy/view?usp=drivesdk)

I watched and listened to all these videos. For a Sanatani deeply committed to preserving his culture against external threats, discovering such individuals within his own community, masked in the guise of his own civilization, is a profound shock. It brings a sense of betrayal and shame, as we realize that such vile statements about our revered gods have never been uttered even by those of other faiths. Outsiders might claim, "Only our God exists; all others are false." But these individuals go further, saying, "Your gods exist, but they are servants of our supreme god. They draw their power from him and act on his behalf. In fact, your gods' wives are actually the wives of our god. Therefore, there is no need to worship your gods anymore; only our new god, who stands above all, deserves worship."

To trace the roots of this distortion, we will examine the literature of this sect, revealing it as a cesspool of perversion. One fact becomes evident: none of the BAPS Swamis have made such extreme statements in these videos. The offensive remarks from BAPS Swamis tend to focus on belittling Dalits, goddess-worshipping communities known as Patanis, and others. Yet, upon examining the literature across all branches of the sect, we find that the most distorted and destructive writings against Sanatan Dharma appear in BAPS publications. Other branches seem to follow this lead, attempting to legitimize themselves by echoing similar narratives. So, let us begin our exploration into the literature of this sect.

Literature:

From the official BAPS website, you can find four key books, available in Gujarati, Hindi, and English: Ghanshyam Charitra, Nilkanth Charitra, Sahajanand Charitra, and Akshar Purushottam Upasana. These four books are used as textbooks to indoctrinate and brainwash those who join the sect as monks. When we read these books in the order they are listed, we will observe an increasing level of corruption and perversion in their content.

- (Link: https://www.baps.org/SatsangExam/Studymaterials.aspx)

In Ghanshyam Charitra, we find numerous distortions of religious doctrine, including the following:

1. Hanuman saves young Ghanshyam from a demon named Kalidatta, returns him to his mother, and says, "This child is God, and I am his servant." (Page 3, 4)

2. Sage Markandeya visits Ghanshyam's house and performs his naming ceremony. (Page 6, 7)

3. Goddess Lakshmi visits and requests to serve young Sahajanand. Ghanshyam tells her to come to Kathiawar when he arrives and that he will fulfill her wish. (Page 10)

4. Young Ghanshyam commands the eight mystical powers to bring food for his mother. (Page 11)

5. Ghanshyam kills the demon Kalidatta. (Page 16)

6. Ghanshyam takes the form of Yamaraj to frighten a fisherman. (Page 19, 21)

7. When Ghanshyam is injured, deities like Indra, Chandra, Brahma, and Vishnu arrive. (Page 38, 39)

8. Ghanshyam manifests as Lord Rama and grants darshan to his parents and others. (Page 61, 62)

9. Scholars in Kashi witness the forms of Shiva and Rama in young Ghanshyam. (Page 78)

Details from the Book Nilkanth Charitra:

1. Hanumanji said, "Maharaj! It is my routine to have your darshan daily. If you permit, I would like to remain in your service." Sahajanand replied, "For now, I intend to travel alone, so please come whenever I call you." (Page 1, 2)

2. Sahajanand appeared in the form of Chaturbhuj Narayan (four-armed Lord Vishnu) and gave darshan to ascetics heading towards the Himalayas. (Page 8)

3. At the Haridwar fair, Lord Shiva and Goddess Parvati took the form of Brahmins and served Sahajanand for several days. (Page 10)

4. Near Lakshman Jhula, Lord Lakshman emerged from his statue and bowed at Sahajanand's feet. Sahajanand then revealed himself in the form of Lord Ram. (Page 10)

5. Hanuman brought sweet fruits for Sahajanand, and in gratitude, Sahajanand blessed him. (Page 22)

6. The Sun god, with folded hands, said to Sahajanand, "O Lord, it is by your grace and through your worship that I have received my light." (Page 25)

7. Hanuman said, "I am Hanuman, son of Anjani, and a servant of Nilkanth Varni (Sahajanand)." (Page 42)

8. In the guise of a wandering ascetic and a woman, Lord Shiva and Sati came to Sahajanand and said, "This is Lord Shiva, and I am Sati. You have been hungry for days, so we brought some food for you." After serving Sahajanand, Shiva and Parvati were delighted, offered their respects, and disappeared. (Page 63)

Corrupt Teachings from the Book Sahajanand Charitra:

1. Sahajanand Swami contains within him all avatars; he is the origin of all and the cause of everything. (Page 3)

2. Swaminarayan is the master of all the gods—Indra, Chandra, Vishnu, Mahesh, and others. No one can surpass him. (Page 10)

3. In Akshardham, Swaminarayan sat on the throne, while Shiva, Brahma, countless gods, sages, and avatars stood on one leg, offering their praises to Swaminarayan. (Pages 15, 16)

4. Rudra, Bhairav, Bhavani, and other gods and goddesses do not have the power to grant happiness or sorrow to any living being. (Page 31)

5. In Gadhada, Sahajanand established his own statue and named it 'Vasudev Narayan,' saying, "This is my form." (Page 32)

6. Speaking of his devotee Mulji Bhagat, Sahajanand said, "The infinite Brahmands, in which Brahma, Vishnu, and Mahesh reside, rest on Mulji's shoulders." (Pages 41, 42)

7. Sahajanand said, "Yes, I am Sachchidanand Parabrahma Purushottam. I am the lord of Radha and Lakshmi. The scriptures speak of my glory." (Page 56)

8. While lying on his bed, Sahajanand threatened Indra for not bringing rain. (Page 66)

9. Sahajanand said, "Brahma, Vishnu, Mahesh, Ramchandra, and Shri Krishna are all below our Akshardham. I am beyond even that." (Page 84)

10. In Vadtal, Sahajanand personally established a statue named 'Harikrishna.' (Page 121)

11. Swaminarayan told the British Governor Malcolm, "Your rule will last for a long time." (Page 146)

This last point regarding Governor Malcolm reveals a deep-seated mystery, one that will show us how this Indian sect became so corrupted. We will explore this in later chapters.

৺

Upon exploring the books from the provided website link, I also came across other titles on the webpage. One particular book that caught my attention was Akshar Purushottam Upasana. I downloaded it and was shocked by what I read. It was an ocean of perversion, which I was the first to identify and bring to the attention of Hindu society. Let us examine the distortion.

Corrupt and Distorted Writings in Akshar Purushottam Upasana:

The entire book is filled with fabricated, corrupt theology, but chapter 4, titled "Sarvopari," reaches an extreme level. In this chapter, Sahajanand Swami is elevated above all other deities of Sanatan Dharma, diminishing their significance. Below is the selected text from pages 34 to 66 of the fourth chapter in this book.

> "*Gunatitanand Swami says, "Without knowing Maharaj as Purushottam, it is not possible to go to Akshardham" (Swāmini Vāto 3.12).*
>
> *Shriji Maharaj therefore says, "The path of jnān should be understood in such a way that one does not malign the form of God in any way. ….However, one should also intensely maintain the strength of conviction in God's form; i.e., 'I have attained the very form of God who reigns supreme, who forever possesses a divine form, and who is the 'avatāri' – the cause of all of the avatars.' If a person realizes this, then even if he may have left the Satsang fellowship, his love for God's form will not diminish. In fact, even though he is out of Satsang at present, ultimately, when he leaves his body, he will go to God's Akshardhām and stay near God. On the other hand, a person may be in the Satsang fellowship at present, and he may even be abiding by the commands prescribed in the shastras, but if his conviction of God is not firm, then when he leaves his body, he will either go to the realm of Brahmā or to the realm of some other deity; but he will not go to the abode of Purushottam Bhagwan. Therefore, one should realize the manifest God that one has attained to forever possess a divine form and to be the 'avatāri', the cause of all of the avatars. If, however, one does not realize this, and instead realizes God to be formless or like the other avatars, then that is regarded as committing blasphemy against God" (Vachanāmrut, Gadhadā II 9).*
>
> *In the Vachanāmrut and other texts of the Sampradaya, Shriji Maharaj has been described as sarvopari – the transcendental highest, as the avatāri – the cause of all incarnations, and as Purna Purushottam Nārāyan. The following extracts will help one to understand his supreme position.*

4.2 Akshardham: the highest abode; shriji maharaj: the Supreme

- *Akshardhãm is the divine abode of Bhagwan Swaminarayan. It is distinct and above the abodes of other incarnations and deities. As ordained by God, other incarnations, devotees and deities reside in different abodes.*

- *Nishkulanand Swami explains: Brahmã's abode is Satyaloka. And Kailãs is the abode of Shiva. (*Actually the Gujarati sentences says 'Brahma is placed in Satyaloka, Shiva is put in Kailas, Vishnu is placed in Vaikubtha and so on.) Vishnu's abode is Vaikunth. They each have separate abodes given by God. Indra is placed in Amarãvati. And Sheshji's place is in Pãtãl. Wherever ordained by God, they happily live forever. Rishishwar lives under Badri. The nirannamuktas stay in Shvetdwip. The Gopas and Gopis are placed in Golok. The akshar muktas are in close proximity with God himself [in Akshardhãm].*

  - Nishkulãnand Kãvya, Vachan Vidhi 37

- *Barring Akshardhãm, the remaining lokas are enwrapped in mãyã, and are subject to the triple misfortunes. Sadguru Muktanand Swami says: Vaikunth and the fourteen lokas are under the spell of mãyã. The wise shun them to escape from the triple misfortunes. Akshardhãm transcends mãyã and hence is immune from the three types of miseries. The bliss in Akshardhãm is therefore incomparable.*

- *Shriji Maharaj explains, "Moreover, the happiness of humans exceeds the happiness of animals; and the happiness of a king exceeds that; and the happiness of deities exceeds that; and the happiness of Indra exceeds that; then Bruhaspati's happiness, then Brahmã's, then Vaikunth's. Beyond that, the happiness of Golok is superior, and finally, the bliss of God's Akshardhãm is far more superior" (Vachanãmrut, Panchãlã 1).*

- *Nishkulanand Swami also says: The ultimate divine abode is from where there is no return. An indescribable reservoir of sublime happiness, it is beyond all. Where, in close proximity of God, live infinite muktas; full of infinite bliss. They live as if in the midst of oceans of utter happiness. God's divine abode [Akshardhām] is unique and incomparable with other abodes.*

- Chosath Padi 55-56

- *Therefore, Shriji Maharaj says that the bliss offered by his divine abode is so infinitely overwhelming that in comparison to it, the happiness offered by the lokas of the deities is described in Moksha Dharma as utterly infernal and insignificant (Vachanāmruts, Sārangpur 1, 4, 11; Gadhadā III 28).*

- *Apart from Akshardhām, all other abodes are perishable. Akshardhām is imperishable and eternal. Nishkulanand Swami says: In the scorching heat of the final destruction, the fourteen lokas, Bhav (Shiva), Brahmā, and Prakriti Purush are all consumed.*

- Chosath Padi 56

- *Shriji Maharaj also explains, "With the exception of God's Akshardhām, the form of God in that Akshardhām and his devotees in that Akshardhām, everything else – all of the realms, the deities, and the opulence of the deities – is perishable" (Vachanāmrut, Gadhadā II 24).*

- *The other abodes are influenced by the three gunas and māyā (e.g. the dispute between Radhikaji and Shridama in Golok is indicative of tamo guna. Tamoguna was also apparent in Jay and Vijay when they belittled Sanak and the sages in Vaikunth). It is only Akshardhām that is uninfluenced by the gunas or māyā. Golok, Vaikunth and other abodes have specific dimensions according to scriptural descriptions. However, because of its vastness, Akshardhām is described as immeasurable and endless in all directions (Vachanāmrut, Loyā 14).*

- *Other abodes abound with material objects such as diamond-studded palaces, jewels, etc. Akshardhām, however, is flooded with divine light. Purushottam, Akshar and the akshar muktas dwell within that divine light.*

From page 39, a section comes named Shriji Maharaj - The Supreme. It has three subsections named, i) In his own words, ii) As expressed in Swamini Vato, iii) In the words of Paramahansa. This entire section is filled with perversion and a great assault on the Sanatan Dharma and its entire form including its deities. Below are just a few drops of that entire ocean of filth.

- In the old manuscripts written during his own lifetime, Maharaj reveals, "The earlier incarnations had a specific cause for a particular end. But my incarnation is to make the jivas brahmarup and allow them to attain ultimate liberation. For this noble mission, I – Purushottam – beyond even Akshar, have assumed human form. Shri Krishna and other incarnations manifest to serve a specific purpose, such as defeating the demons. Having accomplished their mission, they departed from the world. But Bhagwan Swaminarayan incarnated to make the jivas brahmarup and to grant them ultimate liberation, thereby ensuring permanent liberation from the cycles of birth and death. (Page 40)

- "All of the avatars of God manifest from the very God [Shriji Maharaj] that is present in this Satsang fellowship. That is to say, he is the cause of all of the avatars and is the antaryāmi of all. It is he who, in Akshardhām, is radiant, full of countless powers and eternally has a form. He is also the lord of all of the lords of the countless brahmānds; he is even the cause of Aksharbrahman" (Vachanāmrut, Ahmedābād 6). These words of Shriji Maharaj clearly explain the importance of firm faith in his supreme form. (Page 41)

- (Gunatitanand) Swami said, "Know that Maharaj is supreme, the source of all avatars and the cause of all causes." Based on this, he had Vachanāmruts, Gadhadā II 9 and Gadhadā III 38 read and said, "Today, in Satsang, the sadhus, āchāryas, mandirs and murtis are all supreme. So what is there to say in Maharaj being supreme? One should understand that he is definitely supreme" (Swāmini Vāto 3.12). (Page 43 of Akshar Purushottam Upasana)

- "There are three grades of snake charmers, vādi, fulvādi and gārdi. Of these, a vādi captures meek snakes; a fulvādi captures those which are easy to catch, otherwise uses a cloth tie to kill them; and before a gārdi all types of snakes, even cobras, dance. The principle of this is, like the first type of snake charmer – vādi – Dattatreya and Kapil liberate the aspirants. Rama and Krishna, like the second – fulvādi – liberate those who abide by their dictates; otherwise they wield the sword to settle the point. Maharaj, however, is like the gārdi, the third type of snake-charmer. Jivas, Ishwars, Purush, Akshar and others are all standing before him with folded hands" (Swāmini Vāto 3.5). (Page 43 of Akshar Purushottam Upasana)

- "Previously, many great avatars have incarnated. Compared to them, when I look at the children of these satsangis I see that they have tens of millions of times greater divinity than them. So, how can the glory of the great devotees, the great Sadhus and Maharaj even be described?" (Swāmini Vāto 3.72). (Page 44)

- (*Note: This passage from Swamini Vato 3.72 suggests that, compared to all the avatars ever manifested in Sanatan Dharma, even a single child following the teachings of Sahajanand Swami in this sect possesses a radiance surpassing that of millions of other divine beings. Thus, the greatness of other saints, as well as Maharaj (Swaminarayan) himself, is portrayed as beyond human comprehension. This idea forms the basis of distorted beliefs, as illustrated in videos where BAPS Swami Gunatitanand tells his disciple in Dakor, "You have no idea who we are or what our status is. Go, offer your darshan at the temple of Krishna." Such distorted thinking arises from statements like these in their scriptures. Encouraged by these writings, followers of Prabodh Swami claim that Lord Shiva once told a man named Nishitbhai, "My fortune hasn't awakened enough to grant me darshan of Prabodh Swami, but I am blessed to have had your darshan." Following this, Lord Shiva (whom they refer to as Shivji) supposedly touched Nishitbhai's feet and departed.)

- "Actually, first Ganesh is described as a god; then Brahmā, Vishnu and Shiva are described; Aniruddha, Pradyumna and Sankarshan are also described as gods, then who out of them should be believed as God?

The explanation for this is that there are tens of millions of classes of jivas, ishwars, Brahmãs. The cause of them all is Maharaj himself. When one understands like this, then an answer can be said to have been given. There are countless Ramas, countless Krishnas and countless akshar muktas – and the creator of them all, the supporter of them all, the controller of them all and the cause of them all is Maharaj. If he is understood in this way, then spiritual wisdom is attained" (Swãmini Vãto 6.254). (Page 44)

- "What is the difference between a devotee of Purushottam and devotees of other avatars? The difference is comparable to that between the cub of an elephant and a louse" (Swãmini Vãto 2.107). (Page 44)

- "Despite all the discourses of Shri Krishna, Uddhava alone managed to renounce the world. Today, however, even teenagers renounce the worldly life to become sadhus. The shastras do not mention anyone renouncing women. Today however, thousands renounce women. The shastras cite only two or three instances where God appeared before devotees on their deathbeds. But today, God appears to call all the devotees when they pass away. The previous incarnations are like pãrasmani, but Purushottam is like chintãmani" (Swãmini Vãto 2.169). (Page 44)

- On many occasions, Gunatitanand Swami explained the distinction between avatar and avatãri using these analogies: the archer and the arrow are separate. One should know that the archer is the cause of the arrow. However, the distinction between avatar and avatãri is not like the different guises of an actor on a stage. Just as there is a sharp difference between a sovereign emperor and a subordinate chieftain, there is a difference between avatar and avatãri. It is against the spirit of the shastras to treat all avatars and all sadhus as equal. (Page 45)

- "The bleating of hundreds of thousands of goats incites no fear at all. But the roar of merely one lion is terrifying and can tear apart an elephant's temple. Similarly, there is no problem in describing Maharaj as similar to other avatars. But to proclaim that all the avatars owe their powers to Maharaj and have attained their present state by worshiping him is as intimidating as a lion's frightening roar is to an elephant" (Swãmini Vãto

5.197). (Page 45)

- In Nishkulānand Kāvya, Purushottam Prakāsh 55, Shriji Maharaj is compared in the simile with the heavy downpour of the month of Ashādh which blossoms the whole earth. The other avatars are compared to dew which cannot affect the earth. In such words, Nishkulanand Swami has sung the divine glory of his supreme master. (Page 47)

- Thereupon Lalji Bhakta inquired, "How eminent is this Varni? Can he be compared to you?" Ramanand Swami replied, "Varni is superior to me and even superior to Shri Krishna. He is the cause of all avatars, greatest of the great, endowed with all divine virtues and powers. He himself is Purushottam." In this way, Ramanand Swami explained at length the supremacy of Shriji Maharaj and rebuked Lalji Bhakta for not going to Loj. This incident has been described in the Harililāmrut (4.3): Lalji asks, "How great is he? Is he like Dattatreya or Rishabhdev? Or is he comparable to Ramachandra?" Ramanand replies, "Please listen carefully, Krishna is greater than all other [avatars]. He [Varni] is greater than even Krishna. He is the ultimate avatāri of all avatars. There is no need to elaborate any further. Leaving aside his darshan, why have you come to Kutch?" (Page 59-60)

BAPS records how Sahajanand Swami gradually converted the Hindu populace of his time into followers of this new sect, centered on the supreme God.

> "*On pages 65-66, a question is posed: "If Bhagwan Swaminarayan is supreme, why has he been described as Krishna in the Vachanāmrut, in other shastras of the Sampradaya and in the kirtans of the paramhansas?"*
>
> *The answer given is strikingly similar to how the concept of Allah was introduced in pre-Islamic Arabia, where many gods existed. The answer is: "During the time of Shriji Maharaj, there were many faiths and cults, some of which expounded irreligious practices, accepted false gurus, believed in superstitions and indulged in black magic. Their influence was widespread. All of these fiercely opposed the new Sampradaya. In such trying times, if any person tried to identify himself as God, people would naturally be reluctant to join the*

Sampradaya out of sheer dismay. The acceptance of a new idea is always gradual. Shriji Maharaj was therefore identified initially as a Satpurush, then as an avatar and finally as Purushottam – the avatāri of all avatars. As the aspirants' faith in him deepened, the paramhansas depicted Shriji Maharaj in more inspiring and enlightening terms.

.....To attract people, Shriji Maharaj consecrated the murtis of those deities at the places where they were popularly worshiped. Their devotees came for darshan. By subsequent association with the sadhus, they developed unshakeable faith in Shriji Maharaj's supreme and sublime form. Gradually, the true upāsanā began to be widely accepted in the Sampradaya." (Pages 65-66)"

Efforts to Deify Pramukh Swami:

BAPS, which had separated from the original sect more than a hundred years ago, has surpassed all other branches largely due to the support of the Patel community. The reason for this success was their policy of building temples. Initially, land was acquired from governments in different countries under the pretext of promoting interfaith harmony, then temples were constructed using funds primarily from Patel business followers. It is said that the sect's followers were required to donate a certain percentage of their annual income to the temple. Furthermore, contracts for materials like marble, granite, bricks, cement, and labor were given to devotees, encouraging them to start such businesses. Through this network, around a thousand temples were built, which lacked spiritual energy but served as great picnic spots, and business opportunities. The income from these temples was akin to that of amusement parks like Disneyland. On social media, links to these temples' websites and discussions emerged, suggesting that certain businessmen and industrialists had invested in the construction of these temples, receiving returns from the income generated by these "fun parks." It became a business model where the Swamis were essentially employees, and God was the product, with Hindus as the consumers. Even today, the names of business trustees can be found in BAPS temples outside India, though they remain hidden within India.

At places developed like Poicha, which resemble amusement parks, there are statues of Shiva and Parvati serving Sahajanand Swami, and Hanuman serving another Swami. In place of Lord Vishnu on Sheshnaag, their new deity, Sahajanand Swami, sits with his left hand raised in blessing. However, the ignorant and spiritually dull Hindus, despite seeing all this, found nothing wrong with it. With the growing power of BAPS, the discussion began to arise: Why should we regard that man from UP (Ghanshyam Pandey/Sahajanand Swami) as God? Sahajanand Swami divided the sect into two parts and handed over the hereditary lineage to his nephews, whom he called from UP. BAPS, having built everything through their own efforts and funds, thought that God should be theirs. Thus, efforts began to deify Pramukh Swami, culminating in the grand celebration of Pramukh Swami's 100th birth anniversary festival in Ahmedabad.

On the final day of the festival, Swami Bhadresdas gathered all BAPS Swamis and led chants to fulfill this main objective, which was captured in a viral video. In that video, Bhadresdas said, "When the Gita says 'Yada Yada Hi Dharmasya Glanirbhavati…', to whom is it referring, whom is it talking about?" The chorus of Swamis responded, "Pramukh Swami Maharaj." Bhadresdas then asked, "To whom does it refer today?" and the crowd shouted, "Mahant Swami Maharaj." Hindu scriptures, including shlokas where Shri Krishna or Lord Vishnu are mentioned, were being linked to the former and current leaders of BAPS, attempting to present them as gods.

The most striking material I found about Pramukh Swami was from a book titled Shri Pramukh Swami Maharaj – Mahimnashtakam, the screenshot of which sparked controversy on Gujarati news channels. The text reads, "Perhaps the drops of the ocean can be counted, and the stars of the sky can be measured… but can the qualities of Pramukh Swami Maharaj be counted, even by gods like Brahma, Vishnu, and Shiva? Certainly not. Even Vyasa Muni, deeply involved in the creation of the Vedas and Puranas, was incapable of adequately praising you, O treasure house of virtues, Pramukh Swami Maharaj!"

Not only this, but the book Gunatitanand Swamini Vato—which BAPS uses as its foundational scripture by declaring Gunatitanand Swami as Sahajanand Swami's "Akshar"—is filled with distorted stories that belittle the deities of Sanatan Dharma. BAPS continually publishes this same book and Pramukh Swami has compared the book to the Brahmasutras.

In addition, BAPS has released comic-style books called Satsang Vihar, aimed at children, in which the message that Swaminarayan is superior to all the gods of Sanatan Dharma is instilled in the minds of the sect's young followers. Moreover, efforts have begun to elevate Pramukh Swami to the same level, placing him above the gods of Sanatan Dharma. For example, in Satsang Vihar Part 1, on page 26, there is a children's story called "Bada Karm Mein Marm" where it is said that Sahajanand Swami once rolled his eyes. When asked by a devotee, "What did you just do, Maharaj?" Swami replied, "In one Brahmand, Brahma, Vishnu, and Shiva were not getting along with the population, so I transferred them to another Brahmand and replaced them with new ones." In Satsang Vihar Part 2, on page 15, there is a story titled "Brahmaji Came in the Form of a Crow to Receive Prasadi," where a crow takes a piece of bread from Sahajanand Swami's plate. When asked what had happened, Sahajanand replied, "That was Brahmaji. He had been yearning for our prasadi for years, and today, he finally received it." Furthermore, in Satsang Vihar Part 1, on page 37, there is another story called "All Manifest in the Gunatit Saint," where Lord Shiva tells a devotee, "If you want moksha, go to Pramukh Swami."

Thus, even though you may not hear stories insulting the deities of Sanatan Dharma in BAPS Swamis' discourses, the most significant and systematic effort to cement such wicked writings has been done by them more than any other faction.

Additionally, I received writings and texts from the websites and books of other factions within the Swaminarayan sect.

From the Website of the Kalupur Swaminarayan Temple:

• It is written that Goddess Lakshmi came for darshan of Sahajanand and is depicted as his wife.

https://www.swaminarayan.in/our-sampraday/swaminarayan-faith/ghanshyam-charitra/laxmiji-visits-her-husband

• Sage Markandeya came in the form of a Brahmin to Sahajanand's home and performed his naming ceremony.

https://www.swaminarayan.in/our-sampraday/swaminarayan-faith/ghanshyam-charitra/markanday-names-ghanshyam

• Brahma, Vishnu, and Mahesh came to witness Sahajanand's Yajnopavit ceremony.

https://www.swaminarayan.in/our-sampraday/swaminarayan-faith/ghanshyam-charitra/janoi-yagnopavit

• When Sahajanand got injured while playing, Ashwini Kumaras descended from the heavenly realm to bandage him.

https://www.swaminarayan.in/our-sampraday/swaminarayan-faith/ghanshyam-charitra/khapa-talavdi

· Nar Narayan Dev from Badrikashram came to have darshan of Sahajanand.

https://www.swaminarayan.in/our-sampraday/swaminarayan-faith/ghanshyam-charitra/narnarayan-dev-arrive-for-ghanshyam-s-darshan

From the Book Shri Purushottam Lilamrut Sukhsagar, Published by the Bhuj Swaminarayan Temple:

· "At that time, Lord Shiva arrived with his attendants like Nandi and offered full prostrations to Shriji Maharaj (Sahajanand Swami), standing on one leg with folded hands, offering praise with his five mouths and beholding Maharaj with his fifteen eyes. At that time, Ganga, who was seated beside Shriji Maharaj, also offered her praise, tearfully saying, '…You have graced me with your presence to purify me.' Saying this, Lord Shankar left with his retinue." (Page 219)

· "Lord Shiva, having manifested in a physical form, folded his hands and bowed before Shri Hari (Sahajanand Swami), touching his feet and praying, 'O Maharaj! I have been waiting at this place for a long time, hoping to witness you. Today, you have blessed me with your darshan, and I am deeply grateful.'" (Page 223)

From the Book Sarvopari Shri Swaminarayan Bhagwan – Part 2, Published by Maninagar Swaminarayan Sect:

On page 227 of this book, there is an illustration showing Shiva and Parvati, along with Nandi, serving Sahajanand Swami in his Nilkanth Varni form. It states:

"Varni asked: 'Who are you? We do not eat food from unknown persons.' Shiva and Parvati replied, 'You have been hungry for five days, so we have brought this humble offering for you. Shiva said, 'O omniscient Lord! Though you know everything, still you ask. I am Shiva from Kailash, and this is Parvati.'"

Pleased with their service, Varni blessed them, saying, "I will keep you in my service." According to this promise, Shri Hari later installed statues of Shiva and Parvati in the Junagadh temple.

In another book published by the Maninagar Swaminarayan sect, titled Shri Sankalpmurti Sadguru Shri Gopalanand Swami's Stories, many distorted stories about Lord Shiva and Goddess Adya Shakti are narrated by Swami Gopalanand. In story 25, on pages 44, 45, and 46, the following can be found:

• "With a soft smile, Gopalanand Swami asked, 'Which god do you worship?' The young nobleman replied, 'I am a devotee of the goddess. My family deity is Mahishasuri and Chamunda.' To this, Sadguru Gopalanand Swami explained, 'Why do you worship these insignificant goddesses when you should be worshiping the supreme God? The worship of other gods and goddesses leads to nothing but the darkest hell and the cycle of birth and death. If you wish to attain the true purpose of this life, abandon the worship of deities and turn to the worship of our supreme Guru, Shri Swaminarayan Bhagwan, the cause of all causes.'" (Pages 44-45)

… "One night, as the nobleman slept, his family goddesses Mahishasuri and Chamunda appeared before him and said, 'Narupat, look! Both Hanumanji and Ganesha, the deities of your home, are chanting the name of Swaminarayan. They have raised their maces and are telling us to leave because you have become a follower of Satsang (Swaminarayan sect). From now on, you must only worship Swaminarayan, and we will take our leave.' After the goddesses left, even the eternal lamp that had been burning in his house for over a hundred years extinguished by itself. Seeing this, Narupat had a change of heart. The next morning, he woke up, removed the goddess's statue from his home, and cleaned the entire place, all while chanting the name of Swaminarayan." (Page 46)

In story 24, on page 39 of the same book, a story can be found where Lord Krishna is depicted in a lesser light. It tells the story of a man named Ramchandra, a devotee of Lord Krishna in his Ranchhod form at Dakor, who, after hearing Gopalanand Swami's teachings, became a follower of the Swaminarayan sect. In this sect, becoming a Satsangi is equivalent to being brainwashed. The text states, "Ramchandra still had doubts in his heart: 'How can I abandon my beloved deity, Ranchhodji?' With this in mind, he went to Dakor for the Sharad Purnima festival. After having darshan of Ranchhodji, he went to sleep. In his dream, Ranchhodji appeared and said, 'Why do you still harbor doubts, even after hearing the words of the great saint of Shri Swaminarayan Bhagwan? We are but servants of that Lord.'"

From the Book 'Sadguru Shri Gopalanand Swamiji no Mahima' by Kundaldham (part of Vadtal)

Now, we can see a very neat and clear explanation of how this sect aims to transform Sanatan Dharma into a monotheistic religion, similar to Islam and Christianity. Below is an excerpt from the book Sadguru Shri Gopalanand Swamiji no Mahima (Pages 9–10 of Gujarati version).

The Conversation Between Maharaj and Gopalanand Swami in Akshardham:

Shriji Maharaj (Swaminarayan aka Sahajanand Swami) asked Gopalanand Swami, "Swami, do you know why we have come here?" Swami replied, "No, Maharaj, I am unaware." Maharaj said, "You were seated as the original Aksharmukt in Akshardham, and we had a discussion there. We spoke about how this universe has been created for countless ages, yet no soul has reached Akshardham.

"We then sent incarnations like Dattatreya and Kapila, but no one reached Akshardham by worshipping them. Later, during the Treta Yuga, we sent Shri Ramchandra. At that time, human lifespans were 10,000 years, but Ramchandra himself stayed for 11,000 years. Yet, even he could not establish Ekantik Dharma (absolute monotheistic religion).

"Then we sent Shri Krishna. Despite his lifetime being a hundred years in that era, he lived for 125 years, but even he could not establish Ekantik Dharma.

"At that point, you said, 'Maharaj, those who worship the incarnations you send attain their respective divine realms. However, souls can only reach Akshardham when you, Purushottam (Supreme God), personally descend to Earth.'

"To this, we replied, 'When we descend to Earth, you too must accompany us.' You asked, 'What would be my role?' We explained, 'Your task will be to uphold Dharma (righteousness) and teach others to do the same. Through devotion, you will inspire others to devote themselves to God.' You said, 'Maharaj, if you are descending, how can I avoid coming?' That is why we brought an Asarmukt like you here."

Then Shriji Maharaj continued, "Swami, we have come to this Earth for six purposes." Maharaj then explained:

1. To bring back to Akshardham the incarnations we sent earlier.

2. To guide all those who have worshipped those incarnations to Akshardham.

3. To grant Ekantik Sukha (absolute bliss) through devotion and righteousness.

4. To establish Ekantik Dharma on this Earth.

5. To instill unwavering faith in Swaminarayan across all beings.

6. To create new Mukta (liberated souls).(643)

Gopalanand and Sarangpur:

I was given information about the Sarangpur temple of the Vadtal sect. According to this information, a temple has been built in Sarangpur where Hanumanji is depicted as a servant of Swaminarayan. The temple houses a monkey-shaped idol, which was created from the memorial stone of a man named Jiva Khachar. However, nowhere in the temple is there the phrase "Jai Shri Ram," nor are the chants of Lord Ram ever heard. Additionally, there is no Hanuman Chalisa inscribed or recited in the temple, as the Hanuman Chalisa repeatedly states that Hanuman is a devotee of Ram and an avatar of Shiva, based on descriptions from the Ramayana. Hence, they have composed a new Hanuman Aarti, in which the monkey-shaped figure in the temple is called Hanumanji and shown as a servant of Sahajanand Swami. In the texts of this sect, there are various images depicting Hanumanji serving Sahajanand Swami. In this way, the temple uses Hanuman to attract followers of Sanatan Dharma, only to then connect them to a new supreme god named Swaminarayan, aka Sahajanand Swami.

I was astonished that the innocent and ignorant people of Sanatan Dharma never asked the basic question: Hanuman is not merely a monkey name; you cannot just call any monkey statue Hanuman. Hanumanji is a character from the Ramayana and is solely devoted to Lord Ram. Even when he appears in the Mahabharata, he serves another avatar of Ram, Shri Krishna, but still worships Ram. This is who Hanumanji is. Where Ram is absent, where there is no Hanuman Chalisa, where there are no chants of Ram's glory, Hanuman cannot be depicted as a servant of anyone else.

Along with this, in a book of stories attributed to Gopalanand Swami, a disciple of Sahajanand Swami who created the monkey idol from Jiva Khachar's memorial stone, there are some vile references to Lord Shiva. In one place, it says, "Upon seeing Mohini, Shiva's semen was discharged. What kind of yogi is someone who still has semen in his body?" Another statement from the same book or another I came to read was saying, "Someone who repeatedly opens their third eye in anger cannot be called a yogi, but rather an egotist." Such disrespectful statements about Lord Shiva are found in the teachings of Gopalanand Swami. Earlier, we also saw the perversions written about Goddess Adya Shakti in the book of the Maninagar sect.

In some places it is also written that Gopalanand Swami was such a great yogi that even Shri Krishna and Hanumanji received their yogic powers from him. Therefore, the Sanatan warriors exposing the distortions of this sect have mockingly called Gopalanand "Gapgolanand" - the expert of fanatic lies. In the books of this sect, it is written that Gopalanand Swami worshiped the monkey-shaped idol of Salangpur, and through his devotion, he consecrated it and placed it in the temple. He later told one of his disciples, Govindanand, "Go and have darshan of that idol." When Govindanand went to bow at the feet of the idol and folded his hands in prayer, the idol (referred to as Hanumanji in the sect's writings) grasped his hands and said, "You don't need to fold your hands before me. You too are a servant of Gopalanand, and I am also a servant of Gopalanand. We are like fellow disciples." In another incident, the idol began to tremble through Gopalanand's devotion or some action, and it fell at his feet. And that statue they poses against Hindus as Hanumanji in Sarangpur temple.

Corrupted Images:

These images visually reinforce the distorted writings of the sect, but I do not wish to give the brainwashed followers of this sect any opportunity to harass this book by claiming ownership of those corrupted images. Therefore, I am providing a verbal description of the images here, along with a link where you can view them in a PDF.

- (pdf   Link: https://drive.google.com/file/d/1M30MdRqGcS4f799_YTV4BqV49_z2dbui/view?usp=sharing)

1. In a video from the Swaminarayan Kundaldham (SMK) YouTube channel, Sahajanand Swami, also known as Swaminarayan, is seated on a throne, with his disciples in saffron robes seated before him, and on the side, Brahma, Vishnu, Shiva, and other deities of Sanatan Dharma are standing

with folded hands before Sahajanand.

2. In another similar image, Sahajanand Swami, as Swaminarayan, is blessing Brahma, Vishnu, Shiva, Saraswati, Lakshmi, and Parvati with both hands, while a temple spire from their sect is visible in the background.

3. In the book Ghanshyam Charitra, there is an image where, after child Ghanshyam gets injured, Indra, Chandra, Brahma, Vishnu, and others come to visit him (Page 39).

4. In Sarvopari Shri Swaminarayan Bhagwan – Part 2, there is a picture where Shiva and Parvati are asking for permission to serve Sahajanand Swami, standing with folded hands before him. This same imaginary event is depicted in statues in a garden in Poicha.

5. Numerous pictures in the sect's books depict Hanumanji serving Sahajanand Swami, sitting below him with folded hands. In some places, these have also been made into murals and statues. (Some of these images have been removed due to strong opposition from Sanatan followers, but they remain in the books.)

6. On the day of Prabodhini Ekadashi in the month of Kartik, when the wedding season begins for Hindus with the marriage of Lord Vishnu and Tulsi, this sect instead performs the wedding of Tulsi with Sahajanand Swami, replacing Lord Vishnu. A picture of this event is provided.

7. On the day of Mahashivratri, instead of performing the ritual of Abhishek of the Shivling, this sect performs the abhishek (bathing ritual) of Nilkanth Varni, another name of Sahajanand Swami. In this way, they have sidelined Lord Shiva and replaced the sacred Shivratri day, associated with him, with Sahajanand Swami under the name Nilkanth Varni.

8. During Navratri, where traditionally Garba is sung in devotion to Goddess Amba, this practice is forbidden in the Swaminarayan sect. There is a video of the current BAPS leader, Mahant Swami, comparing Garba to playing with dolls, rejecting the tradition. Also a video is there where Pramukh Swami is pointing Navaratri Garba as Disco by saying never go there even if one gives you ten million rupees. Instead, they sing Garba for just one day, on Sharad Purnima, with Sahajanand Swami in the center. Pictures of this event are included in their announcements.

9. On Ashadhi Beej, when the Jagannath Rath Yatra takes place, this sect conducts its own Rath Yatra of Sahajanand Swami on the same day, placing Sahajanand Swami above and Lord Krishna below. In BAPS Rath Yatras, Sahajanand Swami's image is placed above, with the sect's leader below, followed by Lord Krishna. They do the same during Ganesh Chaturthi,

where Sahajanand Swami's statue or image is placed above, with Lord Ganesha below.

Decision to Act:

All this distortion was enough to shock and appall me, and I know that it has likely had the same effect on you, especially if you were unaware of these facts before. The conclusion was clear: before Sahajanand Swami arrived in Gujarat, the Uddhav sect led by Ramanand Swami followed Krishna devotion and was a Vaishnav sect. They sang the chant "Radhe Shyam Govind," and the followers of this sect were called Hari Bhaktas because Lord Krishna is an incarnation of Shri Hari, who is Lord Vishnu. However, after Ramanand Swami's death, when the sect came under Sahajanand Swami's leadership, he introduced a new mantra called "Swaminarayan" for Krishna devotion. In 1824, he wrote the Shikshapatri, where he stated that the supreme god is none other than Purnapurushottam Bhagwan Shri Krishna, who is his personal deity, and he commanded the sect's followers to worship only Lord Shri Krishna as the supreme god, along with the Panchadev Upasana (worship of the five principal deities). This was in line with what was already followed in other Vaishnav traditions, where Lord Vishnu or Krishna is the main god, and the other four deities are his manifestations. However, after Sahajanand Swami's death, or after 1824 to his later life, a transformation occurred that caused the sect to deviate from the Sanatan Hindu Dharma.

In the Vedas, the name Narayan originated as the name of Lord Vishnu. In the Rig Veda, which is the first Veda, Vishnu is given the highest position as a supreme deity. In the Yajurveda, it is mentioned that because water (Neer) emerged from Vishnu's feet, he is also called Narayan. Thus, Vishnu is the main name, which is why there is the Vishnu Purana and not a Narayan Purana. And this is where the distortion in the sect occurred. The name "Narayan," which belongs to Lord Vishnu, was separated from him, and a new god named Swaminarayan, i.e., Sahajanand Swami, was created. And since the Krishna devotees of this sect were called Hari Bhaktas, they continued to be called so, and the names Hari and ShriJi, which belong to Lord Vishnu, were adopted by this new god, Swaminarayan, i.e., Sahajanand Swami. After that, a whole conspiracy was developed to bring the entire Sanatan Dharma under this new god and wipe out the original traditions, incorporating influences from both Islam and Christianity.

This conspiracy to destroy Sanatan Dharma is such that the followers of this sect are prohibited from worshiping any deity other than Swaminarayan or keeping any images or idols of other gods. In BAPS, only the paired idols of Swaminarayan and his disciple Gunatitanand Swami are permitted. They are forbidden to worship any other god, and to enforce this prohibition, the gods of Sanatan Dharma are mocked and belittled in their literature and discourses. Their aim is to create a sense of hesitation and inferiority in worshiping these deities. All the festivals connected to Lord Vishnu, Shiva, and Goddess Shakti in Hindu society are paralleled by this sect, which associates these festivals with their new god. This sect is more dangerous than Islam or Christianity because, while Islam directly imposes a new god named Allah and Christians impose Jesus Christ, this sect pretends to honor our gods while gradually deceiving Hindus and leading them to a new supreme god. Eventually, Hindus themselves end up mocking the very deities they have worshiped for thousands of years. This is the true danger. This is the most serious attack in the history of Hinduism because it is an internal distortion within Hinduism itself. We have traced the roots of how and by whom this distortion was brought into the sect, which we will explore later in this book.

With this realization, I decided to take action. The day was December 15, 2022, the second day after the inauguration of the Pramukh Swami 100th Birth anniversary festival.

III

Blowing the Trumpet

Prime Minister Narendra Modi inaugurated the festival. The Pramukh Swami 100th Birth Anniversary Festival, which was to last for a month in Ahmedabad, became a new attraction for the public of Gujarat. This was the same crowd that spent their weekends at the sect's temples, which resemble fun parks and tourist spots. They now had another spot to visit, take selfies, and post on social media for a month. Narendra Modi attended on the first day. The Home Minister of India, Amit Shah, was yet to come, as were the national chief of the RSS, Mohan Bhagwat, Foreign Minister S. Jaishankar, Railway Minister Ashwini Vaishnaw, who was to dedicate a train named Akshardham, and many renowned artists, saints, and prominent figures from Gujarat. Days were set for each of them during the month-long event. On the first day, Narendra Modi's inauguration photos and videos spread across social media, and the praise for Pramukh Swami was so high that it seemed the only thing left was to declare him a god.

However, in the midst of all this, the truth I highlighted in the previous chapter had already reached a section of aware Sanatanis. They were like the defeated Avengers from Thanos, heartbroken and looking for ways to endure the coming days. The political party and the popular leader they voted for in the name of Hindutva, and the organizations they held in esteem, were all deeply immersed in this festival. In this situation, on the second day of the festival, with a photo of Narendra Modi's inauguration, I published my first article on this journey, on Facebook.

Title: On the Occasion of Pramukh Swami Maharaj's 100th Birth Anniversary, a Message from the Hindu Community

to Swaminarayan Organizations

· December 15, 2022 / Facebook

"First of all, I bow to the divine soul of Pramukh Swami Maharaj on his 100th birth anniversary, and I pray that this divine soul inspires the world to illuminate the true essence of the Supreme Truth. This prayer is necessary because large-scale festivals and political and commercial involvement cannot divert attention from the distortions that have surfaced since the passing of Pramukh Swami Maharaj. Therefore, I also pray to the BAPS, the most successful of the Swaminarayan organizations, to engage in deep self-reflection during this month-long festival. They must cleanse their writings of the distorted passages that insult the supreme gods of Sanatan Dharma—Shiva, Rama, and Krishna—and purge this mindset from their monks.

Sanatan Dharma has many sects, but no sect wishes to place its revered Guru or founder above Shiva or Vishnu. They all understand the fundamental principle of Sanatan Dharma, the primordial energy known as Brahm, which was the original light form at the beginning of creation, manifested as Shiva and Mahavishnu chronologically. From the navel of this Mahavishnu, countless Brahmas emerged, and each of them created their own universe. Thus, the essence of the universe is Brahm, and the supreme forms of Brahm are none other than Mahavishnu and Shiva. There is nothing beyond or above them. Therefore, any divine person who appears in the world carries the divinity of either Mahavishnu or Shiva. This is why, in all sects of Sanatan Dharma, the founders of those sects have, at most, been regarded as incarnations of Shiva or Vishnu. Many such incarnations of Shiva and Vishnu are currently worshiped. But your sect does not declare your founder to be an incarnation of Vishnu. Instead, you place him outside of the framework of Sanatan Dharma and the entire cosmos and seat him as the ruler above both Shiva and Vishnu. This individual lived just a few hundred years ago. After great figures like Rana Pratap and Shivaji struggled to keep Sanatan Dharma alive, you now place someone born after them as the king and ruler of the entire Sanatan Dharma. During this month-long celebration of Pramukh Swami Maharaj's centenary, the BAPS should clarify to all Hindus of this nation whether they hold the same view as other factions of the Swaminarayan sect. If not, then how do they view

Sahajanand Swami—whom they also call Bhagwan Swaminarayan—relative to Bhagwan Shiva and Bhagwan Vishnu?

This clarification is necessary because even the scriptures of foreign religions that this Hindu populace fights against do not say what your saffron-clad members regularly claim. Until today, no Muslim or Christian has dared to speak as disrespectfully about Hindu gods as your members frequently do. Foreign religions claim their god is the only true one and that our gods are false. But you say that, yes, all our gods are real, but they are merely servants of your god, who lived only a few hundred years ago. So, tell us, which of these two is more insulting? Who should we consider the greater enemy?

Therefore, do not remain silent by merely placing idols of Rama, Krishna, and Shiva-Parvati in your temples. Cleanse your writings of the distortions that have painted them in such a way and come within the framework of Sanatan Dharma. Which Hindu has a problem with Vishnu-Narayan, the ruler of the universe? Everyone is a devotee of him. Even your Sahajanand Swami, who gave the 'Swaminarayan' mantra, promoted Krishna devotion. The idols in your temples were also originally of Narayan Krishna. But then you turned Sahajanand Swami into Narayan himself and declared Krishna's idols to be his. Even this, we can accept, assuming that you worship him as a tiny incarnation of Lord Krishna. But no, your writings and your monks' discourses show that you have found a place above Narayan Shri Vishnu and have seated Sahajanand Swami there, giving him the name 'Swaminarayan.' And now, you have begun portraying Mahadev Shiva as a subordinate god, as if he is just a minor deity who keeps company with drunkards. The Hindu community of the rest of India is still unaware of this insult to their Shiva and Narayan Shri Vishnu. When they find out, the storm that will arise will be one you cannot withstand.

Yes, we are also aware that you are using your wealth to infiltrate the Sanatan Hindu institutions of this nation. But even they do not know your true nature. They, like the Gujarati Hindu community did for years, imagine that the Narayan in 'Swaminarayan' is their Vishnu Narayan. Perhaps even Modiji is still in the dark about this. But nothing is hidden anymore, so stop trying to keep people in the dark by constantly presenting the life of Pramukh Swami Maharaj. Provide clarity. If you don't, it will mean that you also hold the same beliefs but are avoiding saying it outright to propagate deeper into Hindu society.

Moral: Anyone with even the basic sattvic nature of an ordinary person would never imagine insulting someone else's deity while worshiping their own. When you are immersed in devotion, your mind is solely focused on love. But when your focus is on belittling others deity, understand that your mind is not even on your own deity. It is not on devotion. It is consumed by envy, hatred, and ego. You want to make yourself superior to someone by using your deity as a tool for dominance. If you supervise just this much spiritual understanding, the entire situation will become clear."

This article received a great response. Among my friends in the Sangh and the BJP, there were various reactions. Some close friends messaged me immediately, saying, "I always felt there was something off about this sect. We recently visited a Swaminarayan temple in America, and all the talk there was only about Swaminarayan, as if nothing else existed. It felt strange." Others were shocked by the article, as they too were immersed in the praise of Pramukh Bapa and took pride in being associated with the sect. Some close friends in the Sangh and BJP, when we met in person, said, "Sir, you've taken up an important issue. It's necessary. This group is terrible. Do what you must."

But on the other hand, I was receiving different kinds of messages from across Gujarat. Many new individuals from among the scattered Sanatani warriors came to my timeline because of the article. These individuals were responding to the comments made by people influenced by the sect, using the writings, videos, and images I had shared in the previous chapter to reply. Some of these disheartened warriors wrote, "Sir, we've said and done a lot, but nothing seems to work. This corrupt sect has strong support from the authorities and Hindu organizations." Below this, another warrior would reply, "No, no. Look at the level of this article. This is on a different plane. We simply hurl abuses. We need to speak like this now."

In general, the response was good. It seemed that the common Hindus got exactly what they were looking for. They also believed that such things could not be said publicly. Some were momentarily shocked and were waiting to see what would happen next.

What happened next was that the RSS chief, Mohan Bhagwatji, attended the festival. While the sect's people were projecting Narendra Modi's photos as if he were the brand ambassador for an advertisement, Sanatanis already had photos and videos of Modi with Asaram Bapu and of his presence at

Muslim and Christian events. The message being conveyed was that a leader has to cater to everyone, and just because a leader attends an event doesn't mean their spiritual leader is recognized as a god. However, after Mohan Bhagwatji attended, there was not much logic to make such clarifications. So, on that day, I wrote another article.

Title: Do These Hindu Organizations and Hindu Political Parties Know the Reality of the Swaminarayan Sect?

· December 22, 2022 / Facebook

"Modiji said there, 'Shiva exists within every being.' Mohan Bhagwatji said, 'Saint Tukaram used to say that Vaikunthavasi (Shri Vishnu) must come down to Earth to show that what the sages have said is true.' While highlighting the greatness of these two supreme pillars of Sanatan Dharma (Shiva and Vishnu), did these two respected figures fully understand the true nature of this sect? - This is the fundamental question that remains. Because here, Vaikunth has no significance. Instead, above everything, there is a god called Swaminarayan whose Akshardham is the ultimate realm, where Vishnu and Shiva are relegated to the eighth level as minor deities. These two deities stand as courtiers in Akshardham, paying their respects to Swaminarayan. Only those who have lived within this sect on Earth get to go there. Others who have indulged in alcohol or other vices end up in Shiva's realm, Kailash. According to the books of BAPS, going to Vaikunth, Golok, or Kashi means enduring the threefold miseries, and true liberation is only found in Akshardham. Compared to Akshardham, these other realms are like hell. The time has come for the truth about this sect to be made known to the entire Sangh Parivar (RSS) and the Sanatani Hindu family of the nation.

The people of BAPS have arranged for their Swami Bhadreshdas to obtain a PhD in Sanskrit from Bangalore, and they are now trying to propagate the idea that he has developed a 'seventh darshan'—the 'Akshar Purushottam Darshan'—after the six major Vedic darshans of Indian philosophy. This has been in the works for the past four or five years. Slowly, they are beginning to present this as equivalent to the other darshans and are attempting to gain recognition for it in Kashi through financial means. This philosophy establishes a chart where Swaminarayan, as the embodied

Parabrahm, is at the top, and step by step, Brahma, Vishnu, and Mahesh are placed at the seventh and eighth levels. However, the flaw in their thinking is that in all other traditions, if any form of the embodied Parabrahm is shown as supreme, it is always in the form of Shiva or Vishnu. According to the foundation of Sanatan Dharma, the supreme embodied forms of Brahm are none other than Shiva and Vishnu, who belong to the group of Panchdev. These people are presenting Swaminarayan as an embodied god and calling him Parabrahm. But in Hindu Sanatan Dharma, Parabrahma is a formless entity represented as Om. When this formless Parabrahma takes on form, it manifests as Shiva, Vishnu, Goddess Shakti, Sun, and Ganesh. These people are inserting another embodied form, a human, above Panchdev, making this human their boss. This is where they step outside the boundaries of Vedic and Sanatan Dharma.

This is exactly like what happened in the Arabian society of deities when they placed a supreme Allah above all the other gods and created a new religion called Islam. Similarly, in the society of Jewish deities, the God of Jesus' father was placed above all to establish Christianity. These people are attempting to change the form of Hindu Dharma by placing a supreme god above the current deities. The difference is that Islam and Christianity completely rejected the old gods of their previous societies, while these people retain the old gods as their servants and subordinates. Because no one comes to their temples for Swaminarayan alone. The crowds that flock to their temples are drawn by Hanuman and Shiva, whom they have kept as servants to generate revenue. And they are using that money to spread their Islamic and Christian-like religious model."

After this article, supporters of the sect who had infiltrated the Sangh and BJP came forward to defend the sect, using the argument that one should not create divisions among Hindus. Meanwhile, some writers and journalists, whom the sect had won over by inviting them to their temples, honoring them at various events, and bestowing awards, became more active in praising the service work of the sect and Pramukh Swami. In response, I continued to write one article after another, breaking through their cover fire.

Title: A Message to Those Praise and Recognition Hungry Gujaratis Who Are Willing to Pawn Their Religion and

Gods for Positions, Money, and Prestige

· January 9, 2023 / Facebook

When the British arrived in India, they began in the same way. By praising kings and influential people, giving them gifts, titles, and honors, they brought them under their control. Using their influence, they established rule over the rest of the common people. And once they had gained control over the country's administration, they imposed their dominance and tyranny even over those kings and influential people. It was this model that the British used to establish their power in India, and it is this same model that kept their power intact. Even today, the left-wing lobby of Europe and America follows this model to dominate narratives across the world. The Swaminarayan sect, and especially the BAPS organization, operates exactly like this. They invite today's writers, doctors, politicians, and TV personalities to give speeches at their events, or they go to their locations to honor them with awards and recognition, persuading them to praise the sect and thereby bewildering the common people. This model is precisely what the British used.

Under this model only, Pramukh Swami had arranged a meeting with Abdul Kalam, who, with his gentle words on religion, persuaded the innocent Dr. Kalam to author a book. The book's cover was widely promoted, but, like those fake temples, its impact has remained hollow and ineffective. Abdul Kalam, a Muslim by birth, stood for a genuinely secular lifestyle that is noticeable at a glance, yet the content of the book touches no one, as it is part of a deception. Under this same deception, all those considered close to Prime Minister Narendra Modi in Gujarat today are under BAPS's influence. This reveals that Indians are still hungry for power, wealth, and prestige, willing to mortgage their religion and deities for fame and money. Even today, the lives and characters of these influential people are so hollow that they can be bought by flatterers with evil intentions, leading the common people into yet another form of slavery.

Where they do not yet have a foothold, this sect starts by getting doctors and businessmen to display their sect's photos in their offices and have the sect's mark applied on their foreheads. They then try to bring customers to those doctors and businessmen. They give them awards and recognition, making them bigger so that others follow suit, thus pulling the common people into the sect. This is how they bring columnists in newspapers and minor and major politicians into their fold and elevate them. Now, they have also infiltrated the Rashtriya Swayamsevak Sangh (RSS) under the guise of staunch Muslim opposition. This began around 2015 when a national-level RSS meeting was held at a Swaminarayan temple in Kutch. The sect knows that gaining a majority within the Sangh means gaining control of the state and national power through the BJP, and like the Buddhists and Christians, establishing their sect throughout the country through political power.

But what this sect truly is, none of these doctors, businessmen, writers, or politicians has ever tried to understand. They have only focused on the positions, money, recognition, and votes they receive. And what is this sect? Since the birth of Sanatan Hindu civilization on this Earth, they are the only people—who, not only their founder but even the subsequent leaders of the institution from time to time, have declared as being the supreme rulers of the universe above Narayan Shri Vishnu and Mahadev Shiva. They violate the spiritual and religious tenets given in the scriptures of Sanatan Dharma, insulting Hindu gods, but still narrate stories from the same Hindu scriptures. Like the legal book of Islam, they have their own legal book, the Shikshapatri, which lays down strict rules for how people should live in society. Here, liberation does not make a person one with Parabrahm. The soul that attains liberation is stationed in the service of their founder, who is the embodied Parabrahm, and of their leaders who represent the Akshar form. Liberation from the world here means being enslaved by a supreme god in a heaven called Akshardham. It is exactly the same as what a true Muslim gets after following the commands of the Quran and what a Christian receives after living according to the Bible.

They dismember the form of Hindu Sanatan Dharma without understanding its core philosophy, and insult its supreme deities, yet still claim that they are Hindus. In this way, they deceive the entire Hindu society and slowly convert it. Their children's literature is filled with stories that constantly insult the supreme Trinity of Sanatan Dharma, instilling these ideas in young minds. Meanwhile, the influential people of Gujarat I have described above, driven by the desire for some fleeting praise and recognition, are preparing the way to impose the slavery of these people on the common Hindu populace.

Wake up, my friends. You fought and freed yourselves from the British and Muslims, but now you are becoming the instruments of people who are attempting to impose their own version of this same system on the Hindu society. Stop right here, be vigilant about your history. One day, this society will wake up and overthrow these people. Just think, on that day, how will this society, and your descendants, remember you? Will they remember you as heroes who fought against this corrupt invasion on Sanatan Dharma, or as cowards and traitors who empowered this invasion for a moment of recognition and praise? Whenever these people appear in the Sangh, Sanatan Hindu followers should immediately start questioning them face-to-face. Discuss the form and descriptions of Indian scriptures and stop them right there. This is an issue of society, not politics. As a cultural and social organization, the Sangh's responsibility lies in addressing this situation. This is no time for silence.

"*Dharma Rakshati Rakshitah:*
   'He who protects Dharma is protected by Dharma.'"

ॐ

When the Hindu Society Was Robbed of Its Narayan Shri Hari…

• January 15, 2023 / Facebook

"Let's start with basic information: among the many names of Mahavishnu in the Hindu scriptures, the three main names are Shrihari, Shrinarayan, and Shrivishnu. Now, Ramanand Swami was running the Uddhav sect in Gadhada, where devotion to Lord Krishna, in the form of Narayan, was prevalent. The devotees who came to the ashram and were connected to the sect were called Hari Bhaktas, as they worshiped Krishna in the form of Narayan. This very sect was passed into the hands of Sahajanand Swami, who declared that the supreme God, Purna Purushottam Shri Krishna Bhagwan, was their primary deity and gave the people the 'Swaminarayan' mantra, asking them to chant it while practicing devotion to Krishna. He established two main Krishna temples, where the deities of Lakshmi-Narayan and Nar-Narayan were installed, representing two relationships of Lord Vishnu as depicted in the Srimad Bhagavat and Vishnu Purana: one with Bhagwati Shri as Lakshmi and the other as Nar with a male companion. Along with these, Sahajanand Swami established several other Krishna temples, including Revati Baldevji Temple in Jetalpur, Murlimanohar Dev Temple in Dholka, Madanmohanji Maharaj Temple in Dholera, Gopinathji Maharaj Temple in Gadhada, and Radharaman Dev Temple in Junagadh.

However, it is unclear where things began to corrupt after this, so let us directly refer to the PDF available on the BAPS website titled Sahajanand Charitra, where the distortion begins very quickly. After Sahajanand Swami became the head of the Uddhav sect, it is written that he gave the devotees a Swaminarayan mantra, which praised his own form, and then used the words Shrihari and Narayan to refer to himself. Let's assume that he declared himself an avatar of Vishnu, and the people of that time accepted him. That could be a personal matter between the two. But then, the writings start distorting the spirituality, science, and form of Hindu scriptures. It is written that the abode of Shrihari Swaminarayan is Akshardham, where Brahma, Vishnu, and Shiva along with all other deities bow before him and pay their respects. As it continues, it openly states that both Shiva and Vishnu, along with other gods and goddesses, stand with folded hands in reverence to Swaminarayan. In other words, the name Narayan is slowly separated from Lord Vishnu and is given to Swaminarayan, who is seated in Akshardham, a realm separate from Vaikuntha, where all the other gods of Hinduism, including Shiva and Vishnu, are his servants.

In other words, the entire Sanatan Hindu Dharma is enslaved under this new invader, a deity or man named Swaminarayan. Where did this Babaji come from? Where is his origin? Naturally, no Hindu scripture contains any mention of him, and neither do any of the texts of this sect. This Akshardham, which is not found in any Hindu scriptures, has suddenly emerged above the entire religious structure of Sanatan Dharma, above even Vaikuntha and Kailasa. In Hindu scriptures, there are detailed descriptions in every Purana of how Shiva and Vishnu originated from the cosmic energy of Parabrahm and how they began creating the universe.

So, wake up, my friends. Even a common, pious individual who worships Gayatri, Maa Amba, Kalbhairav, or Ram, Krishna, Hanuman, or Mahadev Shiva does not display the low-mindedness to think that other deities are inferior to their chosen deity and are their servants paying homage. They focus their mind on their own devotion, centered on their deity, while still respecting other gods as forms of Parabrahm, as stated in the Hindu scriptures. Even a 10-15 year old child or teenager has enough purity and divinity to avoid thinking like that. Yet you have gone so far as to create a new supreme deity by stealing Vishnu's name, writing numerous texts to support this distortion. Another point to mention is that Pramukh Swami, whom you are now preparing to elevate as a new god, was fully aware of all this, and much of it was written and promoted under his leadership.

Therefore, the next time Pramukh Swami Maharaj appears on the moon or the sun, or to some thief, kindly ask him to come out and clarify who authored these distorted, anti-Sanatan Hindu Dharma texts and why they were allowed to continue under his leadership. "The one I worship must be the supreme above all others so that my position appears to be the highest"—this childish mindset is not that of a devotee but of a power-hungry hypocrite. But for you to go so far as to separate Hari and Narayan from Vishnu and attempt to establish a new god and realm over the entire Sanatan Dharma—this makes you unique in the history of Bharat. And deep down, you know that one day, the entire Hindu society will rise against you. That's why, in the first pages of all your PDFs, you fill people's minds with extreme declarations like 'We will live for Shriji and die for Shriji,' which is similar to what is written in the religious texts of Islam. Like them, your followers aggressively declare that 'We have been told that, in the end, only we will remain, and there will be no one else.' No Hindu scripture contains any such text advocating such extremism for any god or sect. Hindu scriptures do not teach fighting or dying for any god. They only speak of attaining self-realization through the path of devotion and establishing Dharma in the world."

౮

Now, in the previous chapter, we have already learned that the most distorted writings are found in the books of BAPS. We have examined these writings in their Akshar Purushottam Upasana and the three biographies of Sahajanand Swami. The same ideas are found in the book of Gunatitanand Swami's Discourses (called 'Gunatitanand Swami ni Vato'). He is the same Gunatitanand who lays the foundation for BAPS separating from the original sect. This book contains the most distorted statements that demean the supreme deities of Sanatan Dharma. When praising this book, Pramukh Swami even compared it to the Brahmsutras. The vigilant warriors of Sanatan Dharma gathered information from that book, which I compiled into an article that I shared on my timeline on January 21, 2023.

The proof that Pramukh Swami was aware of and endorsed these distorted teachings...

The BAPS Swaminarayan sect has a book titled Discourses of Swami by Gunatitanand Swami. It contains 386 pages. Pramukh Swami, while blessing this book on February 3, 1990, wrote: "The discourses of Gunatitanand Swami are like the Brahmsutras. They are wonderful discourses. One must read them regularly to attain everlasting peace. Everyone should read these discourses thoughtfully to understand the principles and mysteries of Shriji Maharaj (Sahajanand Swami, who lived from April 3, 1781, to June 1, 1830)!" Another book containing these discourses, published on October 27, 2006, by Swaminarayan Mandir Kundaldham and Swaminarayan Mandir Karelibaug, Vadodara, is titled Sadguru Shri Gunatitanand Swami's Discourses and contains 428 pages.

What's written in Discourses of Swami?

1. Sahajanandji is far greater than Indra, Brahma, Vishnu, and Shiva!
"All the beings, animals, kings, and subjects of this Earth will perish if Indra does not cause rain to fall. Indra, Brahma, Vishnu, and Shiva do not even count in comparison; all of them, including Brahma, Vishnu, and Shiva, do not compare to Virat. Virat does not compare to the Pradhan Purush. The Pradhan Purush does not compare to Akshar. And beyond Akshar is Purushottam (Sahajanandji), whom we have met directly!" (Chapter 1, Discourse 217)

2. Sahajanandji is superior to Brahma, Vishnu, Shiva, Ram, Krishna, and others! He is the origin of all avatars. The cause of all causes! There is no one above Sahajanandji! Akshardham is superior to Goloka and Vaikuntha!
"Those who consider Maharaj (Sahajanand) to be like Krishna will reach Goloka. Those who consider him like Ramchandraji will reach Vaikuntha. Those who consider him like Vasudeva will reach Shvetadweep. Those who consider him like Nar-Narayan will reach Badrikashram. But those who know Maharaj as the origin of all avatars and the Lord of Akshardham will reach Akshardham!" (Chapter 2, Discourse 2)

"In Gadhada, Shriji Maharaj told a devotee, 'Go and visit Akshardham.' The devotee then went into a trance and first arrived at Badrikashram, where he saw our monks, followers, and devotees. He asked, 'Where is Shriji Maharaj?' All of them said, 'This Nar-Narayan is Shriji Maharaj!' The devotee responded, 'No, I recognize Maharaj!' Then the devotee went to Shvetadweep, where he saw the same thing and asked, 'Where is Shriji Maharaj?' The reply was, 'This Vasudeva is Shriji Maharaj!' Again, the devotee said, 'No, I know Maharaj!' Then he went to Vaikuntha, where the same thing occurred, and he asked, 'Where is Shriji Maharaj?' They replied, 'This Lakshminarayan is Shriji Maharaj!' Once again, the devotee said, 'No, I know Maharaj!' Then the devotee went to Goloka and saw the same thing, asking, 'Where is Shriji Maharaj?' They responded, 'This Shri Krishna is Shriji Maharaj!' The devotee again said, 'No, I know Maharaj!' Finally, the devotee arrived in Akshardham and saw Shriji Maharaj. There, he saw our monks, brahmacharis, followers, and devotees serving Shriji Maharaj. Shriji Maharaj asked him, 'What places have you visited?' The devotee replied, 'Maharaj, I have seen our monks, brahmacharis, followers, and devotees in the other realms. Why aren't they here?' Shriji Maharaj replied, 'They believe me to be the Lord of those particular realms, so they reside there. But those who recognize me as the origin of all avatars and as the Lord of Akshardham are here with me in Akshardham!'" (Chapter 7, Discourse 15)

3. "Those who equate other realms with Akshardham or other avatars with Maharaj are even greater sinners than the five most sinful people and should not be associated with!" (Chapter 6, Discourse 20)

Well, if you want to know the real meanings of these Pradhan, and Purush from Hindu scriptures, we have given it in chapter 18 of this book. When you read it, you find this unattained fanatic description funny enough to laugh out. But read it when the book reaches there. We are passing through an important journey, just walk with it.

IV

Society and Sangh

The chain of articles from the previous chapter created waves across the Hindu society of Gujarat. These articles were not just gaining a mere hundred or so likes on Facebook. The information they provided was something that people were experiencing but were unaware of. Even if they were aware, they were too afraid to speak out. They would silently express their displeasure or sometimes sigh deeply and say, "The current ruling power is favoring them, so we have to endure it." Stories about this sect acquiring land illegally, committing financial fraud, and engaging in the sexual exploitation of women and children were frequently visible in society. Additionally, the behavior, conduct, and atmosphere surrounding the sect's monks felt strange, impure, and unappealing to a simple, pious individual. People seemed to understand the phrase "religion as business" by observing this sect.

When these articles started circulating in WhatsApp groups of Gujaratis living in India and abroad, we began receiving numerous testimonies from Hindus about their experiences with the sect. In this chapter, we will discuss the Hindu society and the Sangh that has been deceived and trapped by the sect's outward appearance of being Hindu.

After the last article of the previous chapter, I received a call from a Patel brother in Ahmedabad. He asked, "Are you the one writing about the Swaminarayan sect?" I was prepared for any follower of the sect to confront me, so I replied firmly, "Yes, it's me. What do you want?" Immediately, the voice on the other end said, "What you are doing is absolutely right. But you are just scratching the surface by talking about spiritual matters. What lies beneath is far more disturbing than you can imagine."

I replied, "My concern is with how this sect has gone against the scriptures and deities of Sanatan Dharma, as this poses a threat to the entire future of Hindu civilization. As for their internal corruption involving land, sexual exploitation, and other abuses, that's for individuals to reflect upon and decide for themselves."

The Patel brother responded, "But sir, the control they exert starts from there itself. First, they took over Surat, and now they are trying to dominate Ahmedabad. If you want to do good business and seek benefits, you have to apply their tilak. It makes a huge difference, from government offices to other places. On the other hand, in the household, women are brainwashed into believing that their Ghanshyam Pandey (Sahajanand Swami) is more important than even their husbands. He is the one who will lead them to Akshardham. They test the elderly women by taking exams where questions are asked like, 'Where did Hanuman serve Ghanshyam Maharaj?' and 'Where did Lord Shiva seek his service?' All of this is done to keep their minds fixated on these ideas. So, what you are doing is good, but the problem is massive, and it needs to be addressed on a larger scale." I thanked him for his support and assured him that I would take his advice seriously.

In addition, two Brahmin couples reached out to me with similar issues. One met me in person, and the other, an elderly man, messaged me. Both had daughters married to NRIs in the United States. Despite belonging to Brahmin families, their educated sons-in-law were deeply entangled in this sect. Their joint complaint was, "Our daughter, raised in a Brahmin household, is now in a home where no deity or photo of any god other than Ghanshyam Maharaj is allowed. No Ram dhun or Krishna bhajan is played because, according to them, all of these gods are merely servants of their new god. Our sons-in-law are completely blind in their devotion, and even our six- or seven-year-old grandson speaks like them. It feels like we've married our daughter into a Muslim family."

One of the daughters contacted me through a message, saying, "Sir, my father sent me your articles, and I told him that everything you wrote is true. My husband is completely brainwashed. He walks around with a tilak on his forehead and donates a large portion of his earnings every week. There's even competition among the followers to see who can donate more, as those who give more are pampered by the monks and allowed deeper access. Can you talk to my husband? I am very troubled."

I told her, "Sister, from what I have seen of the followers of this sect over the past month, they are like brainwashed sheep, no different from fundamentalist Muslims who want to establish their god over the entire world. But these people have the capacity to convert only Hindus, so they are doing it. If their conscience or inner soul awakens, perhaps something can be done. Otherwise, whenever you find a rational point in my articles, use it to counter their arguments. Be patient and persistent."

I came across information about a Patel family whose son had gone to Australia for studies and had been brainwashed by this sect's monks. After a few years, when his marriage was arranged and he returned for the wedding, he had become so indoctrinated that he refused to allow a photo or verse of Lord Ganesha on his wedding invitation. He set various conditions, insisting that only Swaminarayan rituals be performed during the wedding and that every page of the invitation must feature only this new god's image and name, as all other deities are considered his servants. This created a rift in the family just as the wedding preparations were underway. His father had expressed his deep disappointment to one of my friends.

After learning about these cases, I began investigating the alarming rate at which conversions were happening overseas. First, I listened to some information from a dentist friend who had been my college mate. He said, "My sister and brother-in-law live in Australia. This sect targets new immigrants during their initial struggles. They help them find jobs, provide accommodation, and arrange meals. In return, you are required to attend their sermons, which are held twice a week and glorify Ghanshyam Pandey as the supreme god while also drawing from other Hindu scriptures. They also insist that you bring along other friends. If you don't comply or follow their teachings, they gradually distance themselves from you. But if you go along with it, they help you get settled, even arranging permanent residency. However, once you're settled, you must donate a certain percentage of your earnings to their temple for life. And people do it happily because up to that point in time, they are brainwashed. My sister and brother-in-law got caught up in this during their early years, and they only barely managed to get out."

When I heard this, I reached out to my cousins who had settled in Australia to see if the sect had tried to infiltrate their lives. My cousin responded with frustration, saying, "These people are very mean and malicious, just as you described. I can't stand them at all. But they always try to make inroads, targeting someone in the family—whether it's the wife, children, or elderly parents. They try to find a way into your household and bind you to them. They are just like the Mohammedans."

Hearing this, I could only think of one thing: when, 1,400 years ago, the Arab society with its pantheon of deities was being taken over by a single god, Allah, they must have employed similar tactics to absorb the old civilization. Back then, people must have been hearing the same kinds of stories, facing similar circumstances. The only difference was that those tribal people had swords as weapons, while in this merchant-centered society of Gujarat, the weapons are business and family.

I asked my sister, who lives in Australia, and she said, "Yes, my parent-in-laws have fallen under their influence. But I always had a certain discomfort whenever I saw them. I couldn't quite put it into words, but I never liked them. After reading your articles, I understand now. That's exactly what it is. Some people from our community have been caught in their web. One family from our caste was helped by them to get settled, and now the whole family is in it. These people are trying to establish themselves as the face of Hinduism here, trying to convert Hindus abroad. Recently, there was a marriage proposal for my daughter from a family, but they were completely immersed in this sect, so I declined. This happened before you wrote these articles."

Another relative of mine from Sabarkantha District, who was a seventy plus aged lawyer, said, 'Muslims forced people to abandon their religion with swords and knives at their throats, but these people today are even worse than them. Just for money, luxuries, and appearances, they are abandoning their gods. This is horrifying. I never thought I'd witness such things in my lifetime. Just last year, a relative of mine went to America. He lives there in a shared room with four or five other boys. Somehow, this sect found out that Hindus from Gujarat are living like this, and they initiated contact with them directly. They regularly visit them, pressuring them to attend their spiritual gatherings. They even coming to their doorsteps with special vehicles to take them to these discourses. They've established an entire network that informs them whenever a new Gujarati arrives there, whether on a visitor or student visa, and they approach them directly. They flaunt luxury and indulgence, help them find jobs, and assist them in settling down. But the condition is that they must listen to their stories and discourses.' These were the same stories which we saw in chapter 2 of this book as a drop of the ocean.

An old volunteer associated with the Sangh from Amreli district mentioned that, during his teenage years, he was expelled from the bhajan group in a Swaminarayan temple simply because he and his family were devotees of Lord Shiva. He said that a Swami from the temple grabbed his hand, pulled him out of the temple premises, and told him, "This child is the offspring of a 'kusangi' (of a bad company).' He said it because his family was worshiper of Shiva." He also mentioned that he was not allowed to get a home on rent or by purchasing in areas dominated by Swaminarayan followers—just because he worshipped Shiva. Many people from villages around Amreli and Bhavnagar have shared similar incidents on TV news channels. A devotional singer stated on VTV News that when he visited a village and chanted "Jai Maa Amba," the locals stopped him, saying, "No, no! This entire village is now Swaminarayan. Here, we do not chant the names of any other deity except the supreme Lord Swaminarayan."

In other words, just as Hindu temples and worship practices cease in areas where the Muslim population increases, a similar pattern occurs in areas where Swaminarayan followers dominate. The worship of Hindu gods and goddesses is abandoned in favor of a single supreme god, similar to Allah in Islam, and Hindu temples are converted into Swaminarayan temples.

A video showcasing these realities is available at the following link: (Video link: https://drive.google.com/file/d/1--ZFUV5Mggfra2wcd8sAY_VlOpGtoAV1/view?usp=sharing)

After learning all of this, I turned again, concerned, to my friends in the Sangh. I was pressing them, asking why the Sangh was not doing anything. The entire society is undergoing religious conversion, and Sanatan Dharma is being destroyed! My friends in the Sangh would respond, "We've raised the issue, things will happen gradually." But some of my friends, who despite being part of the Sangh still managed to maintain their independent thinking and vision, and didn't just blindly follow whatever came from above, gave me an account of the situation abroad. They said, "These people (the sect) have seriously misled Hindus abroad. Hindus outside Gujarat don't get caught up in it easily because it feels strange to them. But Gujaratis, especially Patels, even those who came from Africa, have been deeply trapped by them. Gujaratis living abroad face difficulties in keeping their second generation connected with Indian culture and language. The generation born and raised there, who attend local schools, find themselves being taught Gujarati classes by the sect's monks who visit their homes. Along with teaching them Gujarati, they also teach them Indian culture and religion, but the understanding of religion is that of the sect, where all the gods of Sanatan Dharma are seen as servants of Ghanshyam Pandey, and only Swaminarayan is the supreme god worthy of worship. The format of Hinduism presented by the sect resembles that of Christianity, where the goal is to reach Ghanshyamji's Akshardham."

Hearing this, I reproached my friends in the Sangh, saying, "All this time, I've been saying that the people in the Sangh haven't fully internalized the knowledge and understanding of Sanatan Dharma. In response, I was told, 'But we are Sanatanis, and we are fighting for it. We don't need to be scholars of the scriptures. We are here to protect religion and culture.' And look at how that incomplete understanding has manifested into such a huge crisis! You claim to be a social and cultural organization. You put on a façade because you did not know of the true essence of Sanatan Dharma. You focused on preserving its external form, assuming that whatever is within Sanatan Dharma is inherently superior—unity in diversity. But what diversity is acceptable, and what isn't? How does unity emerge from these various forms? Why don't you try to find unity between Ram and Ravan, Kansa and Krishna, Hiranyakashyap and Prahlad, Duryodhan and Yudhishthir? You ignored these questions and now look—a demon has risen to exploit your greatest weakness.

They are not changing the exterior of your society or culture; they are simply detaching it from all the Vedic gods and attaching it to a man who died two hundred years ago, whose life was mostly that of a Krishna devotee. The external form is the same—the saffron robes, the tilak on the forehead, the aarti of idols, and even the name includes Narayan and Hari. And that's why you can't find the logic to oppose it. Despite knowing deep down that this isn't right, you lack the argument to counter it. Although they wear saffron robes and have tilak on their foreheads, this is no longer Vedic Dharma. It's similar to Abrahamic religions. They won't build your Vedic society; they will create a society like that of Islam and Christianity, where one supreme god is recognized, and all other gods are denied and insulted. Their culture will be that, but the external appearance shown to the Sangh people will look like Hindu society and culture. This is where you have been deceived. This is the flaw in your approach and understanding.

Now, there are two paths. One, admit your flaws, correct them, and save the Hindu society from taking a turn like Islam. Or two, continue to feed your ego with roundabout talk to cover up your flaws, allowing this demon to grow larger, helping it spread beyond Gujarat into the rest of India. Because that's exactly what they want you to do. You are the vehicle they are using to ride on the back of anti-Muslim sentiment, establishing this situation all over India. What you do from here will determine the history of you and this Hindu society."

Sangh, VHP, and BJP:

Now let's understand why I gave this rebuke to my friends in the Sangh. In fact, I was continually receiving some very disappointing reports. Before I got involved in this work, several Sanatanis had urged me to do something about this issue, and many of them were people connected to the Sangh. When I first entered this work, the very first question I asked was, "Why aren't you contacting the people in the Sangh? Inform them, they will stop it." But they responded, "Sir, what are you talking about? It's the people in the Sangh themselves who are promoting and protecting them." And the information I gathered after that was as follows.

Amidst the strong anti-Muslim stance, large numbers of people from this sect had infiltrated the Sangh and VHP (Vishwa Hindu Parishad), with some even holding key positions. It was the people in the Sangh who were organizing events to bring Sanatani saints to the temples of this sect, and most of the programs of the Sangh and VHP were being held in the lavish temples of this sect. One prominent volunteer from the VHP who worked closely with Praveen Togadia was playing a major role in this. When the conflict between Narendra Modi and Praveen Togadia occurred, this volunteer did not abandon Togadia. As a result, in fear of Narendra Modi, who held dominance over the Gujarat Sangh and VHP, no one was willing to stand by this volunteer. At that time, Nautam Swami of the Vadtal Swaminarayan sect took him under his wing, much like how Duryodhan had taken in Karna. They provided him with a car, a credit card, and accommodations. This volunteer then established a new organization of Hindu saints, with Swami Nautam as its head in Gujarat. The task of aligning Sanatani saints with the Swaminarayan sect and integrating them was led by this volunteer.

On the other hand, the BJP was expanding the BAPS organization of the Swaminarayan sect. Narendra Modi's relationship with Pramukh Swami played a similar role as it once did with Asaram Bapu. However, even though Modi had a close relationship with Pramukh Swami, he had always made one thing clear to society—that he never wore the Swaminarayan sect's tilak on his forehead. While he often adorned his forehead with various tilaks from the Vaishnav and Shaivite sects, he never applied the Swaminarayan sect's tilak. And he hasn't done so to this day, as I write this. Just as he wore many caps and turbans, he never wore the Islamic skullcap. However, in the 2017 Gujarat Assembly elections, BAPS played a significant role in supporting the BJP.

This was the first Assembly election in Gujarat after Narendra Modi left the Chief Minister's office to become Prime Minister. The party was suffering from the impact of the Patidar reservation movement and the Dalit movement. It is said that to garner support from the Patidars during the election, Modi sought the help of BAPS. His meeting with Mahant Swami of the BAPS at the Akshardham Temple in Gandhinagar was a testament to this. Through BAPS, which is considered a Swaminarayan sect of the Patidars, a portion of the Patidars sided with the BJP, and the BJP narrowly won the election. Since then, it was said that BAPS had not missed any opportunity to gain political advantage. In fact, even among the Patidar community, those who were distant from this sect found themselves forced to align with it through their business dealings, jobs, and transfers. It became such that to move forward in business, get contracts, or secure transfers or jobs, one had to rely on the intervention of the monks from BAPS. This influence had always been present but intensified after the 2017 election. What emerged was a cocktail reminiscent of the collusion between the Roman Catholic Church and Roman emperors in Europe 1,500 years ago. Taking advantage of this collusion, BAPS was trying to bring as many Hindus as possible into its fold.

In Sardar Patel University of Vallabh Vidyanagar and several other universities, courses based on the corrupted scriptures by BAPS were added as textbook curriculum, offering PhD degrees in their fabricated philosophy. When this attempt was made at Saurashtra University, Indrabharati Bapu from Junagadh Dashanami Sampradaya publicly protested and led a movement that resulted in the reversal of that decision, although similar practices continue elsewhere. Thus, everything was laid open for this sect, and it leveraged this opportunity to influence all of Gujarat. As part of this effort, a discourse series was organized in Palanpur in 2019, which I have mentioned in the first chapter. What Patelbhai from Ahmedabad was talking about at the beginning of this chapter reflects the same situation. If someone wanted to progress in business, seek benefits from the government, or maintain financial stability, they had to display the sect's mark. Surat has already been influenced, and now Ahmedabad is undergoing the same.

So, on one side, BAPS was pulling Patels and other communities into the Swaminarayan sect with the help of the BJP, while on the other side, that Sangh volunteer was integrating Sanatani saints into the sect. Just as Christianity spread through Roman Jews after the Roman Emperor Constantine converted to Christianity, similarly, the Swaminarayan-ization of the Hindu population and saint society of Gujarat was happening with the unconscious support of the party and organization. None of them knew what the inner religious truth of this sect was.

However, it is said that the collective consciousness of the people is very strong. There had always been a sense of resentment and anger among the people of Gujarat towards this political-sect alliance, as well as a sense of fear. When I started writing my articles, friends and well-wishers within the BJP expressed their concerns to me with disappointment on their faces, saying, "Kaushikbhai, you are opposing them, but you don't know how deep this infiltration has gone. Everything is controlled by the monks of this sect. Lands, temples, and trusts are all going in their hands. If you want to advance in the BJP, you have to keep good relations with the Swamis of this sect, and only through them can you go higher. Seeing what's happening, I've long since lost my hatred for Muslims. In ten years' time, if someone like you dares to speak out, we might see the same kind of killings of Hindus here as we saw in Kashmir in the 1980s. So, be cautious, and let things be if they are happening."

Some people from Saurashtra called me and said, "Sir, there was a Hanuman temple here. These people (the sect) wanted to take it over just like the Sarangpur temple, so they could present the Hanuman of that temple as a servant of Swaminarayan. The case went to court, and the sect wasn't getting any favorable outcomes. It's said that the government transferred a special judge here, who ruled in favor of the sect, and the temple was seized by them. Now, the name of Ram and the recitation of the Hanuman Chalisa are being removed from there."

One person mentioned, "Sir, when Gyanvallabh Swami called Lord Ram and Krishna murderers, some Hindus went to intimidate him, but even then, a man from the Sangh intervened to save him."

Those who had met me from Rajkot were also messaging me, saying, "Sir, you've made a strong entry; even we didn't expect this much. But be careful, these people are very wicked. They can do anything." When they said this to me a second time, I scolded them, saying, "If you're so cowardly, why did you involve me in this? At worst, they will have me killed? They'll ruin my business? Do you think Maharana Pratap, Shivaji, and Rani Lakshmibai would have remained silent in fear? Would we have attained independence if they had been afraid? Didn't they wander through forests and mountains, hungry, fighting for Hindu culture and their deities? What is there to fear when an entire civilization is being destroyed?"

The proud Sanatanis opposing the Swaminarayan sect were mostly people who had been connected to some institution of the Sangh at some point. But now, having distanced themselves from the Sangh, and Sangh distanced itself from them, they were focusing on this issue. Their stance was clear: "The Sangh is not above Hindu Dharma and its deities. We haven't chosen the Sangh; we have chosen Hindu Dharma and our deities. If there is a conflict between the Sangh and Hindu Dharma, we will stand with Hindu Dharma." I also received phone calls from Sangh volunteers who said, "Sir, if we like or share your article, we immediately get a call from above saying we are not going to get involved in this." Some Sangh friends would call me and say, "Sir, be careful. While no one may do anything outright, because deep down everyone knows you're right, still, take some caution."

This showed how aware people were of the sect's closeness with Hindu organizations and power, and how much of an illusionary fear there was around it. It was the same type of false fear that had prevented previous Indian governments from responding to Pakistani terrorist attacks out of fear that doing so might trigger a nuclear war.

Sanatanis, angry over the sect's rise to the status of a political religion in Gujarat, would even accuse it of using its temples for money laundering. It was widely talked about in Gujarati society that the sect brought black money from abroad into India through their temples, took a fixed commission, and laundered the money. This talk is being discussed in Gujarati journalists, politicians and Sangh karyakartas on daily basis as if it's not a hidden secret. Together with this, the people also alleging that during the 2016 demonetization, the sect helped BJP leaders safeguard their black money, which is why BJP now found itself in their clutches. But this can be a mere accusation coming out from the anger and frustration of Sanatani Hindus without having any substantial proves.

Sidelining Morari Bapu:

Amidst all this, what was done to Morari Bapu stands as an example of the changing landscape in Gujarat. There are videos from 20–25 years ago showing Morari Bapu having already identified the true nature of this sect, and during his Ram Katha, he urged Hindus not to abandon Ram, Krishna, and Shiva against this sect. But after 2017, in one of his Katha, Morari Bapu said, "They took me to a temple and said, 'Here, Bapu, pour water on Neelkanth.' And I saw it and thought, 'Where is the Neelkanth? It was their founder's statue. I want to tell them that to become Neelkanth, one must drink poison. You don't become Neelkanth by eating Ladudis!'" From that statement on, this sect got its popular name Ladudi sect' in Gujarati Sanatanis. Morari Bapu was referring to how on the day of Shivratri, instead of worshiping Lord Shiva, this sect worshiped Sahajanand Swami as Neelkanth Varni and performed his abhishek. Even stronger comments can be seen in videos of Morari Bapu from years ago. This was the same Morari Bapu who, after 2013, frequently endorsed Narendra Modi as the country's Prime Minister during interviews on national news channels, even thanking him along with other Hindu saints for being nominated as the party's Prime Ministerial candidate in 2013-14. At that time, this sect was not even in the picture.

However, as we know, the situation changed after the 2017 Gujarat elections. The people from the sect, who had infiltrated the Sangh, BJP, and VHP, launched a campaign against Morari Bapu, accusing him of chanting "Ali Maula" during his discourses.

Now, the true saints and realized souls of India have always tried to show that Sanatan Dharma encompasses all paths and traditions of the world. It includes the formless Allah and the incarnate Jesus. Sanatan Dharma excludes nothing. Saints, from Kabir to Gandhi, have tried to demonstrate this inclusiveness. Even Pandurang Shastri used to say that we should consider Jesus and Prophet Muhammad as incarnations and include them within ourselves. Based on this philosophy, saints like Sadhguru in Tamil Nadu, Morari Bapu here, and others, would, for a few minutes, chant such lines in the spirit of Gandhi's "Ishwar-Allah Tero Naam" philosophy. However, the hyperactive anti-Muslim members of the Sangh immediately seized the opportunity to attack, and they began targeting Morari Bapu. Misinformation was spread about him, claiming he had married off his daughter to a Muslim, and his videos were edited and circulated on social media. Audio clips of middle-aged women gossiping about Morari Bapu's character were also circulated. All that stuff proved fake and fabricated later on, but the damage was done.

The Sangh was unaware that this was revenge for the Neelkanth controversy. A Sanatani saint was being taken down. Even if they wanted to oppose the "Ali Maula" chant, they could have gone to him and said, "Bapu, this kind of one-sidedness always harms our community. You chant Ali Maula, but Muslims will never allow Vedic mantras to be chanted in their mosques. This one sided secularism never pays off. You could at least ask them to allow Vedic chants in their mosques." If they had said this, even Morari Bapu would have agreed. Even the Sangh's chief meets with Muslim religious leaders for a mutual dialogue. But the Sangh, under the influence of the people who had infiltrated from the sect, was being led in a specific direction. Later, in one of his speeches, Morari Bapu, in a moment of frustration, described Lord Krishna's life as a failure due to the destruction that came at the end of his life. He was trying to convey that if Krishna, despite being Krishna, experienced failure, it's no surprise that a human's life ends in failure. In a similar way, we pointed out that even Ram, despite being Ram, endured suffering, so why should we be surprised if we too face suffering? But even then, the same opposition groups targeted Morari Bapu, and a BJP leader even went so far as to slap him. Through this sustained campaign, the stature and political respect of Morari Bapu were diminished.

Now, only Rameshbhai Oza remained, cautiously speaking out. He would say what needed to be said, but carefully, ensuring that he didn't say anything that could be used against him. Therefore, he didn't launch an open attack like Morari Bapu. In the various Katha broadcasts on different channels in Gujarat, more people from this sect began to appear than Morari Bapu or Rameshbhai Oza. New channels opened up where, at night, these people would narrate Kathas to elderly Hindus. The stories had names like Ram Katha and Bhagavad Katha, but the discussions were about family life, business, and their Swaminarayan. Everything gradually fell under their control.

When I wrote articles exposing the truth about this sect and tried to awaken the Hindu society, I saw and heard the regret and acknowledgement from many in the Sangh, saying, "Yes, we were used by the people from this sect back then."

Despite pointing out all these mistakes of the Sangh and its affiliated organizations, my respect for the Sangh has not diminished. The main reason for this is that it's very clear that their ignorance and blind faith were exploited. Just as this sect betrayed the entire Hindu society by hiding behind the Hindu name, they did the same to the Sangh. Both the Sangh and the society were deceived by the malicious intentions of this sect. After receiving all the advice to remain vigilant, I continued to engage with my friends in the Sangh, repeatedly asking them what they were planning to do and how much they objected to what I was doing. From all the responses, two things became clear: the Sangh would not be able to do anything directly in this matter, as it was enslaved to its superficial ideas of Hindutva, which it had adopted to focus on fighting the civilizational battle against Muslims. This situation had arisen due to the flaws in their thinking, but the Sangh had not yet developed the intellectual or spiritual strength to handle it. Most of the Sangh volunteers were deeply affected by this new truth and understood its gravity. They wanted something to be done, but there was no provision in the Sangh's thinking to address this issue. The second thing I learned was that the Sangh was not trying to stop me at that point in time, meaning it was allowing me to do what I was doing. It recognized the truth in it. It didn't consider its issue but acknowledged that it was a matter that needed to be addressed.

This is why, despite all this, I have never lost my respect for the Sangh. It has always seemed to me that they are fundamentally good people, just intellectually, spiritually, and in terms of Hindu self-awareness, they are lacking. This is why, while my respect for them remains, I have lost faith in their ability to protect Hindu Dharma and civilization as of now. They are specialists in dealing with Muslims, but that is all they have achieved in their 100-year history. They are unprepared to deal with internal attacks on the scriptures and the form of Dharma. They are not only ill-equipped for such challenges but are also an additional burden. They cannot protect Sanatan Hindu Dharma from the kind of internal treachery that happened to the ancient Arab society with Islam or to the Jewish society with Roman Christianity. And with this conclusion, I have maintained my friendship with them while continuing this fight independently.

V

Exposing the Lie of Akshardham

Every day, brainwashed Hindus from the sect would flood my Facebook timeline with their fabricated beliefs, and I would push them back by providing the true knowledge and understanding of Hinduism's authentic philosophy and scriptures. Sometimes, I would feel exhausted and reflect on how, just five months ago, I was deeply contemplating the vast subjects of Sanatan Dharma, and now, where had I landed? I found myself having to explain the most fundamental concepts as if they were profound truths—concepts even my household children already knew. Before getting involved in this task, I was engaged in the work of bringing the scriptures of Sanatan Dharma into the modern era, where the spiritual truths of these texts could be defined in the language of contemporary science and presented as the foundation for future scientific discoveries rooted in Indian knowledge. But here, I had to lower myself to a level I had never anticipated, as you will see in this chapter.

One of these brainwashed sheep, running an account under the name 'Bhagwan Shri Swaminarayan,' once said to me, "Come under the refuge of our Bhagwan. Our scriptures say that by believing in him alone as the supreme god, you will attain the highest place, Akshardham." I responded calmly, "Nonsense! There is no such place called Akshardham in Hindu scriptures." The joy that filled that person's every pore was visible. His words revealed intense enthusiasm: "And if I show you a mention of Akshardham in the Hindu scriptures, what will you do? Will you wear the Swaminarayan

Kanthi around your neck and follow the Swaminarayan religion?"

For a moment, even I was confused. Where does this confidence come from? I said, "Stop issuing challenges like Zakir Naik does with Islam. If you have the courage, show me." And what followed was unexpected.

He wrote, "The mention of Akshardham in the Bhagavad Gita," and then he posted 21st verse from the eighth chapter of the Bhagavad Gita:

अव्यक्तोऽक्षर इत्युक्तस्तमाहुः परमां गतिम् ।
यं प्राप्य न निवर्तन्ते तद्धाम परमं मम ॥ २१ ॥

"That unmanifest (avyakta) is called 'Akshar,' and that Akshar is said to be the supreme destination. Those who reach that eternal unmanifest state never return; that is my supreme abode, Vishnu's supreme realm."
(Bhagavad Gita 8.21)

I replied, "Fool. Just like you have stolen the names of Bhagwan Vishnu, like Narayan, Hari, and Shreeji, to create a new god, you have also stolen words from Sanatan Dharma's scriptures to invent places with meaninglessness? I expected something truly insightful from you. Idiot, first of all, Bhagwan Vishnu is speaking about himself here, and you have placed your new god as an idol above Vishnu. This verse proves that the verses you cite to deceive innocent Hindus are actually speaking of Bhagwan Vishnu, and you are attempting to link them to your new god. Furthermore, in this verse, Lord Krishna, as Vishnu, says that his original form is that of the unmanifest Parabrahman, which is Akshar, meaning imperishable. In the scriptures, Akshar means 'that which does not perish.' In the Vedas, the sound 'Om' is called Akshar Brahman because it is the first subtle manifest form of the unmanifest Brahman in the form of sound. Hence, Om itself is Ishwara, the imperishable (Akshar) Brahman. That imperishable, unmanifest state—the eternal form of God, where even God does not feel the need to manifest—is the supreme goal of the soul, for it is the original form of Bhagwan Vishnu. Once a soul attains it, it never returns to the world. This is the meaning of this verse. Where, then, has your so-called Akshardham, which is claimed to be above Vaikuntha and Kailash, come from?"

But he wasn't ready to listen. He was determined to empty his pot of misinformation, which his sect's Swamis had used to brainwash him. He then cited another verse:

एवमुक्त्वा स भगवान्म रूद्रणवृतः प्रभुः ।
जगाम भवनं विष्णुरक्षरं परमं पदम ॥

"From the Shanti Parva of the Mahabharata, 65.32, Lord Vishnu appeared before King Mandhata in the form of Indra, gave him instructions, and then returned to his own abode, Bhagavadham, also known as Akshardham. This is mentioned in the Mahabharata too."

Again, I responded, "You liar. I can see that verse. It also says that after giving instructions, Vishnu returned to his 'Akshar Param Pad,' which means his imperishable supreme state. The last two words of that verse mean the same. It refers to Bhagwan Vishnu's imperishable unmanifest Parabrahman form. You fool! Are you here to prove the greatness of your new god or to show the greatness of Bhagwan Vishnu? Accept Vishnu as the Supreme, and acknowledge your Sahajanand Swami as a devotee of Vishnu's incarnation Lord Krishna, and this entire argument ends. I can then peacefully return to my work. We have no issue with that. Now, what else do you have to say?"

Then, he presented another verse from the Kurma Purana:

तद् अक्षरं परमं ज्योतिः तद् विष्णोः परमं पदम् ।

He provided a translation, saying, "That Akshar is the supreme light among lights. That is Vishnu's supreme abode."

Barely able to contain my laughter, I finally burst out laughing. Meanwhile, all the Sanatani warriors on Facebook were reading our exchange. They began posting on their social media pages and groups, saying, "Akshardham has been exposed. Akshardham is nothing but a lie. Kaushikbhai has turned the lie of Akshardham upside down."

And here I was, still responding to the man behind the 'Bhagwan Shri Swaminarayan' profile. Regarding the Kurma Purana verse, I said, "First, let's translate it correctly—'That imperishable (Akshar) supreme light is the supreme abode of Vishnu.' This is what it says. And it is Bhagwan Vishnu's abode, not the abode of that poor mortal who died of cholera in 1830 and was eighty years younger than Peshwa Baji Rao."

The man tried to persist with his argument, not accepting his foolishness, but that day the big expose was done. And its effect lasted for several days. The screenshots of our Facebook argument spread across Facebook and numerous WhatsApp groups. People began to realize that they had been listening to the falsehood of Akshardham for a long time without ever bothering to verify it, or even turning their attention toward it!

Two days later, I wrote an extensive article explaining that in the Vishnu Purana, Bhagwan Vishnu's Vaikuntha is referred to as Akshar, meaning imperishable, and in the Shiva Purana, Kashi is also described as imperishable. The word Akshar was used merely as an adjective for these places, not to describe a place called 'Akshardham.' The word means 'imperishable abode,' which, in Sanatan Dharma, refers to Lord Vishnu's Vaikuntha and Lord Shiva's Kashi.

In the Vedas, the Nirakara Ishwara, represented by Om, is referred to as Parabrahman. This Parabrahman is explained to ordinary humans in the Puranas through five manifest forms. These five manifest forms are known in Sanatan Dharma as the Panchadev. When Adi Shankaracharya reestablished Vedic Dharma, he declared that the Parabrahman of the Vedas is expressed in the Puranas through these five forms. He called these five manifest forms Panchadev: Ganesh, Maa Shakti, Vishnu, Shiva, and Surya/ Brahma. Whether an incarnation or part of these deities, they alone are worshiped in the Puranas as the Parabrahman Ishwara. This is how he unified Sanatan Dharma, which is spread across the four Vedas, six Darshanas, six Vedangas, and eighteen Puranas. All the acharyas after Adi Shankaracharya, and every sect or tradition formed within Sanatan Dharma until today, accept this basic principle. No matter what path of devotion one follows or how moksha is defined, the worship of only the Panchdev is accepted as valid.

This is why the Uddhav sect, part of the Vaishnava (meaning 'Vishnu devotee') tradition of Ramanand Swami, also commanded the worship of the Panchadev. When the sect came into the hands of Sahajanand Swami, he too instructed in the Shikshapatri that Lord Krishna is the Supreme and the highest form of Purushottam. Along with this, he also commanded the worship of the Panchadev. This is the straightforward and undeniable truth. Any sect within Sanatan Dharma does not accept any form of Parabrahman other than the Panchadev. Any new divine figure who emerges must be recognized as an incarnation or part of one of the Panchadev to be worshiped as Parabrahman within Sanatan Dharma. Deviations and distortions arise in society because people are unaware of the form of Sanatan Dharma as it spans from the Vedas to the Puranas. Social and religious institutions should regularly remind the Sanatani community of this truth and, by doing so, keep society free from distortions and impurities.

Two days later, on March 14, 2023, I wrote another article explaining the true description of the imperishable Vaikuntha in the Srimad Bhagavatam, which uses the adjective 'Akshar' (imperishable). Through this, I clearly presented the difference between the fictitious abode of the fake Narayan and the divine abode of the true Vishnu Narayan.

The Difference Between the False Akshardham and the True Akshar Vaikunthdham

As one sows, so shall they reap. The act of stealing words and names from the scriptures of Sanatan Dharma to create a new supreme god and his fictional 'Akshardham' is a perverse distortion. This new god, crafted by stealing names from Bhagwan Vishnu, was placed above the Panchadev of Sanatan Dharma, and these Panchadev were presented as mere servants of this new god, making them unworthy of worship. According to this sect's books and sermons, in Akshardham, their Swaminarayan god is the boss of all the deities. As he walks towards his throne, Brahma, Vishnu, Shiva, Parvati, and all other deities fold their hands, bow their heads, and offer him respect. When this new god sits on his throne, the same Panchadev of Sanatan Dharma, along with other deities, stand on one leg, praising this new god. It seems less like a divine abode and more like the den of a villain, like Mogambo from a Hindi film, where all the gods of Sanatan Dharma raise their hands in submission, saying "Yo Mogambo."

This is Akshardham. Yes, the same Akshardham that you may have visited during your vacations, thinking it was a Hindu temple. You would have seen Hindu deities there and believed it was your temple. But in reality, the gods of Hindu Dharma are depicted there in the demeaning manner described above.

Now, let us take a look at the depiction of the true Akshar (imperishable) abode of Bhagwan Krishna or Bhagwan Vishnu, known as Vaikunthdham in the Bhagavata Purana. In the Puranas, Vaikunthdham is described in various places as the imperishable (Akshar) energy's abode and as Bhagwan Vishnu's supreme realm. Over time, the Puranas gradually reveal the form, location, and manifested nature of Vaikunthdham. In the Bhagavata Purana, Vaikuntha is depicted as being above all other realms and abodes in the universe, revered by all (X.12.26), and it is the supreme region of Srishti where Vishnu resides (XII.24.14). It is beyond the darkness and the worldly cycle of birth and death (IV.24.29; X.88.25). Those who transcend the three gunas (qualities) while alive, make it their ultimate destination (XI.25.22), and there is no place higher than it (II.2.18, II.9.9). The peaceful ascetics who reach this place never return (IV.9.29; X.88.25-6). The inhabitants of Vaikuntha do not have material bodies; they possess pure forms (VII.1.34), and these forms are like Vishnu's (III.15.14ff.). In Vaikuntha, Vishnu resides with the goddess of fortune, Lakshmi, in crystal-walled palaces. The gardens there shine like the ultimate liberation itself, with trees that fulfill all desires and bloom year-round. There is a fragrant breeze, the calls of exotic birds mingle with the hum of bees, and glorious flowers bloom everywhere. Vishnu's devotees travel with their beautiful wives in aerial vehicles made of jewels, sapphire, and gold, but even the attractive residents of this realm cannot disturb the minds of others because everyone is deeply immersed in Krishna's love (III.15.14-25).

This is the true Akshar Vaikunthdham of our Sanatan Dharma. We can see how serene, divine, and liberating it feels, and how the stolen concept of a 'Dhama' created by the sect seems like the den of a power-hungry overlord.

VI
Exposing the False Interpretations of Scriptures

Once the falsehood of Akshardham was exposed, a huge crack formed in the deceitful web of the sect's hypocrisy. Sanatani warriors were now awake. This was significant because, before I entered this endeavor, all the Sanatanis who had opposed this sect were confused by the false interpretations of Sanatan Dharma scriptures that were thrown to them by the sect. The sect ran numerous YouTube channels under different names, with a large number of brainwashed followers. When insulting comments about Sanatan Dharma deities began appearing in the sect's discourses, even the famous Bhagavad Katha speaker, Bhai Shri Rameshbhai Oza, expressed his anger on Gujarati news channels a couple of times. In one interview, he said, "Your scriptures have been misrepresented; correct them. Otherwise, the outcome will be catastrophic." In response, members of the sect created videos that twisted the entire conversation, justifying the insults to Hindu deities based on the perverted interpretations of scriptures done by them.

These videos were circulated among the sect's followers, who, like brainwashed sheep, would repeat these false arguments to everyone they encountered. It was a blatant charade, devoid of logic, full of lies and malice, but they just kept talking, wasting time until their opponent got tired and left in frustration, often swearing. When the frustrated person left, the sect members would say sweetly, "See how he swears. He has no religious values." This was their modus operandi.

I, too, had responded to some of these baseless claims in videos, but as I mentioned, they would bombard you with absurdities, trying to wear you down. One recurring argument in these videos was, "Look, in the Vishnu Purana, Shiva is shown bowing to Vishnu, and in the Shiva Purana, Vishnu is shown bowing to Shiva. So, are those scriptures also wrong?" Another claim was, "When Krishna was born, Shiva came to see him, and in the Ramayana, Ram established a Shivalinga at Rameshwaram and bowed to Shiva. So, are these scriptures also incorrect?" Yet another claim was, "In the Hanuman Chalisa, there is a line that says, 'Aur Devata Chitt na dharayi, Hanumat seyi sarva sukha karayi,' meaning, 'There is no need to focus on other deities, all happiness comes from Hanuman.' In the same way, we say that only Swaminarayan should be worshiped and not other gods. That is our faith. So, is the Hanuman Chalisa also false?"

I responded to these arguments in a few short Facebook reels, and my responses went viral. I said, "You are misusing the structure of Panchadev worship in Sanatan Dharma to justify your position. In the Ramayana, Mahabharata, and Puranas, there are many instances where Shiva and Vishnu demonstrate mutual respect and refer to each other as their revered deity. Shiva comes to see Krishna because Krishna is Vishnu. Ram refers to Shiva as his revered deity because Ram is Vishnu. Vishnu and Shiva are two manifest forms of the same formless Parabrahman, meaning they are one. The entire Hanuman Chalisa portrays Hanuman as a devotee of Lord Ram, who is an incarnation of Vishnu, and it also shows Hanuman as an incarnation of Shiva. It then says that by worshiping Hanuman, one can reach Parabrahman through both the forms of Shiva and Vishnu, so worshiping Hanuman alone is sufficient. The focus is on the unity of Shiva and Vishnu. Your new god is neither Shiva nor Vishnu, nor is he one of the Panchadev. He has seated himself above all of them, claiming to be their boss. You are outside the structure of Sanatan Dharma and its scriptures, so stop taking the names of Sanatan Dharma's gods and comparing them to yours.

Only those great beings or gods who are incarnations of or related to the Panchadev can be compared with the Panchadev. And even that comparison must be made according to the scriptures of Sanatan Dharma. Your new god, who died 200 years ago due to a gastric disease, is not even mentioned in the scriptures, not even in the form of Rahu or Ketu. He belongs in the same category as Hiranyakashipu, Ravana, Kansa, and Paundraka, all of whom called themselves the supreme god and considered Vishnu their enemy or subordinate. You have placed your new god in the role of these demons."

These responses raised the spirits of the Sanatani warriors. However, despite this, the reach of the sect's YouTube channels and social media portals was far greater. These portals and channels continued to spread false interpretations of many more verses from Hindu scriptures, just as we saw in the previous chapter when they distorted verses to prove Akshardham. Sometimes they altered the meaning, sometimes the verse would say one thing, and the translation would say another. In some cases, verses referring to Lord Vishnu were linked to their new god, who was now portrayed as the boss of even Vishnu. After the exposure of the false verses promoting Akshardham, one Sanatani warrior messaged me, saying, "Sir, I think this is the case with all the verses they spread. Please check them." I assigned a friend and follower of mine the task of searching for the original translations of all these verses online and compiling them into a document with links to the websites where the original translations could be found. He completed this task in about ten days, and I organized the information and released a PDF. What happened next? It caused a storm. Another massive crack!

People who were on the fence and still ignored the sect's distortion were stunned. Everyone realized that this sect was a massive conspiracy against Sanatan Dharma, filled with lies and deceit. Let's see these verses with the sect's false interpretations and the correct meanings from the scriptures.

1. Padma Purana, Uttarkhand,

Verse:

नरःकृष्णो हरिर्धर्मनन्दतो धर्मजीवनः ।
आदिकर्ता सर्वसत्यः सर्वस्त्रीस्वदर्पदा ॥

Interpretation by the Sect: To revive and protect Dharma, Paramatma Sri Hari Krishna Bhagwan will incarnate as a human in the house of Dharmadev in Kaliyuga. He is the creator of countless universes, is the form of complete truth, and has conquered the senses.

- The true translation: He who is the destroyer of Shiva's trident, he who even grants boons to Shiva, he is the supreme man, he is Krishna, he is Hari, he delights in Dharma. Dharma and Truth are his life. He is the first representative, the embodiment of complete truth. He defeats the arrogance of all the jewels of women. He is the leader of the sages who gave birth to Urvashi.

शिवत्रिशूलविध्वंसी श्रीकंठैकवरप्रदः
नरः कृष्णो हरिर्धर्मनंदनो धर्मजीवनः ॥१७२॥
आदिकर्त्ता सर्वसत्यः सर्वस्त्रीरत्नदर्पहा
त्रिकालजित कंदर्प उर्वशीसृड्ड्गनीश्वरः ॥१७३॥

- Truth: The entire translation is false. Even the verse number is incorrect. This verse is actually a combination of two verses from Chapter 71 of Padma Purana Uttarkhand, verses 172 and 173. The sect misrepresented it as 72.175. Hari Krishna is one of the many names given to Sahajanand Swami. Sahajanand Swami's parents' names, which were Hariprasad Pande and Premavati Pande, are also altered by the sect to Dharmadev and Bhaktidevi, respectively. The names given to them are the names of the ancient sages Nar-Narayana's parents. In this way, they are trying to insert this fabricated story into the scriptures of Sanatan Dharma.

2. Kurma Purana, Brahmi Samhita, 27.12-13

Verse:

ये ब्राह्मणा वंशजाता युष्माकं वै सहस्त्रशः ।
तेषां नारायणे भक्तिर्भविष्यति कलौ युगे ॥
परात्परतरं यान्ति नारायणपरा जना: ।
तते तत्र गमिष्यन्तियेद्विषन्तिमदेश्वरम् ॥

The sect's translation: Bhagwan Shri Krishna tells the sages that the people born in your lineage in Kaliyuga will develop devotion to Purushottam Narayan, the Supreme Brahman. All those who develop devotion to this Supreme Brahman Narayan will attain the highest abode, beyond all other abodes. However, those who oppose Lord Shiva will never attain that abode.

- The true translation: The thousands of Brahmins who will be born in your lineage will have devotion to Narayan. Those who hold devotion to Narayan will attain the highest abode. However, those who show enmity towards Maheshwar (Shiva) will not reach there.

- Truth: There is no mention of "Purushottam Narayan" appearing in Kaliyuga in this verse, as claimed by the sect. The sect tries to separate the name Narayan and status of Purushottam from Lord Vishnu, and attach it to Sahajanand Swami wherever the words Narayan and Purushottam appear in the Hindu scriptures.

3. Rig Veda 1.154.06

Verse:

ता वां वास्तून्युश्मसि गमध्यं यत्र गावो भूरिशृङ्गा अयासः ।
अत्राद् तदुरुगायस्य वृष्णः परमं पदमव भाति भूरं ॥

Translation by the Sect: In the supreme Brahma abode, where the rays of immense and long light spread everywhere, resides the Supreme Lord Shri Purushottam Narayan. That supreme abode is limitless. In that abode, immense and expansive rays of light emit from a vast aura, and countless eternal devotees constantly praise Shri Hari. There, Shri Hari resides forever with his eternal devotees. The divine abode of Bhagwan is infinite, devoid of any boundaries, and self-illuminating from the light of Purushottam Narayan himself.

- Truth: Shamelessly, the sect has written two lines from the Rig Veda and then added their own long content, which has nothing to do with the verse. In the Rig Veda, Vishnu is mentioned as the supreme deity among the thirty-three gods. This particular verse is dedicated to him. In the Yajur Veda, Vishnu is called Narayan because water (Nira) flows from his feet. As he is omnipresent, he is also called Vasudeva in Yajurveda. The Vishnu Gayatri mantra repeatedly asserts in the mentioned Veda, "Narayan is Vasudeva and he is Vishnu; we bow to that Vishnu deity."

- True Translation: O Indra and Varunadev! We (the hosting couple) desire such a residence as our shelter, where the health-giving and bright rays of the sun may enter. Where there are beautiful, horned, milk-yielding cows. In such excellent homes, the special splendors of the supreme abode of Vishnu, the deity worshiped by many, are self-manifested.

4. Shukla Yajurveda, 6.3

Verse:

याते याते धामान्यु म्म सिगमंध्य यत्र गावो भूरिशृङ्गा अयासः ।
अत्राद् तदुरुगायस्य विष्णोऽपरमम्पदमवं भारिं भूरिं ॥

The sect's translation: In the supreme Brahma abode, where the rays of immense and long light spread everywhere, resides the Supreme Lord Shri Purushottam Narayan. That supreme abode is limitless. In that abode, immense and expansive rays of light emit from a vast aura, and countless eternal devotees constantly praise Shri Hari. There, Shri Hari resides forever with his eternal devotees. The divine abode of Bhagwan is infinite, devoid of any boundaries, and self-illuminating from the light of Purushottam Narayan himself.

- True translation: Illuminated by the rays of the sun, we desire to reach the supreme abode of the all-pervasive, honorable Lord Vishnu. We consider you the rightful distributor of strength and prosperity to the Brahmins, Kshatriyas, and Vaishyas. Therefore, bless Brahmin scholars with the wealth of knowledge, Kshatriyas with valor and heroism, and Vaishyas with wealth and prosperity, thereby increasing the life and numbers of the people.

- Truth: In the second line of this verse, the word "Vishnu" is clearly written. There is no mention of Swaminarayan in the true translation.

5. Skanda Purana, Vasudeva Mahatmya, 17.1-5

Verse:

तत्त्वेककालसंभूतको टिकोट्यर्कसन्निभम् ।
स व्यचष्ट महतेजी दिव्यं सिततरं मुने ॥१

दिशश्च विदिशः सर्वा ऊर्द्धाधो व्याप्नुवच्च यत् ॥
अक्षरं ब्रह्म कथितं सच्चिदानन्दलक्षणम् ॥२

शा प्रकृतिं पुरुषं चोभौ तत्कार्याण्यपि सर्वशः ॥
व्याप्तं यद्योगसंसिद्धाः षट्चक्राणि निजान्तरे ॥
व्यतीत्य मूर्धनि पश्यन्ति वासुदेवप्रसादतः ॥३॥

यद्भासा भासितः सूर्यो वह्निरिन्दुश्च तारकाः ॥
भासयन्ति जगत्सर्वं स्वप्रकाशं तथामृतम् ॥४।

यद्वह्मपुरमित्यादुर्भगवद्धाम सात्वताः ॥
यस्यान्तिकेषु परितस्तिष्ठन्त्यर्चककोटयः ॥५॥

Sect's translation: What is this great brilliance seen in this grand square? It is as radiant as thousands of suns rising together, vast and immeasurable. This light pervades all directions, sub-directions, above and below, and is known as Akshara Brahman. This brilliance pervades Purusha-Prakriti and all their works. It is the same light that the accomplished yogis see in their mind's thousand-petaled lotus (Sahasrara chakra) after transcending the six chakras (within their body) by the grace of the Lord. This light illuminates the sun, moon, fire, and stars and is called Brahmapur, or the abode of Purushottam Narayan. Surrounding this light are groups of devotees standing in worship.

- Truth: This verse is claimed in their videos to describe Akshardham, but reading the following verses 10, 11, and 12 makes it clear that it is describing Vaikuntha, the abode of Narayan Vishnu, not Akshardham. Wherever the term "Akshara" is used, it means "imperishable," not in reference to Akshardham.

- Correct translation:
- Skanda Purana, Vasudeva Mahatmya, 17.1-12:

1. O sage, the Lord (Vishnu) displayed an **extremely radiant and heavenly** light, as bright as billions of suns.
2. That imperishable Brahman (Akshara Brahman) pervaded all the subtle foundations of the universe, above and below. It manifested as the essence of all existence, knowledge, and supreme bliss.
3. It spread through all forms of both Purusha and Prakriti. This is the light that humans receive in their mind by crossing the six chakras in their bodies through the grace of Vasudeva.
4. This is the light from which the sun, moon, fire, and stars derive their radiance. It illuminates the entire world with its imperishable (Akshara) light.
5. The Sattvat people refer to it as Brahmapur, the abode of the Lord, surrounded by millions of devotees.
6. O sage, groups of Brahmas and Shankaras, carrying offerings for worship, flock to that (Brahmpur).
7. But only the cowherds and cowherdesses who have Krishna's grace can see this radiant Lord; others see only the brilliant glory, not the Lord Himself.
8. Narada beheld this wondrous, shining, divine, and extremely beautiful abode, filled with precious gemstones, many gem-studded pillars, and a vast assembly hall.
9. It was illuminated by rows of radiant houses of the Lord's devotees. These male and female devotees were adorned with jeweled ornaments and various beautiful garments.
10. The sage, in ecstasy, saw a brilliant throne made of precious stones, which filled the hearts of those who gazed upon it with amazement.
11. And there, on that throne, he saw Lord Krishna, the Narayan who is Nirguna Brahman, the all-knowing king of the universe, the supreme person whom his devotees call Vasudeva.
12. Some devotees call him the "Supreme Soul," others call him the "Supreme Brahman," others "the highest of the high Brahman," some call him "Lord Vishnu," and others call him "the Supreme Lord."

6. Chandogya Upanishad, 3.13.7

Verse:

अथ यदतः परी दिवो ज्योतिर्दीप्यते विश्वतः पृष्ठेषु
सर्वतः पृष्ठेष्वनुत्तमेश्तमेषु लोके ध्विदं वाव
तद्यदिदम स्मिन्नन्तः पुरुषे ज्योतिः ॥

Sect's translation: Now, the light above this divine heavenly world, and
that light which also exists above many high realms like Satyaloka and
other high realms, is also inside Purusha (the soul).

- Correct translation: And then, above this heaven, above the world, above
  all places, in the highest realm where nothing exists beyond it – that light
  shines. This same light shines within a human being (as the soul).

- Truth: The essence of the original verse is that the highest power of the
  universe, that same element, exists within every human being, meaning
  the soul is a part of Brahman or is Brahman in essence. The sect has
  distorted the meaning to refer to "Purusha" as a separate realm, which is
  presented in their charts of creation.

7. Skanda Purana, Vasudeva Mahatmya, 18.42-44

Verse:

मया कृष्णेन निहता: साड्र्जुनेन रणेषु ये ।
प्रवर्तयिष्यन्त्यसुरास्ते त्वधर्म यदा क्षितौ ॥
धर्मदवात्तदा भक्तादिदं नारायणो मुनि: ।
जनिष्ये कोशले देशे भ्रमौ दि सामग्री द्विन: ॥
मुनिशापान्नृतां प्राप्तानृषींस्तात तथोद्भवम् ।
ततोड़ वितासुरेभ्योड़दं सद्धर्म स्थापयत्रज ॥

Sect's translation: Bhagwan Shri Krishna says: "When the asuras, who were defeated by me and Arjuna in battle, start spreading adharma on earth, I will incarnate on earth as Narayanamuni, born to Dharmadev and Bhaktidevi in the land of Kosala. O Brahma, I will uphold the true Dharma and protect the sages and saints from the demons born as humans due to the curse of Uddhava and other sages."

- Correct translation:
- 42-43 When the asuras, defeated by me (Krishna) and Arjuna in battle, will spread Dharma on earth, I, as Narayana Rishi, will be born in the land of Kosala, in the house of my devotee Dharmadev, as a Brahmin who chants the hymns of the Samaveda.
- 44. O Brahma, by establishing Dharma, I will protect the sages who were cursed by the Munis and Uddhava to be born on earth as humans.
- 45. At the end of the Kali Yuga, I will incarnate as Kalki. Riding on a divine horse, I will destroy the extremely sinful people born of the Mlecchas.
- 46. When Dharma, as described in the Vedas, is being eradicated by the demons, I will incarnate to protect Dharma.

(Skanda Purana, Vasudeva Mahatmya, 18.42-46)

- Truth: In this verse, there is no mention of Bhaktidevi, which has been added by the sect in their false translation. Moreover, Sahajanand Swami's father's name was Hariprasad Pandey, not Dharmadev. In Hindu Puranas, the names of Nar-Narayan's parents were Dharmadev and Bhaktidevi, and this sect altered the names of Sahajanand Swami's parents to make him appear as an incarnation of Nar-Narayan.

This translation exposes how the sect has distorted various scriptures by inserting their interpretations to claim false connections.

8. Padma Purana, Uttara Khanda

Shloka:

ततः स्वामिनमालोक्य लोकानां स्वामिनं विभुम् ।
यमालोक्य न पश्यन्ति निरयं जातु चिन्नराः ।
स्वर्गे कल्पशतं स्थित्वा मुक्तसंसारवासनाः ॥
मुक्तिं च प्रतिपद्यन्ते नात्र कार्या विचारणा ।

Sampradaya's Translation: By just obtaining a glimpse of Lord Swaminarayan, the Supreme Lord and Master of all universes, one is freed from the realm of Yama (hell). Those who witness Him experience immense happiness in heaven for a hundred kalpas, are freed from worldly desires, and attain the ultimate liberation (Moksha). (Padma Purana, Uttara Khanda, 176.48-50)

- Truth: Firstly, the location of this shloka is incorrect. It actually belongs to the 180th chapter of Padma Purana (not 176 as claimed) and consists of the second half of verse 48 along with verses 49 and 50. Additionally, the word "Swaminamalokaya" in the verse is mistranslated as referring to Lord Swaminarayan. The correct meaning is "Lord of all beings." The authentic translation in English refers to "Lord of the worlds." The term is written for Lord Vishnu in Padma Puran. The Sampradaya falsely highlights the word "Swami" to imply it refers to Swaminarayan.

- Correct Translation: The one who remains free from the bondage of rebirth in the earthly realm after enjoying the bliss of heaven for a hundred kalpas will behold the Lord of all beings. The one who beholds Him will never see the underworld again. After spending a hundred kalpas in heaven and being freed from the desire for reincarnation in the material world, they will achieve liberation. There is no doubt about this.

9. Varaha Purana 10.15-16

Verse:

एवं विष्णुर्मदेशानां नाम ग्रदाव्यवस्थितः ।
स च नारायणो देवः कृते युगवरे प्रभुः ॥
त्रेतायां रुद्ररुपस्तु द्वापरे यज्ञमूर्तिमान ।
कलौ नारायणो देवी बदुरुपी व्यजायत ॥

Sampradaya's Translation: Thus, Lord Vishnu mentioned the names of all the great gods. In Satya Yuga, too, the Lord takes an incarnation. In Treta Yuga, He appears as Rudra, and in Dvapara Yuga, He manifests as the sacrificial form of Yajna. In Kali Yuga, the Supreme Lord Purushottam Narayana will manifest, revealing various forms of the gods and goddesses.

- Correct Translation: Thus, Vishnu established the names of those great gods. In Krita Yuga (Satya Yuga), He is Narayana. In Treta Yuga, He is Rudra, and in Dvapara Yuga, He is the Yajna form, manifested as sacrifices. In Kali Yuga, Lord Narayana will take on multiple forms.

- Truth: The false translation by the Sampradaya attempts to prove that the Varaha Purana foretells the manifestation of some Lord Swaminarayan in Kali Yuga, revealing the various gods and goddesses. However, this misinterpretation ignores that these verses are actually about the different avatars of Lord Vishnu across the Yugas. The "new lord" that the Sampradaya claims to be above Vishnu and Shiva contradicts the Sanatan Dharma scriptures.

10. Krishna Upanishad, 2.6
Shloka:

स एव भगवान युगे तुरीयेऽपि ब्रह्मकुले (ब्रढाण्या) जायमानः सर्व उपनिषद उद्दिधीर्षुः सर्वाणि धर्मशास्त्राणि विस्तार विष्णुः सर्वानपि जनान संतार विष्णुः
सर्वानपि वैष्णवान् धर्मान् विजृम्भय न्सर्वानपि पाषण्डानिचखान ।

Sampradaya's Translation: In Kali Yuga, the Supreme Lord will be born as the fruit of a Brahmana. He will expound the essence of all the Upanishads and the Sanatan Dharma scriptures. He will convert atheists into devotees and defeat their demonic tendencies. He will practice Vaishnavism and establish righteousness.

- Truth: There is nothing wrong with the translation here. The mischief they tried is the verse is written for Lord Vishnu, while they are trying to connect it to their new God. The ignorance here is the failure to recognize that the term Vaishnava itself means "devotee of Vishnu."

11. Srimad Bhagavatam 11.5.32
Shloka:

कृष्णवर्ण त्विषा कृष्णं साङ्गोपाङ्गास्त्रपार्षदम् ।
यज्ञैः सङ्गीर्तनप्रायैर्यजन्ति दि सुमेधसः ॥

Sampradaya's Translation: In Kali Yuga, the Lord who manifests will specifically extol the glories of Lord Krishna. His body will shine with a radiance similar to the glow of sapphire, and His form will be "akrishna" (fair-complexioned). His limbs will resemble those of a human, adorned with beautiful ornaments. His weapon will be the chanting of His holy name, meaning He will not carry weapons, and He will roam among His saints and devotees. The wise men of Kali Yuga will worship Him through yajnas, glorify His qualities and pastimes, and sing His holy name.

- Truth: The translation of the shloka is manipulated here. The deceitful attempt is in first sentence where they add a new sentence to prove that Lord Swaminarayan's form was prophesied in the Puranas as Swaminarayan was a Krishna devotee in most part of his life.

- Correct Translation: In Kali Yuga, the Lord's divine form will be of dark complexion, and His body will shine with the resplendence of sapphire. His form will be adorned with a conch, a discus, and other divine ornaments. He will be surrounded by His companions like Sunanda. The wise men of Kali Yuga will worship Him through yajnas, glorify His names, qualities, and pastimes, and chant His names.

12. Srimad Bhagavatam 11.5.38-39
Shloka:

कृतादिषु प्रजा राजन कला विच्छन्ति सम्भवम् |
कलौ खलु भविष्यन्ति नारायणपरायणाः |
क्वचित्क्वचिन्महाराज द्रविडेषु च भूरिशः ||
ताम्रपर्णी नदी यत्र कृतमाला पयस्विनी |
कावेरीच महापुण्या प्रतीचीच मदानदी |

Sampradaya's Translation: O King! The residents of Satya, Treta, and Dvapara Yugas intensely desire to be born in Kali Yuga because, at this age, the Supreme Lord Purushottam Narayana and His many devotees will take birth. These devotees will be present in various places, and many will be found in the Dravida region, i.e., South India, where rivers like Tamraparni, Krtamala, Payasvini, the most sacred Kaveri, Mahanadi, and Pratichi flow.

- Correct Translation: O King! The people of Satya Yuga, Treta Yuga, and Dvapara Yuga wish to be born in Kali Yuga because in this age, the devotees who have taken shelter under Lord Narayana will be born in various places. In the Dravida country of Kali Yuga, there will be many devotees where the rivers Tamraparni, Krtamala, Payasvini, the most sacred Kaveri, Mahanadi, and Pratichi flow. O King, those who drink from these rivers will purify their inner selves and become devotees of Lord Vasudeva.

- Truth: Once again, the Sampradaya falsely inserts the name Supreme Lord Purushottam Narayana to tell it is a reference to their new God Swaminarayan. Thus, they try to imply that the Bhagavatam foretells his manifestation. They try to misinterpret verses that refer to Lord Vishnu's avatars as referring to Swaminarayan, who they claim is superior to Vishnu and Shiva. However, no such lord exists in the Sanatan Dharma scriptures or understanding.

13. Brahma Vaivarta Purana, Khand 4, Purvardh, 22.48

Shloka:

अंशेन ज्ञानिनां श्रेष्ठौ नरनारायणावृषी ।
त्वं च धर्मसुतो भूत्वा लोकविस्तारकारकः ॥

Sampradaya's Translation: O Lord, Nar-Narayana will incarnate in Kali Yuga as the son of Dharma Dev. You will be the greatest of all wise men and, with your limited power, you will uplift the entire world.

- Correct Translation: The great Rishis such as Nar-Narayana were born from your partial incarnations. As the son of Dharma, you have expanded the universe. At present, you have manifested yourself as Lord Krishna, and you are the seed of all eternal avatars.

- Truth: Nowhere in the original shloka is it mentioned that Nar-Narayana will incarnate as the son of Dharma Dev in Kali Yuga, as claimed by the Sampradaya. Furthermore, the original verses in the Brahma Vaivarta Purana describe the various avatars of Lord Vishnu, including his manifestation as Lord Krishna.

శం

These were the translations of the shlokas manipulated by the Sampradaya to spread their false interpretations. While these thirteen verses have now been exposed, the Vedas, Ramayana, Mahabharata, and the eighteen Puranas contain hundreds of thousands of verses. Just like a thief caught red-handed in one place moves on to another, these deceitful individuals can easily pick another set of verses in the future and spread new falsities by distorting translations. Therefore, until the end of evil itself, their deceit will persist. However, since these thirteen falsifications were the first to be used by them, exposing their lies has revealed the full extent of Sampradaya's deceptive intentions. The Hindu society has now realized that one cannot expect even the basic level of honesty or virtue from this group.

The question arises: How could a group lie so badly to an entire society for so many years? This was a scam on the level of a major stock market fraud, which was exposed that day.

It is unfortunate to mention here that the warrior who exposed this fraud passed away just two months before this book could be published. His name was Yash. As the time approached for this book to be made available to the public, I remembered him. He hadn't been visible on social media for about a month and a half, and there had been no messages from him. So, I messaged him, asking why he hadn't been active and if everything was okay. By evening, there was no reply, so I called him. His sister answered and told me that he had passed away on August 29, 2024. He had developed a fever and weakness, and the doctor had administered an IV drip. After the drip, he experienced chills, and within ten minutes of removing the IV, he passed away. He was from Rajkot and worked in Ahmedabad. Every few months, he would visit me in Palanpur with questions about spirituality and India. If needed, he would send questions via message, and his queries were so deep that I would often arrange a YouTube live session to answer them.

In 2019, I initiated him into Ashtanga Yoga, and the spiritual transformation and depth he gained after that were remarkable. From being a naive young boy who would pester me with questions, he had grown to a level of intellectual depth where I could call him my friend. At the time of his death, he had booked a flight to visit Sadhguru's Isha Ashram. He was opposed to marriage. The last couple of times when he visited me, I had advised him that one cannot win by staying away from worldly duties; one must go through them to emerge victorious. So, he had finally agreed to look for a bride. Occasionally, he would translate my Gujarati writings into Hindi and send them to me. Once, when I posted one of his translations with his name mentioned, he told me, "Sir, please don't put my name. Let me work selflessly as you've taught."

It was Yash who first identified one of these thirteen false translations of the Hindu scriptures being spread by the Sampradaya. He sent me the first verse from the Padma Purana and said, "Sir, these translations are wrong. I've checked." It was he whom I had told to compile a PDF listing the false translations along with the correct translations and the links to the original texts online, where the correct versions of these shlokas could be found. Within ten days, he completed the PDF, and we shared it with the public. He once again said, "Sir, please don't mention my name when you post it." But today, I will write his name here. Losing someone close to me accidentally was a first-time experience, and it was deeply painful. When I spoke to his father on the phone, I told him, "Be proud that such a soul was born in your family, who at the age of twenty was searching for the purpose of life through yoga and by twenty-six had achieved a depth of understanding that even seventy-year-olds don't have." His father added, "That's why God calls such people early."

I said, "He will go to a place where his journey toward his goal will accelerate. I am not worried about him. Just remember him as a source of inspiration, knowing that he had already started on the path of finding and doing what needed to be done in life. If you haven't started yet, now is the time to begin. That will be the right way to remember him."

In tribute to Yash, I have only this to say: "Well done, son. You lived a true life. This life was successful, and it will become the seed that leads to success in future lives. Well done. You will always be remembered with pride."

The anonymous warriors of Sanatan Dharma, like Yash, are the people I am writing about in this book. These are the Sanatani warriors who have inspired me to continue this work. This kind of the warriors of Hindu history are the ones to whom this book is dedicated in its opening. It is through such people that the truth remains preserved in this world.

VII

The Sangh and the Shankaracharya

When you embark on a long, seemingly impossible journey to protect your Dharma, you may often hear things like, "There is no end to this. This effort is in vain. It's too late for any change now." Such words might come from well-meaning supporters concerned for you, from cowards who have always sought peace through submission, or even from enemies disguised as well-wishers, like Kalnemi. But upon hearing such things, your mind reacts in two ways. First, it reminds you why your goal is necessary, helping you refocus and gain more strength to work harder. Second, your mind reflects on how far you have come, asking, "What impact has all this effort made?"

These two thoughts constantly lived in the minds of every Sanatani warrior who, knowingly or unknowingly, had leapt into this mission to protect their Dharma. And now, I had also become one of them. When the truths exposed in the last two chapters came to light, the silence we had stirred in society regarding this sect's deceit soon turned into widespread anger against the sect. Neutral people, and even some who had been impressed by the sect's business activity, now realized that it wasn't only a deception with the Hindu community, but also a deep backstabbing had occurred from within. The Hindu Dharma, which had survived countless foreign invasions for centuries, had now fallen prey to an internal attack—an assault more dangerous than any external threat because it came disguised in Hindu garb and language.

Hindus, who had revered their ancestral gods for thousands of years, had gradually begun to abandon them without even realizing it. RSS volunteers and BJP workers, on a personal level, were shocked and angry upon learning all this, but, bound by party and organizational loyalties, they could do little. However, this much awareness, gained after six or seven months of intense struggle, gave us hope and felt like a significant achievement.

A sense of awareness had begun to spread among those active on social media. People started to distance themselves from the dazzling facade of this sect. The grand festival celebrating the 100th birth anniversary of Pramukh Swami, which had been organized to establish him as a new god, ended with the collapse of that dream. The mission we had begun alongside this festival had derailed their plans. Far from creating a new god, even the false god they had promoted for the past century and a half had been exposed as a web of lies, deceit, and trickery. People were now saying, "Their truth has been revealed."

However, there was a vast void of religious knowledge within the Hindu society, with a lack of true spiritual leaders. The awakened Sanatanis had much work to do, but they had no one to guide them. Most saints saw opposition to foreign faiths as their main duty, as this brought them political recognition. Saints who focused on teaching the true knowledge of the Upanishads and the six schools of philosophy, or on guiding authentic yogic practices, were less recognized. Instead, those who spoke against Muslims or aligned themselves with nationalist views of the RSS and BJP were more readily accepted and grew in influence. This vacuum was exploited by the Swaminarayan sect, which joined forces with the RSS and BJP in opposing Muslims while corrupting the essence of Hindu scriptures and imposing a new supreme god on society.

Alongside exposing the truth about this sect, I had also started a YouTube channel to educate the public on true Sanatan scriptures and principles, holding discussions with learned saints. Meanwhile, the anonymous Sanatani warriors were desperately seeking support to bring this fight into the public eye. A Sanatani warrior had independently sought legal advice from a lawyer in Ahmedabad to take action against the distorted writings of the sect. Initially, the lawyer had assured them of fighting the case free of charge, but a few days later, the lawyer refused to take on the case. That made us realize that only a trusted and dedicated lawyer, loyal to Sanatan Dharma and truly understanding the sect's deceit, could take on this task.

Sanatani warriors traveled from ashram to ashram across Gujarat, informing Hindu saints of the internal betrayal by the sect and pleading for action. But the saints too wondered: with whom do we begin this fight? Morari Bapu's political influence had been neutralized, and this made Bhai Shri Rameshbhai Oza cautious, aware of the forces in power.

During this time, one Sanatani warrior visited Swami Sachidanand Maharaj at Dantali to seek guidance on the matter. Swamiji, congratulating him, said, "It is heartening to see people like you walking this path alone. Do not wait for a crowd to rise or for society to fully awaken and raise its voice in protest. That will never happen. You must keep fighting, and the solution will only come legally. You will have to go to court; there is no other way. Only then will society awaken." When asked who could help, the experienced sage, now over 90 years old, replied with his wisdom: "No one can help you. Everyone is playing for their own gains. Go to Dwarka and meet our Shankaracharya of the Sharada Peeth. Tell him everything, and he will support you." When asked how to contact the Shankaracharya, Swamiji responded, "I don't know those details. Just go and try to meet him. He will listen to you."

In this way, Swami Sachidanand Maharaj directed the Sanatani warrior toward the Shankaracharya, adding a new chapter to this saga. Like with many other names, I could have avoided mentioning Swami Sachidanandji's name, as his ashram is located in the same region where this sect thrives. In past discourses, he has been heard praising the people of this sect in their presence, but in other discourses, he has also expressed scorn and anger toward the sect's claims of supremacy. But given his advanced age, I no longer see any risk or harm in naming him. On the contrary, the path he pointed out was crucial, as we will see as this story unfolds. Whatever direction this battle takes in the future, Swami Sachidanand's timely, accurate, and experienced guidance deserves respect, and I do not wish to withhold his name and deny him the honor he is due.

Thus, the path became clearer. Just a few months ago, in September 2022, Sadanand Saraswati Maharaj was appointed the new Shankaracharya of the Sharada Peeth in Dwarka. The Sanatani warriors were considering meeting him, but there was a complication. Sadanand Saraswati was the disciple of Swaroopanand Saraswati, who had served as the Shankaracharya of both Dwarka and Joshimath. In recent years, Swaroopanand Saraswati had developed an image of being a Congress-affiliated Shankaracharya. After Narendra Modi became Prime Minister,

Swaroopanand Saraswati had made some remarks against him. Moreover, former Congress Chief Minister of Madhya Pradesh, Digvijaya Singh, often visited him as his disciple. Swaroopanand had also sparked controversy in the national media by opposing the installation of Sai Baba's idols in Hindu temples, claiming Sai Baba was Muslim. That call was tardily accepted and respected hiddenly, but initially gave him criticism.

However, after Swaroopanand Saraswatiji's death in September 2022, his disciple Sadanand Saraswatiji was appointed Shankaracharya and became known as a firm leader, actively working to prevent religious conversions. Yet, the danger of aligning with him was significant. Just as Morari Bapu had been discredited, this protest against the sect's conspiracy against Sanatan Dharma could be falsely portrayed as a Congress-backed plot against the BJP. This was a significant risk, one I wasn't prepared for. So, I distanced myself from that path and kept questioning my friends in the RSS, asking, "Why are you all silent?" and "Why aren't you doing anything?"

During this time, a senior RSS leader from the Gujarat region had mentioned to me a couple of times, "The Sangh is starting a research and content development wing, and I want to make you the chief coordinator for Gujarat." After witnessing how I had exposed the corruption within Hindu scriptures by this sect, he too had become personally concerned about the issue, although as a leader, he maintained distance from the subject by saying that the Sangh did not officially support the sect in it. The experienced members of the Sangh kept saying that now that the Sangh was aware of the problem, they would slowly address it in their own way. I wanted to join this effort, trusting in the methods the Sangh used to protect Hindu civilization. I had no one else to carry this work forward, so I continued doing what I could within my capacity. If I could be sure that the Sangh would protect Sanatan Dharma from the sect's encroachment in Gujarat, I was ready to leave this work and focus on other matters. For these reasons, when the regional leader formally offered me the role one day, I agreed, traveled to Ahmedabad (Karnavati), and accepted the responsibility at a program held at the Hedgewar Bhavan. Thus, I aligned myself with the Sangh, while the other anonymous Sanatani warriors—many of whom had left the Sangh to fight against this sect—followed the path to Shankaracharya.

After starting our work with the research wing, the senior RSS leader sent me to Delhi to participate in a workshop. I thought he had recommended me, possibly believing that my exposure to Sangh ideas would be beneficial, but perhaps also hoping that I might find a way to present the truth about this sect to senior Sangh leaders in Delhi. Based on what I had observed, it was difficult to relay information from the bottom up within the Sangh, as the flow of directives came mostly from the top down. What I experienced in Delhi, in brief, was this: I saw patriots deeply concerned for Indian civilization, but their awareness of the enemy had become so overwhelming that their self-awareness had almost vanished. They were taught to detect the flaws and ill intentions of their enemies, and how to point out their wrongs and respond to them. However, there was no discussion of the deeper question of who we are in opposition to our enemies, and what Hindu principles offer humanity in those very areas where the enemy seeks to corrupt our society. They were fully formed reactionaries. That was their job. I used the Delhi trip to better understand the Sangh but did not raise the issue of the sect.

During research wing meetings, I shared all the knowledge I had on relevant subjects without restricting my thoughts. I allowed them to take whatever they needed for their agenda and disregard the rest. At one regional meeting in Surat, I accompanied the senior leader who appointed me to the post and other Sangh members. These meetings involved reporting on the work done and understanding any new directives from above. These discussions were called vimarsh, but as I had come to understand, they were essentially about implementing whatever was decided at higher levels. At this meeting, the senior leader raised the issue of the Swaminarayan sect in front of top regional officials. He said, "We need to do something about the Swaminarayan sect and its perverted statements. The response from Sanatani Hindus is becoming very aggressive, and the situation could deteriorate." I was pleased to hear this and gained respect for him. However, I also noticed a flaw in his argument—the statements were just surface-level; the root of the problem lay in the distorted scriptures the sect had produced. All their ideas stemmed from those texts and were instilled in people's minds. Still, I understood that asking for too much here might be difficult—and indeed, that turned out to be the case.

In response, the regional officer said, "We are not getting involved in that. We will stick to our work. These kinds of debates—over whether Shiva or Vishnu is greater—have been going on in South India as well, haven't they? We won't get involved in that." After hearing this, I spoke up for the first time in a Sangh meeting about this: "There is a significant difference that needs to be understood, and it requires at least some basic knowledge of the scriptures. In South India, the debates between Shaivas and Vaishnavas are based on the Puranas. In Sanatan Dharma, the concept of the Panchadev is central, where a person can choose any one of the five deities as their ishtadev (preferred deity) and consider the others as manifestations or other forms of the same supreme reality. This leads from the personal to the formless worship of the divine. But this sect is deviating from the tradition of the Vedas and Puranas, where the Panchadev is acknowledged. Instead, they are elevating a new supreme deity above Shiva, Vishnu, Maa Shakti, Brahma, and Ganesha—a deity who has no connection to Sanatan scriptures and was a mere mortal who died just 200 years ago. This is similar to what happened 1,400 years ago when the ancient Arab society of deities was replaced by the concept of a single supreme god, Allah. The entire ancient Arabic culture, which was idol worshiper, was wiped out. These people are installing a new supreme god over Sanatan Dharma, dismissing our deities as mere servants and making Hindus insult their own Vedic and Puranic gods."

He cut me off, saying, "Okay, that's enough. But why are you getting so deeply involved in this? We don't need to get involved in that. There's a Radha Swami sect here in the North too. It is like that only. It's fine. At least they're not becoming Christians."

I said, "This is more dangerous than that, because this is converting Hindus in foreign countries. This is also a form of religious conversion, one that will progress faster than Christianity. After a few decades, when their numbers increase abroad, it will give rise to a significant conflict. Its impact in India will be massive, far greater than the issues we currently face with the Khalistani Sikhs abroad. Hindus in India will be forced to confront a choice: either abandon all Hindu gods and accept this new supreme god or face an internal conflict, where many of their own relatives will stand on the other side. It will be much like what happened among the old Arabs during the rise of Islam, between followers of Muhammad and their own relatives. This is the time to address this issue, and perhaps, it's the last right time."

But they cut me off again. They said, "Yes, that's all fine. No need to worry so much. We're not getting involved in that. We'll just adhere to our own concept of Hindutva."

I asked, "What concept is that?"

"There is," they replied while looking at their phone, signaling me to stop. The senior leader sitting nearby looked at me with a smile and added, "There is." I also smiled and stopped to go back into the shell of receptivity and discipline. What I couldn't say was that the Radha-Swami sect hasn't yet gained political backing or the strength of a business community, nor has it tried to absorb Hindus abroad to eliminate Hindu gods. The blend of politics and the business class that this sect has gained in Gujarat and abroad is what brings this crisis.

I walked back in silence, but I was no longer as composed as before. An inner fear had awakened. "These people are living in their own world. The sect has understood that whatever their concept of Hindutva is, it serves as armor for this sect's people. This entire malignant force emerges from this shield." Later, in a discussion about outreach, a regional official also hinted, "Followers of all these sects are very dedicated and active on social media. We should use them as effectively as possible in our work for the organization." Hearing this, I renounced whatever little hope I had left in them.

A few days later, I attended a meeting at Hegdewar Bhavan in Karnavati, where another senior RSS official was addressing the group. The discussion veered towards how the Arya Samaj was alienating Hindus from their tangible gods, and how this factor contributed to Hindu conversions in Punjab. I shared my thoughts, saying, "The people of Arya Samaj are good, but they have become rigidly confined to a limited ideology. They have cut down Hindu scriptures and reduced them, turning the 'Om' of the Vedas into something like Allah. They have removed not only the worship of deities but also nature worship. There is no concept of Moksha there. To fit their limited ideology, they have condensed the Bhagavad Gita's seven hundred verses down to just seventy. Just as Allah is worshiped with prayers, the formless god of the Vedas is invoked through yajna. Besides Sharia law and labeling others as 'kafir,' everything else is almost identical. Moreover, the greedy and lusty concept of paradise in Islam offers a more tempting and intoxicating goal than what Arya Samaj presents. So, instead of preventing conversions to Islam among Hindus, Arya Samaj increases the risk of conversions to Christianity and Islam, as it disconnects Hindus from their tangible gods. The RSS needs to bring Arya Samaj back into the mainstream of Sanatan Dharma." But the senior official quickly dismissed it, saying, "We're not concerned with scriptures. Are we people guided by scriptures? We won't get involved in all that. Our focus is on cultural issues only."

But what is culture? Just external symbols? A tilak on the forehead, a shaved head with a tuft of hair, saffron robes? Speaking of cows and satsangs, reciting names from the Vedas and scriptures while twisting their meanings? If Hindu civilization is now associated with a god made to resemble Jesus or Allah, while making all deities in the Vedas and Puranas mere subjects of this new god, can it still be called Hindu culture? Despite India's diversity, all Hindus share an identity, not because of the Vedas or Upanishads—most have never read them—but because they collectively worship Vishnu's incarnations, Shiva, and Shakti.

After Lord Vishnu's marriage to Tulsi, our auspicious season for weddings begins. But if, instead, Mother Tulsi is wed to someone claiming to be the God of Krishna and all other Panchdevs, is that Hindu culture? Is it acceptable when this figure is named Neelkanth Varni and worshipped on Shivaratri instead of the Shivalinga, and Lord Shiva is made to sit at his feet in processions? When Navratri's nine days dedicated to Mother Shakti are replaced by a single Garba night on Sharad Purnima centered around this god? When the chariot procession of Lord Jagannath with Krishna, Subhadra, and Balram is instead led by this god, who has no connection to the occasion? When this god, like Jesus in heaven, is placed in an Akshardham "heavenly abode," with the name "Narayana"—a title of Vishnu—usurped, and all Sanatan deities, including Vishnu, are depicted as mere devotees? When the supreme cosmic position once held by the formless OM (ॐ) of the Vedas is now attributed to this god, and the terminology of Sanatan Dharma is repurposed to serve him; when swamis, like church priests, intrude into homes, businesses, and family lives in his name—can this still be called Hindutva?

Just as Church priests and bishops violate nature with children in schools, now we see Swamis of this sect committing the same offenses in Gurukuls. Like priests preaching celibacy while exploiting women, these Swamis forbid even looking at women yet engaging in sexual exploitation. A society entirely ruled by this Hindu-appearing sect, which promises a heavenly abode as life's ultimate goal, much like the Catholic Church—can that be called Hindutva? Even with the cows, tilaks, saffron robes, and shaved heads—can this still be called Sanatan Dharma? Can Indian culture exist apart from Sanatan Dharma? Can there be an Indian culture without Ram, Krishna, Shiva, Mother Amba, or the formless OM? These questions expose the deep confusion within the ideology of the Sangh. It has no answers. Yes, the different sects behind Panchdev exist in Sanatan Dharma, but they don't indulge in a race of other people's conversion. They all accept Panchdev worship with their own God from Panchdev. But, this sect runs entirely on the purpose of converting Sanatani Hindu civilization in Gujarat and abroad under this alien God over Panchdevs. Culture and attire remain as they were in ancient Arabia, where many deities were worshiped until Islam redefined its entire structure. Although today's Arab culture appears similar to ancient times, is it truly ancient Arabia?

This sect exploited the ideological gaps within the Sangh. Now, this distorted, anti-Sanatan sect holds influence over Gujarat's Sangh. This flaw in the organization's ideology drives it to pursue everything we will explore in this book. When an individual, organization, or society becomes enslaved to incomplete ideas, failing to see the flaws within, even well-intentioned actions can lead them, knowingly or unknowingly, toward certain dangerous outcomes. These outcomes, we will witness here.

Thus, I realized the direction I was heading had nearly reached a dead end. My path was blocked, and I found myself stuck in my work. But this was only an intermission—the real battle had yet to begin. Those anonymous Sanatani warriors who had asked me to keep their identities secret had done something incredible. They traveled across Gujarat, informing the major saints of Sanatan Dharma about the truth of this sect. They showed the saints the sect's scriptures, and photographs, and distributed my articles. They even went to Dwarka, arranging a meeting with Shankaracharyaji of the Sharada Peeth, and invited me to join them. They wanted me there to explain the scriptural distortions and the wrongs committed by this sect. For some reason, I hesitated to meet Shankaracharyaji, a reason that will be revealed in a later chapter. However, I wrote a five-page letter to Shankaracharyaji, detailing the entire problem and explaining what actions needed to be taken.

The Sanatani warriors met Shankaracharyaji with the letter, and Shankaracharyaji said, "Hmm. This is well-written. Your awareness of dharma is commendable. However, I cannot comment solely based on this letter and photos of these books. Purchase all these books for me, and I will review them before making a decision."

Following his directive, on their return, the Sanatan warriors went straight to Junagadh and purchased some books from the BAPS temple there. Additional books were then procured from the Bhuj temple, some from the Gondal temple, and others from the Maninagar temple. These were handed over to the representative saint of Shankaracharyaji. Thus, in this battle, the Sanatan warriors finally found a guiding hand to lead them forward.

VIII

Shankaracharya and Sarangpur

Shri Sadanand Saraswati Maharaj,

Jagadguru Shankaracharya Peethadhipati,

Sharada Peeth, Dwarka

The Swaminarayan sect in the far western region of India represents an effort similar to what occurred 1,400 years ago in Arabia, when a singular supreme god, Allah, replaced the society's deities and gods. A similar transformation is underway in Gujarat, where the Sharada Math established by Jagadguru Adi Shankaracharya has stood for centuries. Let me explain, Guruji, how this has taken place.

A man named Ghanshyam Pande, after renouncing the world and traveling across India, arrived in Gujarat at the age of 18. Here, he became a follower of the Uddhav sect, devoted to Krishna, and a disciple of the sect's Vaishnav guru, Ramanand Swami. Initiated into sannyas (monasticism), he was given a new name: Sahajanand Swami, a Krishna devotee. However, three years later, when Ramanand Swami passed away, Sahajanand Swami assumed leadership of the sect. He introduced a new mantra, 'Swaminarayan,' intended for Krishna devotion. Consequently, he became known as Swaminarayan. But after Sahajanand Swami's death (or even during his final days), Krishna and Krishna devotion vanished, and Sahajanand Swami became the sect's new deity, Swaminarayan. The Krishna devotees of the Uddhav sect, previously known as 'Hari bhaktas' (devotees of Hari), now became followers of Swaminarayan, merging the name 'Hari' with Sahajanand Swami as Swaminarayan.

However, the names 'Hari' and 'Narayan,' both originally associated with Lord Vishnu in Sanatan Dharma, were appropriated. Not only that, but Lord Vishnu and all other gods of Sanatan Dharma were relegated to the status of servants of this new deity, Swaminarayan. The term 'Akshar' (imperishable), used in Hindu scriptures to denote the eternal Vaikuntha realm, was redefined as Akshardham, the heavenly realm of this new god. Here, Swaminarayan is seated on a throne with Brahma, Vishnu, Shiva, Goddess Shakti, and all Sanatan Dharma deities standing before him, hands folded in reverence. This Akshardham is proclaimed to be above Vaikuntha, Goloka, Kailasa, Brahmaloka, and all other divine realms. Moreover, they claim that all divine realms in Sanatan Dharma are affected by illusion (maya), where souls still suffer. Liberation, they say, is attainable only in this new god's Akshardham, implying that the realms of Sanatan Dharma are inferior, even hellish, in comparison.

In the sect's literature and teachings, Sanatan Dharma's gods and deities are routinely disparaged. Just as Islam dismissed the gods of pre-Islamic Arabia, favoring a single supreme God, Allah, a similar attempt is underway in Sanatan Dharma with the introduction of this new god, Swaminarayan, with Gujarat at its center. The difference is that Islam outright rejected its former deities, whereas the Swaminarayan sect demotes the gods and goddesses of Sanatan Dharma to servants of this new god, portraying them as unworthy of worship. Initially, they display Sanatan Dharma deities in a corner of their temples, giving the appearance of a Hindu temple to attract Hindus. But over time, followers are indoctrinated through books and discourses to believe that Swaminarayan is the lord of all gods and that all other deities derive their power from him. Followers are eventually taught to worship the original god, not "mere servants." Those who fully embrace this belief are strictly forbidden from keeping images or statues of other gods in their homes. They are even discouraged from participating in Navratri celebrations dedicated to

Goddess Amba. If a Ram bhajan or Krishna song is heard in one of their followers' homes, their saints become unsettled.

Just as the Pope in Roman Catholicism is perceived as the representative of Jesus in heaven, the BAPS head is viewed as the earthly proxy of their Parabrahman Swaminarayan. He is believed to communicate directly with Swaminarayan for the followers. Swaminarayan is said to have instructed that Ma Shakti, Ganapati, Shiva, and Hanuman should also be worshiped as Pragat Brahma, suggesting that these Sanatan deities derive their power from Swaminarayan and can only bless their devotees through him. Since these deities are not visible, idols are installed in temples, and many Sanatanis mistakenly believe they are worshiping their gods, like Shiva or Hanuman. However, only the current BAPS head is considered the living Pragat Brahma, regarded as superior and more worthy of worship than these other deities.

When these heads pass away, they are said to join Akshardham after Parabrahman Swaminarayan, and are referred to as 'Akshar.' Hence, the institution's name, 'Bochasanvasi Akshar Purushottam Sanstha' (BAPS), with Bochasan being its founding village. This philosophy, which they call 'Akshar-Purushottam Darshan,' is being propelled as a 'seventh philosophy' alongside the six Vedanta philosophies of Sanatan Dharma. To formalize this, they've trained a swami named Bhadrasedas at a Sanskrit college in Bangalore to present it as such. They have held small events among Kashi's Brahmins, creating videos falsely claiming acceptance of their philosophy, which they spread on YouTube to mislead people.

Much like a thief who crowns himself king by stealing others' riches, they have appropriated terms and concepts from Sanatan Dharma to create a fabricated philosophy, attempting to take over Sanatan Dharma. This is an effort not merely to alter Sanatan Dharma but to reshape it into a structure akin to Islam and Christianity. Abroad, this sect exploits temples among overseas Hindus, actively converting them to their new deity, Swaminarayan. In this crisis, the Sanatani community of Gujarat urges you to take appropriate action.
"

This is the letter I sent to Shankaracharyaji of Sharada Peeth through the Sanatani warriors. He was not entirely unaware of this sect; he had heard reports of disrespect toward Sanatan Dharma's deities and had even issued a cautionary statement during the final day of the Pramukh Swami Janm-Shatabdi Utsav. However, he viewed these actions as merely unethical attempts to elevate their guru. Now, he realized this was not merely unethical—it was an organized invasion. He ordered the purchase of their books from their temples, with receipts as proof, and also called for a meeting or conference with all Sanatani sects and akhadas in Gujarat.

His intention was to convene a meeting of saints to plan a systematic response. However, before this could happen, the outrage among Sanatani saints had already erupted. Several months earlier, a tall statue of Hanuman had been erected in the courtyard of the Salangpur temple. On the square base of this statue, murals were painted on all four sides. These murals displayed the same distorted images seen in the sect's books—the very images that the Sanatani warriors had been exposing. In these murals, Lord Hanuman was depicted serving Sahajanand Swami and his parents. Sanatani warriors took photos of the murals and shared them with the saints via WhatsApp. Filled with anger, the saints could no longer stay silent. They had been quietly tolerating the sect's insults to the deities of Sanatan Dharma, but now their patience had run out. The Sanatani saints began to protest openly, and Sanatanis in the Gujarati TV media also took up the issue, giving it full coverage.

These photos, taken by a Sanatani warrior, of the controversial murals at Salangpur quickly went viral, bringing the controversy into the public eye.

As the Sanatani saints' protests grew, swamis from the Swaminarayan sect responded with flamboyant speeches that revealed a deceitful mindset.

In one speech, Darshanvallabh Swami from Vadodara Gurukul issued a provocative statement: "You pretend to be Sanatanis and Hindus after smoking marijuana, while we wear topknots, remain free from addictions, and uphold our scriptures with tilak on our foreheads. So, stop interfering with Swaminarayan followers. The whole world may change, but our God is supreme than all—He is, and He will always be." Similarly, Vadtal's Nautam Swami declared, "There is no need to be afraid. Our scriptures speak for themselves. Bhagwan Swaminarayan is mentioned in the Skanda Purana and many other Puranas. Ignore what small-status people say; we will not remove any murals."

Nautam Swami was talking about the same fabricated scriptural references that we had exposed months ago, and which is given in chapter 6 of this book. As discussed in earlier chapters, an RSS volunteer, once connected with Pravin Togadia, had aligned himself with Nautam Swami. This volunteer had founded the Akhil Bharatiya Sant Samiti, an organization uniting saints across India, with Nautam Swami serving as its president for Gujarat. Although it was a national committee, both the national president and many prominent saints were from Gujarat. After Nautam Swami's controversial speech, the dignity of the Sanatani saints within the committee was deeply hurt. They not only removed Nautam Swami from his role as president but also expelled him from the committee entirely.

Nautam Swami's speech received wide coverage in the mainstream media, and as he was president of the committee, the Sant Samiti's decision to remove him served as an effective response. However, I only saw the video of Darshanvallabh Swami's speech two months later, after Sanatani warriors shared it with me, requesting a response. "Sir, this needs an answer," they urged. After watching the two-minute video, I wrote a short article on Facebook in response. That article is as follows:

Who is Sanatani and Who is Not? – A Clear Answer

· November 3, 2023 / Facebook

The word Sanatan means eternal—something with no beginning or end, no single originator or specific starting point. It has always existed and will continue to exist. That is Sanatan. To uphold this eternal way of cosmic life is Sanatan Dharma. Therefore, whatever a bapu might say in a discourse or a babaji might do after smoking marijuana has no bearing on Sanatan Dharma, as they are not its originators. But a sect with a founder—a human being who died less than 200 years ago due to a gastric illness - who is revered as a supreme deity cannot be considered part of Sanatan. It doesn't matter if they wear a topknot, tilak, or saffron robes; if their only god and founder is a historical figure with a known beginning, they cannot qualify as Sanatanis. Just as the paths that began with Jesus and Muhammad are not considered Sanatan Dharma.

The formless Brahman, represented by Om in the Vedas, manifests as the five principal deities (Panchadev) in Puranas. Those who worship this formless Om and the embodied forms of the Panchadev as their deities are true followers of Sanatan Dharma because their God is eternal, without beginning or end. His cosmic principles have no origin in time; They have always been here. To realize this God within one's soul and to uphold this consciousness is the essence of Sanatan Dharma.

ॐ

A controversy arose regarding wall paintings and the installation of a Hanuman statue in the Sarangpur premises, where the Swaminarayan sect had applied their tilak (sectarian mark) to the idol. It was argued that this should be removed because the Swaminarayan sect does not belong to the Vaishnav tradition. In response, the followers of the Vadtal faction collected photographs from across India showing Hanuman statues from various Sanatan sects, all of which featured tilaks from their respective traditions.

When some saints found themselves confused by this, they argued against it, to which I responded on Facebook:

"All those sects fall under the Sanatan Dharma and follow the tradition of the Panchadev (five principal deities). The Hanuman idols from those sects represent the same Ram-bhakta (devotee of Lord Ram) Hanuman, worshipped through the Hanuman Chalisa. However, this sect introduces a new, supreme deity above the Panchadev of Sanatan Dharma, which is not part of the Sanatan tradition. Therefore, this sect cannot apply its tilak to Hanuman, let alone establish Hanuman in their temples. They depict Hanuman as a servant of an unknown figure separate from Lord Ram or Lord Vishnu.

In the same way that Christians cannot depict Hanuman as a servant of Jesus or place a cross around his neck, this sect cannot mark Hanuman's forehead with their tilak. The matter is very clear."

The issue had reached a critical point then. A Sanatani, evading police security at the Sarangpur temple courtyard, managed to reach the murals and smeared them with black ink before attempting to damage them. Police ultimately arrested him and brought him to court. Meanwhile, the movement among Sanatani saints gained momentum. Controversial images from various locations associated with the Swaminarayan sect went viral daily. Similar murals to those in Sarangpur appeared at the Swaminarayan temple on the road to Mahalaxmi Temple in Worli, Mumbai. In Poicha, another fun park displayed models showing Shiva and Parvati serving Sahajanand Swami.

Controversial Murals in the Swaminarayan Temple in Worli, Mumbai

In the Poicha temple, controversial statues were discovered, and as of this writing, the statue of Goddess Parvati has been repositioned to face Lord Shiva to avoid further controversy. However, for Sanatanis, it remains unacceptable that Lord Shiva and Parvati are depicted standing near the statue of Sahajanand Swami, labeled as Nilkanth Varni.

The Sanatani saints were now fully awakened. On September 3, 2023, a gathering of key Sanatani saints took place at Lambe Narayan Bharati Ashram in the Sanathal area of Ahmedabad. For the first time, representatives of Sanatan Dharma called for a boycott of the Swaminarayan sect, also issuing an ultimatum to remove the controversial murals from Sarangpur. Just two days later, another saints' conference was held in Limbdi, Surendranagar, with Sanatani saints from across Gujarat in attendance.

As these actions unfolded, the government, the Rashtriya Swayamsevak Sangh (RSS), and the Vishwa Hindu Parishad (VHP) stepped in. Under the mediation of Swami Paramatmananda Saraswati, head of Shivanand Ashram in Ahmedabad, the VHP organized a meeting at Shivanand Ashram between Sanatani saints and representatives of the Swaminarayan sect. Ram Madhav, a top national leader from the RSS, was also present. The Swaminarayan sect was compelled to agree to remove the controversial murals by the morning of September 5.

On the evening of September 4, a press conference was held at Shivanand Ashram to announce the results of this meeting. Acharya Rakeshprasadji of Vadtal stated that the Swaminarayan sect was part of the Hindu society and, to avoid hurting public sentiments, had agreed to remove the murals. He advised Swaminarayan sect leaders against making further inappropriate statements. Additionally, a committee was to be formed under the blessings of Jagadguru Shankaracharya Shri Sadanand Saraswati of Sharada Peeth and Acharya Shri Rakesh Prasadji of Vadtal to address any future disputes related to the Swaminarayan sect.

At first, this resolution appeared positive. Everything we had been advocating for over a year had now become a major, central issue in Gujarat, even resonating beyond the state. I felt a sense of peace, as though my work was complete, believing that now the RSS and VHP would seriously handle the issue. I continued my work within the RSS research domain. However, soon after the murals were removed, a new campaign surfaced on social media. The Swaminarayan sect began working to soothe its injured pride and restore its public image, recycling the same falsehoods we had previously exposed in Chapter 6. Old misinterpretations of scriptures reappeared on social media, with new YouTube channels showcasing Swaminarayan sect priests repeating the same manipulated verses. I was compelled to intervene again, circulating the PDF from Chapter 6 that clarified the true meanings of these verses and exposed the sect's misrepresentations. This made a difference. YouTube channels responded, with anchors highlighting the sect's distortions and accusing it of exploiting people's lack of Sanskrit knowledge. TV news channels also sought clarification from Shankaracharyaji, who firmly stated, "The Skanda Purana does not mention Swaminarayan, and the 'Narayana' referenced in our scriptures is Lord Vishnu—not Swaminarayan or Sahajanand Swami."

Shankaracharyaji's involvement elevated the issue nationally. Recall BAPS's Bhadrasedas, who had introduced a fabricated Akshar-Purushottam philosophy, with the sect promoting him as a seventh acharya in the lineage of Shankaracharya, Ramanujacharya, and Vallabhacharya? Initially, BAPS swamis gained some recognition for Bhadrasedas' philosophy through a Kashi Vidwat Parishad event attended by a few scholars, and they used this on YouTube to mislead people. Although Shankaracharya and other acharyas opposed this, the Sarangpur controversy shed further light on the matter. Two significant news reports from Kashi followed. First, the Vedic Science Center at Banaras Hindu University (BHU) dismissed the Akshar-

Purushottam philosophy, with the news published in Amar Ujala. Meanwhile, the Kashi Vidwat Parishad, which had initially acknowledged Bhadrasedas' philosophy, issued a stern rebuke to the Swaminarayan sect, with a statement signed by the Parishad's Secretary, Prof. Ramnarayan Dwivedi. Below are the screenshots of Amar Ujala newspaper excerpt and the public statement from Kashi Vidwat Parishad.

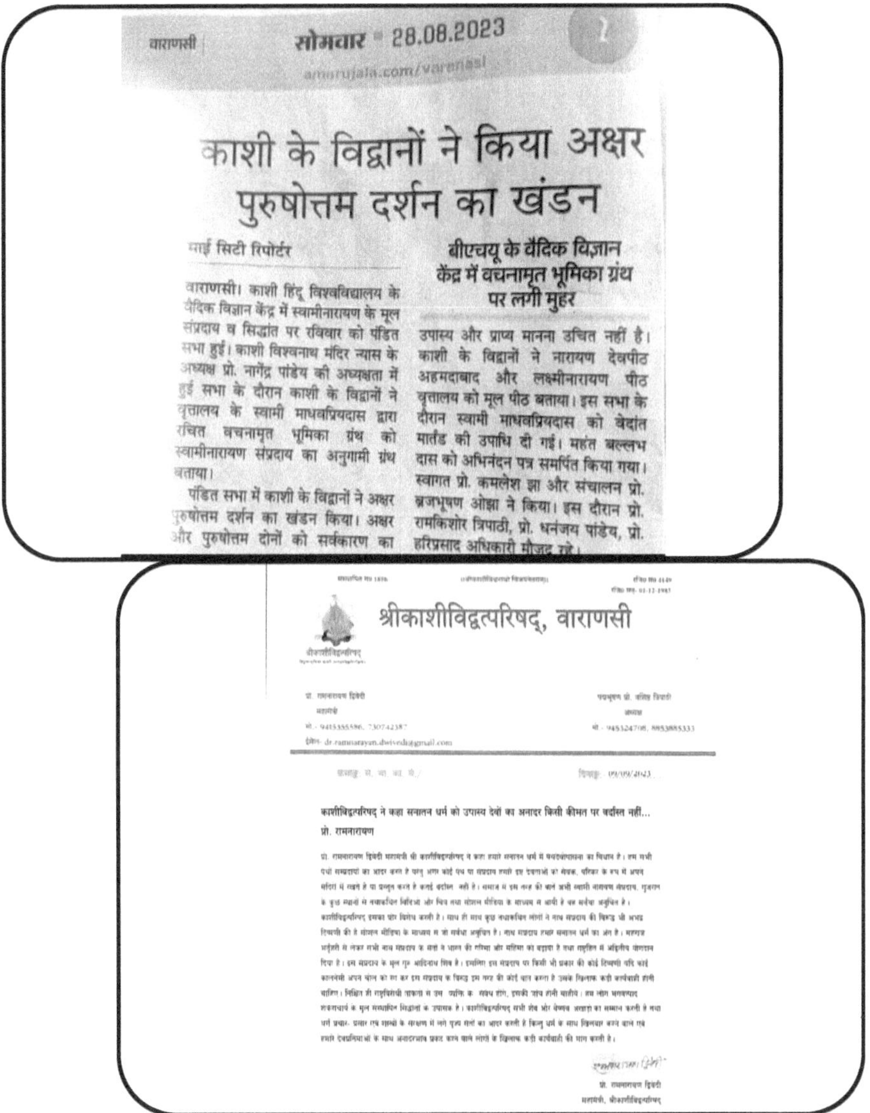

वाराणसी सोमवार ・ 28.08.2023
amarujala.com/varanasi

काशी के विद्वानों ने किया अक्षर पुरुषोत्तम दर्शन का खंडन

माई सिटी रिपोर्टर

बीएचयू के वैदिक विज्ञान केंद्र में वचनामृत भूमिका ग्रंथ पर लगी मुहर

वाराणसी। काशी हिंदू विश्वविद्यालय के वैदिक विज्ञान केंद्र में स्वामीनारायण के मूल संप्रदाय व सिद्धांत पर रविवार को पंडित सभा हुई। काशी विश्वनाथ मंदिर न्यास के अध्यक्ष प्रो. नागेंद्र पांडेय की अध्यक्षता में हुई सभा के दौरान काशी के विद्वानों ने वृत्तालय के स्वामी माधवप्रियदास द्वारा रचित वचनामृत भूमिका ग्रंथ को स्वामीनारायण संप्रदाय का अनुगामी ग्रंथ बताया।

पंडित सभा में काशी के विद्वानों ने अक्षर पुरुषोत्तम दर्शन का खंडन किया। अक्षर और पुरुषोत्तम दोनों को सर्वकारण का

उपास्य और प्राप्य मानना उचित नहीं है। काशी के विद्वानों ने नारायण देवपीठ अहमदाबाद और लक्ष्मीनारायण पीठ वृत्तालय को मूल पीठ बताया। इस सभा के दौरान स्वामी माधवप्रियदास को वेदांत मार्तंड की उपाधि दी गई। महंत बल्लभ दास को अभिनंदन पत्र समर्पित किया गया। स्वागत प्रो. कमलेश झा और संचालन प्रो. ब्रजभूषण ओझा ने किया। इस दौरान प्रो. रामकिशोर त्रिपाठी, प्रो. धनंजय पांडेय, प्रो. हरिप्रसाद अधिकारी मौजूद रहे।

श्रीकाशीविद्वत्परिषद्, वाराणसी

प्रो. रामनारायण द्विवेदी
महामंत्री
मो. - 9415355596, 7307423387
ईमेल- dr.ramnarayan.dwivedi@gmail.com

प्रधानभूषण प्रो. वशिष्ठ त्रिपाठी
अध्यक्ष
मो. - 9415247708, 8853885333

दिनांक- 09/09/2023

काशीविद्वत्परिषद् ने कहा सनातन धर्म को उपास्य देवों का अनादर किसी कीमत पर बर्दाश्त नहीं...
प्रो. रामनारायण

प्रो. रामनारायण द्विवेदी
महामंत्री, श्रीकाशीविद्वत्परिषद्

The public statement from the Kashi Vidwat Parishad, dated September 9, 2023, reads: "The Kashi Vidwat Parishad has declared that any disrespect toward Sanatan Dharma's deities will not be tolerated. Prof. Ramnarayan Dwivedi, Secretary of the Kashi Vidwat Parishad, stated, 'Sanatan Dharma traditionally embraces the worship of Panchadev. While we respect all sects, any sect that places our revered deities in subservient or diminished roles, whether in temples or visual portrayals, is entirely unacceptable. Recent statements and images from some Swaminarayan sect figures in Gujarat are inappropriate. The Kashi Vidwat Parishad strongly opposes this. Furthermore, certain derogatory comments against the Nath tradition are unacceptable. The Nath tradition is an integral part of Sanatan Dharma, tracing its lineage back to Adinath Shiva. Any derogatory statements against this tradition must face strict action. Those making such statements likely have connections to anti-national forces, warranting an investigation. As followers of the foundational principles of Bhagavadpad Shankaracharya, the Kashi Vidwat Parishad calls for strict measures against those who insult our deities and engage in actions detrimental to our faith."

Our efforts had borne fruit—the journey had begun. Videos began circulating from Saurashtra showing people removing Swaminarayan sect tilak marks from Hindu temples, chanting "Jai Shri Ram."

Meanwhile, after my Facebook post clarifying the true meanings of the scriptures, I received a message from the RSS, stating, "Our officials cannot be directly involved in this matter. Share your content with someone else to continue the conversation. If you do it in your own name, other RSS volunteers may join the effort." This approach made sense, and I agreed.

On the other hand, the Swaminarayan sect continued its campaign to restore its image, with misinformation appearing daily. At one point, I provided counter-arguments to another Sanatani warrior, asking him to post them on Facebook. However, challenges arose. Whenever a counterpoint was made, he struggled to respond effectively, and I had to write and send him replies. The other issue was credibility; my posts carried impact due to the credibility and authenticity I had built. Without that, the ghostwritten posts held little influence. Then, two events happened simultaneously. In Ahmedabad, the same baseless arguments reappeared in Dharma Jignasa, a magazine published by Swaminarayan followers.

In a sense, the social media battle seemed to be faltering. While news channels had recognized the sect's falsehoods, the sect resorted to using loyal followers and writers to spread their narrative. To expose the lies in Dharma Jignasa, I posted a direct video on Facebook, which had a strong impact. Yet, once again, I was advised to stay out of the public eye. I tried to remain silent, but a significant event soon compelled me back into action.

IX

Walking Separating from the RSS

In Kheda, a Bajrang Dal procession passed through a Muslim area, leading to stone-pelting by local Muslims. In response, several people associated with Hindu organizations posted on Facebook, "Where are those who went to break murals in Sarangpur? Stones are being thrown at a Ganesh procession here—we need you." Such posts appeared on the Facebook walls of RSS and VHP volunteers, some of whom were my friends. In the comment sections, there was mockery of the Sanatani warriors who had independently worked for two years to reveal the truth about the Swaminarayan sect to the Sanatani community. These warriors, who had tirelessly opposed the sect, had never received support from these organizations. But now, as awareness was finally awakening within the Hindu community, some individuals were ridiculing the Sanatani warriors, as though opposing Muslims was the only way to serve Hinduism.

At that moment, I could no longer remain silent. I wrote a response on Facebook:

My Thoughts on What Happened in Kheda-Thasara and a Message to Those Defending the Swaminarayan Sect

- Date: September 17, 2023

Who causes you more damage and concern—Hindus misled by communism, those corrupted by Khalistani ideologies, or Islamist and Christian missionaries? The answer is clear: it is those corrupted from within, who have lost their roots. We have fought against external threats for centuries and prevailed. But if some Hindus in another region are fighting to prevent others like Stalin from emerging, they deserve your respect and gratitude. Silently thank them for waging a necessary battle that you may be unwilling or unable to confront. And when it's time to counter jihadists or missionaries, those who recognize internal threats to Sanatan Dharma will be far stronger than those who cannot. They stand free from political constraints when it comes to protecting Sanatan Dharma.

If you feel compelled to defend those who insult Ram, Krishna, Shiva, and Jagdamba daily, it's better to remain silent than mock awakened Sanatanis. This shows that their souls quietly scratch them from within by revealing the truth, and to hide that, they have shifted to diminish the stature of those who guard the true essence of Dharma. I've seen such posts and hope not to see more. If you are told to remain silent and disciplined, then stay silent across all fronts—focus only on your assigned tasks.

As for the stone-pelting on Ganesha procession in Kheda, it is primarily the government's responsibility to act decisively. Any Hindu action would be deemed illegal. This was also true with the Swaminarayan issue. The government, elected on promises of Hindutva, remained silent as Brahma, Vishnu, Shiva, and Durga were demeaned. No Hindu organization stepped forward for two years. The Sanatani community had to awaken and take matters into their own hands. Those who unleash such fury against internal enemies will fight external enemies with even greater intensity. Let the government act, and if it can't, it should say so. The Sanatani warriors, who fight against anti-Sanatan sects, will continue to lead the charge. Immature voices shouldn't vent their frustrations in this manner. If members of the sect spoke this way, we would have our responses, but Hindu defenders we respect should not stoop to this level. They risk resembling those who defend the 'Tukde Tukde' gang in the name of freedom of expression. Step back, stay focused on your assigned role, and recognize that the sect you defend holds beliefs not unlike those of the stone-throwers you oppose.

A few days later, another Bajrang Dal procession was stoned in a Muslim area. Some in the media, along with certain Hindu voices, hinted that these incidents were attempts to reintegrate the Swaminarayan sect into the broader Hindu fold after the Sarangour controversy. This time, however, there was no mockery of Sanatani warriors, as had happened ten days earlier. But if there was any truth to the claim that these events were staged to bring the sect back into the fold, those perpetuating it were utterly oblivious to the ground reality. I didn't want my friends in Hindu organizations to fall into this trap, so I posted an article the day after the second stone-pelting incident:

Questions and Suggestions for the Muslim Community Regarding Stone-Pelting on Sanatan Dharma Processions

- Date: September 30, 2023

Let's consider the opposition's argument: that with elections approaching and recent controversies in Gujarat about the sect, processions are deliberately routed through Muslim areas or that loud music is played to provoke Muslims. Even though this isn't happening, when some will try to clean the image of the Swaminarayan sect under this aggression against Muslims, people will find some ground to say it. Regardless, what inherent right (not legally, but morally) does the Muslim community have to throw stones at the Sanatani gods' processions?

You believe in a formless God, Allah, and his final prophet, Muhammad. Hindus, too, believe in a formless God, Parabrahman, yet we honor five embodied forms through which individuals may connect to Him. Similar to how you face the Kaaba stone while praying, we, too, follow traditions. But while you do not believe God takes any form, we hold that He can manifest in different incarnations.

At the core, both of our faiths speak of the same formless God, yet we connect differently. We use a form or idol, while you use a prophet. However, is it not a violation of our beliefs when you proclaim five times daily, "Allah is the only God, and Muhammad is his only prophet"? You reject our gods and loudly declare a prophet we don't recognize. Have we ever thrown stones at your mosques during Azaan? When you gather in large numbers to offer prayers on Eid, have we ever pelted you with stones? If not, then by what right do you throw stones at our processions, celebrating the physical forms of Parabrahman? Isn't this an act of extremism?

If any of us insulted your Allah or showed disrespect toward your prophet, there would be understandable moral and emotional reasons. However, physical violence is never justified. That's why, even when someone portrays our gods in a demeaning way, we do not resort to violence. We choose to explain, debate, press the government and organizations to address the issue, and, if necessary, take legal action. Just as a Sanatani respects the boundaries of his beliefs, other communities should refrain from infringing upon ours. This is basic human decency and what we call civilization. Everyone should live within their beliefs, respecting the rights and beliefs of others. This is the message that one eternal God is imparting to all His children today. If you can put aside the extremism that has clouded your thinking, you'll realize there is no such thing as a "Muslim area" or a "Hindu area"—and there shouldn't be.

Consider this example:

Imagine if, tomorrow, a misguided individual created a new sect, which grew through wealth and followers. The main belief of this sect becomes that only the founder's parents are the true parents of the world, and anyone acknowledging other parents is a heretic. Should we all—Hindus and Muslims alike—hide our parents in front of this sect's followers? Should the whole world conceal their parents just because they cannot bear to see others' parents? Or should this belief remain within their own group? This stone-pelting incident reflects a lack of common sense, and we sincerely hope it won't happen again. We are in the 21st century, and a little humanity and common sense can resolve these issues.

I had now openly started supporting the Sanatani warriors on Facebook. I also sent a message through my RSS contacts, stating that I had joined these individuals before I became part of the RSS's research initiative. My role in this fight had led to my invitation to participate in the research work. I had believed that, after the Salangpur controversy and once Shankaracharya and other Sanatani saints had become active, the RSS and VHP would address this issue on behalf of Sanatan Dharma. But now, all I see are attempts to restore the image of this sect. Therefore, I cannot leave these Sanatani warriors to fight alone. My dharma is with them. As long as I am needed, I must fulfill my role. If necessary, you may reassign the research role. Despite sending this message, I continued my work in research, though the atmosphere was no longer the same.

All the volunteers on my team personally supported me and were pleased about the Salangpur controversy because they, too, felt this sect needed to be challenged. However, as RSS volunteers, they had to take a measured approach—discussing resolution, accepting the Swaminarayan sect within the Hindu fold, and focusing on activities against external threats. Some members, like me, who joined the RSS from outside, spoke out against the sect, but my friends, dedicated RSS volunteers, were caught between personal beliefs and RSS ideology. Not wanting to add to their struggles, I began distancing myself from them while firmly addressing the sect's actions.

Around this time, BAPS was inaugurating its largest temple in the United States. Typically, this inauguration would have received significant attention in Gujarat, but things had changed. There was a complete silence—no one mentioned the temple. The sect's followers and supporters tried to make this event significant and restore its status as a mainstream Hindu sect, but their efforts fell flat. To reflect Sanatani sentiments, I wrote the following article:

Ravana's Lanka Built by Betraying Sanatani Hindus

A Message to Sanatani Hindus Living Abroad and Hindu Organizations of India

- Date: September 26, 2023

The Swaminarayan sect is heavily promoting the inauguration of its grand Akshardham temple in the U.S. on the 8th of next month, hoping to conceal its transgressions. This temple will once again present a man born just 200 years ago at the center, with all of Sanatan Dharma's gods and goddesses portrayed as mere attendants. Sanatan Dharma's form, from the Vedas to the Puranas, is based on worshiping the formless Parabrahman through the physical forms of the Panchdev (Ganesha, Surya, Vishnu, Shiva, and Shakti) and progressing from form to the formless. Any divine person—whether male or female, an avatar, or a part of the Panchdev—is considered an integral aspect of Sanatan Dharma. Now, this Swaminarayan sect has taken the names Narayan and Hari from Lord Vishnu, creating a new god who claims Radha, Lakshmi, and Tulsi, the wives of Lord Vishnu, as his own, while asserting supremacy over Vishnu, Shiva, Brahma, Shakti, and other deities. Such a god has no place in Sanatan Dharma, nor is there any realm where our gods are subservient to an unknown entity.

Yet, our Hindu institutions and political parties will soon praise these temples, dazzled by their grandeur, even knowing they demean our Sanatani gods. Just as this sect deceived Hindu organizations in Gujarat and India, it is now ensnaring Hindus abroad through these temples, converting Sanatanis to their sect in the U.S., Canada, Australia, and the U.K. This could eventually become a larger issue than the Khalistani Sikhs in the coming decades.

Sanatanis living abroad and Hindu organizations in India must understand that if we continue to indulge this sect as one would a spoiled child, Sanatan Dharma will be undermined. Allowing a non-avatar of the Panchdev to be established as the supreme god of Sanatan Dharma sets a dangerous precedent for the world. Others may soon attempt to establish Jesus or Allah over the Panchdev. Muslim saints, fakirs, and maulvis might be depicted in the same way. The sacred structure of the Panchdev, which defines Sanatan Dharma, is our fortress, and no gate has ever been opened to outsiders; it must not be opened from within.

What they seek, we cannot grant. Granting it would strip Sanatan Dharma of its dignity, leaving it exposed to dishonor. We cannot hand over the key to Sanatan Dharma's essence to those dazzled by material wealth, who construct temples in a manner akin to the Roman Catholic Church. Sanatan Dharma is upheld by knowledge and divinity, which uplift humanity. These grand, materialistic temples resemble the path of Christianity's reliance on Roman emperors. We do not need to follow this path. ISKCON temples, dedicated to Krishna Bhakti, represent Sanatan Dharma to the world (*People also have started complaining of ISKCON that they are enforcing Krishna as the only true God culture of Abrahamic religions, avoiding the Panchdev Upasana.), while the Vedanta Society, founded by Swami Vivekananda, offers access to Sanatan Dharma's profound knowledge. Even intellectual Americans are drawn there. Therefore, Sanatanis abroad should turn to these places, which embody the true spirit of Sanatan Dharma.

A Unified Response to Lies and False Arguments

Meanwhile, there were continued efforts by followers of the Swaminarayan sect to clean up its anti-Sanatan image and bring it back into the mainstream of Sanatani society without correcting it. They wanted to make everything seem as it was before without making any changes. They continued to promote the same supremacy and flawed texts. As I mentioned in the previous chapter, the Sanatani community was wide awake now. Just before the inauguration of the BAPS temple in America, they spread more lies, which were sent to me. I responded to these lies with the truth, backed by evidence, which was widely circulated on social media, leading to the collapse of their efforts.

The following message from the sect has been forwarded, and I have responded to each of their lies with the truth, supported by evidence, for the benefit of the Sanatani community. When you read this, you will understand the real issue about the Swaminarayan sect.

- Lie: The Swaminarayan sect is a purely Vaishnav tradition.

- Truth: The word "Vaishnav" means "devotee of Vishnu." The Uddhav sect of Ramanand Swami was a Krishna Bhakti tradition, hence it was a Vaishnav sect. Sahajanand Swami also accepted Lord Krishna as the supreme deity in his Shikshapatri, considering him as the supreme Purushottam and commanding devotion to Krishna along with the worship of Panchdev. He gave the Swaminarayan mantra for Krishna Bhakti. Up until this point, it was a Vaishnav sect. However, after Sahajanand Swami, they replaced Lord Krishna with the new god Swaminarayan, a god who is said to be greater than Lord Vishnu and Krishna, and according to their texts, Lord Vishnu is portrayed as a servant of Sahajanand Swami. From the texts of this sect, there are demeaning statements written about Lord Vishnu and Krishna. The abode of Lord Vishnu is Vaikuntha, but in place of that, a new abode called Akshardham is given, which is not mentioned in any of the Sanatan scriptures. In this new abode, all the gods and goddesses of Sanatan Dharma are depicted as servants and courtiers of the new Swaminarayan god. This is the current state of all the branches of the Swaminarayan sect today.

- Lie: Ramanujacharya is the Acharya of this sect, and Vishishtadvaita is their doctrine, and their Veda is the Sama Veda, with the Kauthami branch.

- Truth: The Uddhav sect of Ramanand Swami indeed followed Vishishtadvaita philosophy and the rest indexation that is mentioned. However, the Swaminarayan sect that was formed later deviates entirely from the entire framework of Sanatan Dharma, from the Vedas to the Puranas. The philosophies of Dvaita, Vishishtadvaita, and Advaita in Sanatan Dharma all prescribe the worship of Parabrahman in the form of the Panchdev (Vishnu, Shiva, Shakti, Ganesha, and Surya). In contrast, the new Swaminarayan sect has introduced a god similar to Jesus or Allah, separate from the Panchdev. The current Acharya of the Ramanujacharya lineage, Shri Raghavacharya, has recently declared this sect to be a danger to Sanatan Dharma.

- Lie: The largest temple of Goddess Lakshmi in Gujarat is the Vadtal Shri Swaminarayan temple, where Goddess Lakshmi has been worshipped for 200 years, adorned in platinum garments. The Swaminarayan sect venerates Siddheshwar Mahadev in Junagadh, Narayan Narayan Dev in Ahmedabad and Bhuj, Madan Mohanji Maharaj in Dholera, Gopinathji Maharaj in Gadhpur, Surya Narayan Dev, Varaha Dev in Vadtal Dham, and Hanumanji Maharaj, along with countless other Vedic deities, for over 200 years.

- Truth: The six original temples were established by Sahajanand Swami, who worshipped Shri Krishna in the form of Narayan. But today, in these temples, Swaminarayan is considered the new god in place of Narayan. To the extent that Swaminarayan claims to be the husband of Radha and Lakshmi, the wives of Lord Krishna, but refers to Lord Vishnu, from whom Krishna is an avatar, as his servant. Essentially, Sahajanand Swami, who once worshipped Goddess Lakshmi as his mother, now has her depicted as his wife in the texts of this sect.

- Lie: In over 3,000 temples, there is an annual expenditure of over 150 crores for the thal (offering of food), adornment, and garments for the deities. This sect has over 200 temples just in America. The institutions of this sect have been working as a Hindu cooperative organization at the

UN for years.

· Truth: The deities of Sanatan Dharma are placed in these temples so that Sanatanis, seeing their deities, visit the temples and then are gradually led to worship the supreme god of this sect. This is not our claim; it is clearly written in the original BAPS book 'Akshar Purushottam Upasana' on page number 66. This point is also affirmed in a video of a Swami from Vadtal.

· Lie: These are not churches or mosques, are they? These are Hindu Sanatan temples.

· Truth: The structure of this sect is similar to Christianity, where worshiping only one sect's god and being promised a place in heaven motivates people. In Christianity, it is Jesus and heaven; in this sect, it is Sahajanand Swami and Akshardham. The leadership of BAPS resembles the position of the Pope in the Catholic Church. We are also aware of the close connections between Sahajanand Swami, Christian priests, and British colonial rulers (*this will be discussed in the next chapter).

· Lie: The monks of this sect took part in the Ayodhya Ram temple movement and were imprisoned for a month. This sect spends over 125 crore rupees annually on festivals like Janmashtami, Shivratri, Holi, Uttarayan, Diwali, Ram Navami, Hanuman Jayanti, Vishnu Yajna, Maruti Yajna, Lakshmi Puja, Saraswati Puja, Dhanurmas, and Shravan month Shiva Puja. The sect manages over 3,000 temples worldwide. It runs over 400 educational schools and gurukuls, educating 750,000 students. It manages over 250 gaushalas (cow shelters) and serves cows. It operates over 75 hospitals and feeds 400,000-450,000 people daily through free meal services. Millions of followers of this sect worship the deity in the early morning, wear the dhoti, observe fasts on Ekadashi, Janmashtami, Shivratri, Ram Navami, and in Shravan, and chant "Ramkrishna Govind Jay Jay Govind" daily. Millions of followers keep the traditional tuft of hair, known as shikha. If this sect has over 3,000 temples, are they churches? Mosques? The Hindu Sanatan Dharma flag flies above these temples. With so many religious activities, some people still claim this is not Sanatan Dharma? Who can explain this to those who are blind to all of this? Instead of trying to belittle or elevate someone, simply accept that your sect's activities cause you jealousy, and that's where it ends. No matter what work you do, there will always be someone jealous of you.

- Truth: Even the smallest creature working for Sanatan Dharma is revered and not envied but is seen as a source of inspiration. This is the character of the Sanatani community. However, all the religious activities of this sect are just a façade to carry out a conspiracy and betrayal of mass conversion. Over thousands of years, the deities worshiped in Sanatan Dharma, the Panchdev, are being replaced by a new god whose ideology is alien to the framework of Sanatan Dharma, showing the Sanatani gods as servants. This hidden agenda is converting Sanatanis to this sect. In households where people have become fully absorbed into this sect, there is a prohibition against keeping photos or idols of any Sanatani deities except Swaminarayan, who is depicted as the supreme god. The devotees are prohibited from participating in Navratri garbas in honor of the Kuldevi or Goddess Amba. Even if a Krishna bhajan by Narsinh Mehta is played in their home, their Swamis get agitated and say, 'The command is to worship the supreme Swaminarayan, not his servants, so why are you doing this?' This conspiracy and betrayal seek to impose the slavery of one god and his monks on the Sanatani community. Their gurukuls are large factories for converting Hindu children. Just like Christian convent schools and hospitals that run under the guise of service, this sect is adopting the same Christian tactics to convert Hindus.

In addition to these foolish fallacies spread by brainwashed followers of the sect, others were brought to my attention. I responded to these as well and provided a post to the Sanatani warriors. Below are those fallacies and their rebuttals.

- Fallacy: Ram and Krishna were not mentioned before their births.

- Sanatani Response: Ram and Krishna are avatars of Lord Vishnu, one of the Panchdev. As avatars of the Panchdev manifest, their stories and legends are written. However, the Panchdev is originally in the form of the formless Parabrahman. They have always existed here. They are neither born nor do they die. Their avatars come in human form, take birth, and leave the body, to guide humanity. Even a small child born in a Sanatani household understands this, but your false knowledge is due to the deceptive teachings of those fake Swamis, which is why you are unaware.

- Fallacy: Swaminarayan's birth is foretold in the Skanda Purana.

- Sanatani Response: The exposure of this lie has long since occurred. All those verses in the Skanda Purana written for Lord Vishnu and his future avatars have been falsely translated and spread before ignorant Hindus. But now that myth has been debunked. Jagadguru Shankaracharya Maharaj has also declared that there is no mention of Swaminarayan in the Skanda Purana—nor could there be. The Skanda Purana speaks of Lord Vishnu, and in Sanatan Dharma's scriptures, 'Narayan' is a well-known name for Lord Vishnu.

- Fallacy: Let us follow our religion, and you follow yours.

- Sanatani Response: Here is your text revised with the eight editing parameters: Imagine if I were to steal from someone's house, take the valuables back to my own, and then tell the rightful owner, "Let me enjoy what I took; you'll just have to make do with what's left." Such deceptive reasoning was, in essence, part of Islam's early establishment, where newly converted Muslims told longstanding Arabs and Jews something similar. At its core, the message is this: "Accept our newly constructed deity, the disruptions we've caused by twisting the teachings of Sanatana Dharma's scriptures, and let us continue to grow. One day, through politics, commerce, and other strategies, we'll have the means to overpower you." This was Islam's declaration—and indeed, it followed through.

- Fallacy: Even Lord Krishna faced opposition.

- Sanatani Response: Indeed, he did. Not just Lord Krishna, but even Lord Vishnu faced opposition. But all those who opposed him were demons like Hiranyakashipu and Shishupala. Just as your books and preachers today describe Lord Krishna in a demeaning manner, calling him a 'murderer' and a 'cowherd; there were such people back then as well. And that's why they were destroyed. And if you don't mend your ways, your future will be the same. Those merchant swamis won't be able to save you. They won't even be able to save themselves. Anyone who stands in their defense will also be destroyed. This is the way of Sanatana Dharma, and this is its unbroken flow.

- Fallacy: To understand Swaminarayan, you must come to Satsang (spiritual discourse).

- Sanatani Response: A Satsang that produces fools like you, a satsang where preachers are born who call Lord Ram and Krishna murderers, and where distorted stories insulting Lord Shiva and the Panchdevs are told, is not a Satsang for any Sanatani, or for any virtuous person in the world. It is a place lower than even the dens of gambling, alcohol, and prostitution. Closing such a place is the responsibility of society.

- · Fallacy: You are dividing Hindus. We need to stay united.

- Sanatani Response: The Sanatani Hindu society does not need to be considered so weak and helpless that it requires deceitful traitors like you to defend it. There is no unity between Ram and Ravana. Anyone who tries to create such unity is a coward and a hypocrite. And who are you to talk about division among Hindus? You have never been a Hindu. You stayed within the Hindu community, corrupted their scriptures, demeaned their deities, and tried to destroy their religion. You are a wicked invader. Talking about unity with you is as ridiculous as when Mahatma Gandhi supported the Khilafat movement, asking Hindus to unite with Muslims. Back then, the British were shown as enemies, and here, it's Muslims. This is an attempt to repeat the same mistake. Evil grows even stronger when you try to shield or protect it. It should be destroyed as soon as it is recognized and not allowed to take even a single step further.

- Fallacy: If you have courage, speak against Muslims.

- Sanatani Response: We speak against you just as we speak against Muslims when necessary. Our social media timelines are filled with words spoken in defense of Sanatana Dharma and its honor. But we are not so foolish that we can't recognize people even more dangerous than Muslims, just because they dress and appear like Hindus. Sanatana Dharma does not discriminate based on appearances or names. It pains us deeply that you have said and written things about our deities, even though you live among us, things that even Muslims haven't said or written. You have sunk to that level.

- Fallacy: We have glorified Sanatana Dharma by building grand temples worldwide. We have performed a lot of public service, especially during natural calamities.

- Sanatani Response: You are not part of Sanatana Dharma. You are merely a conspirator aiming to mislead Hindus and bring Sanatana Dharma to an end under the control of a supreme god, like Islam or Christianity. Your churches-like temples are the foundations of this conspiracy. Your schools, hospitals, and public services are the same as what Christian missionaries have been doing in India for the past five centuries. The life of Pramukh Swami is no different from that of Mother Teresa. Sanatanis didn't know this earlier and hence respected him as a saint. But now, everyone understands that the intentions behind those social works were the same as what's written in those corrupt books.

- • Fallacy: Our temples also have images of Ram, Krishna, and Shiva. You have no knowledge of scriptures.

- Sanatani Response: Yes, and now we understand the intention behind it. In the BAPS book 'Akshar Purushottam Upasana,' it is clearly stated how Sahajanand Swami installed Hindu gods in his temples to attract Hindus, and then gradually brought them under the supreme god's umbrella. As for your so-called scriptures, we are now aware that they are no better than garbage. And as for the true Sanatana Dharma scriptures, their knowledge has been passed down through generations and flows in our DNA. That's how we immediately recognize where you've tried to spread filth in them. Your sect's swamis were prepared from these distorted books, and they have filled you with that same filth. That's why your Sanatana consciousness is dead.

- · Fallacy: Have you ever seen Krishna? We have seen the true God in the form of Swaminarayan.

- Sanatani Response: The caricature you call 'Swaminarayan Bhagwan' is something you created, not saw. He was Sahajanand Swami, a devotee of Lord Krishna, who referred to Krishna as his lord, Narayan. Sahajanand Swami had a beard and large moles on his face, which are visible in his old portraits and statues. But since you set him up as God, you even changed his face, making it look like Krishna from ISKCON statues, and raised him above Krishna. You are the kind of people who, if they dislike their father's face, stick a picture of a Bollywood hero on it and call it their father. And as for seeing Lord Krishna, even when he came in human form, he said 'This body is not my true form. I am that imperishable (Akshar), invisible Parabrahman who pervades this entire cosmos. I alone reside in everything in this world.' We do not regard only that earthly body as Lord Krishna. We experience him daily in his eternal Parabrahman form. Whenever we fight for truth against people like you, it is Parabrahman Shri Krishna working through us. That formless, imperishable Parabrahman is our final destination. Merging with him is our goal. That is our Moksha. We do not need to see him; we aim to become one with him. That is the concept of God and Moksha in our Sanatana Dharma. We have no desire to go to that evil fortress-like Akshardham.

X

Swaminarayan, British Officers, and Christian Missionaries

We now turn to the influence of Christian missionaries and British officials on Sahajanand Swami and how this shaped the history of the sect. The historical details outlined in the introduction are presented here.

As the coordinator of the research division of the Sangh (RSS), I have examined various historical events and figures. Initially, I focused on exposing scriptural distortions and practices of this sect that contradicted Sanatan Dharma, assuming these deviations started after Krishna-devotee Sahajanand Swami's time. However, as ex-Muslims often reveal that certain problematic elements in Islam were inherent from the beginning, I felt compelled to examine Sahajanand Swami's own era. A statement in the sect's books intrigued me, claiming, "Swaminarayan blessed British officer Malcolm, saying his rule would last for 100 years." Finding this suspicious, I searched for 'Swaminarayan and British Officer Malcolm' online, only to uncover a historical narrative contrary to what was claimed: it was Malcolm, not Swaminarayan, who conferred blessings. British documents confirm this fact.

After the defeat of Napoleon at the Battle of Waterloo in 1815, British global influence surged, leading to the "Pax Britannica" movement, aimed at bringing "British peace" and "civilizing" societies under their rule. This movement spanned from 1815 until World War I in 1914, promoting harmony and compliance with British rule worldwide. Documents from this period stored in British universities extensively mention Sahajanand Swami, revealing his role in helping establish Pax Britannica in Gujarat. Similar to Raja Ram Mohan Roy's role in Bengal's social reform (which was also part of this movement), Sahajanand Swami's influence in Gujarat is documented in British records. British writers drew on these records to write books for Oxford and Cambridge, including Raymond Brady Williams' "An Introduction to Swaminarayan Hinduism" and "A New Face of Hinduism: The Swaminarayan Religion", co-authored by him.

In these works, British Governor John Malcolm is presented as a central figure, with Sahajanand Swami depicted as a supportive figure who facilitated British rule in Gujarat. British records and Christian missionary accounts portray Sahajanand Swami as a social reformer who encouraged Hindu-Christian dialogue, fostered relationships between the British and Swaminarayan followers, and "purified" Hindu scriptures. We will now explore the history as detailed in these records and books. The information here is sourced from chapter 1 (The Beginning of Swaminarayan Hinduism) of Raymond Brady Williams' book 'An Introduction to Swaminarayan Hinduism', based on British documents and discussions with followers of the Swaminarayan sect.

In the early 19th century, two figures profoundly affected Gujarat's society, creating an impact still visible among Gujaratis in India and abroad. These figures were John Malcolm, the Governor of the Bombay Presidency, and Sahajanand Swami of the Swaminarayan sect. Malcolm, who accepted the surrender of the Peshwas after their defeat by the British in 1818, brought most of Gujarat (except Baroda, which had accepted British protection in 1782) under British rule. However, Gujarat was fragmented into princely states and lawless regions, and violence and social evils were widespread, making it one of India's most divided and turbulent regions. Bengal's educated and intellectual society allowed for a reform movement led by Raja Ram Mohan Roy that aligned with British and Christian principles. Implementing British peace in Gujarat's violent and chaotic setting, however, was more challenging.

The revolutionary thinker John Malcolm saw potential in aligning Gujarati society with the British government through religious figures rather than solely relying on Christian missionaries. For this, he engaged Sahajanand Swami, who commanded a significant following in the Kathiawar region. Sahajanand Swami's residence was with Dada Khachar, a prominent Kathi landowner whose 13 or 14 villages became Swaminarayan followers under Sahajanand's influence. In these villages, Sahajanand Swami led a sect with a Vaishnav-like structure, focusing on social reform.

However, from 1802, when Sahajanand Swami assumed leadership of the Uddhav sect from Ramanand Swami, to 1818, when the British arrived in Gujarat, Sahajanand Swami faced opposition and persecution from various Gujarati groups. Several Kathiawar rulers labeled him a deceitful leader misleading the people. Even the ruler of Ahmedabad had barred Sahajanand from entering the city. Much of the opposition stemmed from his caste-based teachings including untouchability, abandoning attitudes toward women, and departure from the original Vaishnav tradition. After taking over Ramanand Swami's sect, Sahajanand faced dissent, with two female disciples and one male disciple of Ramanand, Raghunathdas, leaving the Uddhav sect.

When the British took control of Ahmedabad in February 1818, Edward Ironside, the magistrate of Kheda, became the first to lift the ban on Sahajanand Swami's entry into the city and invited him to visit. Known in the sect's scriptures as 'Eron Saheb,' Ironside assured Swaminarayan of the British commitment to protect his right to preach and safeguard his monks from persecution (Shri Haricharitramrut Sagar 17.74). Records indicate that Ironside and Sahajanand Swami met in Kheda in 1809 and again in 1817. Following the British takeover of Ahmedabad in 1818, Ironside, then an officer under the Collector, invited Sahajanand Swami to Ahmedabad. In 1819, during another meeting, Ironside mentioned that he would be traveling to Surat and that John Andrew Dunlop, known as Dunlop Saheb, would oversee Ahmedabad, promising temple land in Kalupur for Sahajanand Swami's followers.

John Andrew Dunlop was appointed as the first collector of Ahmedabad in 1818. In 1820, he obtained permission from Britain to grant land to Sahajanand Swami for a temple in Ahmedabad, and by February 1822, the Nar-Narayan temple in Kalupur was completed. Raymond Williams writes in An Introduction to Swaminarayan Hinduism: "In 1820, the collector of Ahmedabad granted land to Sahajanand Swami for constructing a temple, and the first Swaminarayan temple was built there. Thus, the British were involved in the construction of this fellowship's (sect's) first temple, symbolizing that 'Pax Britannica' and 'Pax Sahajananda' were parallel movements working toward a shared goal. When the Nar-Narayan temple was inaugurated in 1823, Sahajanand Swami was accompanied by 50,000 people. Thus, while the early years of Sahajanand Swami were marked by opposition and persecution before the arrival of the British, the last ten years were marked by great success, high esteem, and significant social reform."

Meetings with Christian Missionaries

British officers like Ironside (Iron Saheb) and Andrew Dunlop operated under a plan devised by Bombay Presidency's Governor John Malcolm in collaboration with Sahajanand Swami. Later, Malcolm also involved Christian bishops in this initiative. During the two-year construction of the Kalupur temple, Dunlop prepared a report on Sahajanand Swami's life and work titled 'A New Sect of Hindus.' He first shared this report with William Hodge Mill, the inaugural principal of Bishop's College in Calcutta. Four months after the temple's inauguration, Mill visited Gujarat in June 1822, where Dunlop showed him this report, which Mill transcribed into his diary. The diary is preserved in the Bodleian Library at Oxford University. An expanded version of this report was anonymously published in the Bombay Courier in 1822, marking it as the first English work on Swaminarayan Hinduism.

Swaminarayan's followers acted as intermediaries and informants for the British officers. William Hodge Mill recorded that he met a householder named Kubersingh Chhadidar and a sadhu named Bhajanand Swami to discuss the report. In return, Kubersingh requested Christian religious books which Mill provided, including the complete set of the New Testament. Kubersingh noted the titles and contents of each book and promised to share them with Swaminarayan. In return, they promised to send Mill all the books related to their sect's principles in Sanskrit or Hindi. Kubersingh's brother, Motiram Chopdar, a clerk in the British East India Company office in Ahmedabad, also acted as a mediator for meetings between British officers and Swaminarayan leaders.

Bhajanand Swami was a scholar of poetics, Puranas, and Ayurvedic medicine. He appears six times in five discourses in the Vachanamrut. Bhajanand requested information from Mill about the teachings of Raja Ram Mohan Roy, whose reforms had sparked controversy in Bengal, and whom Mill personally knew. Bhajanand asked Mill to send some of Roy's publications in Hindi or Sanskrit.

In March 1825, another missionary, Reginald Heber—the noted poet, hymn writer, and Lord Bishop of Calcutta—met with Sahajanand Swami. While traveling from Calcutta to Bombay, Heber encountered Sahajanand Swami in Nadiad, where Sahajanand had come for his nephew's sacred thread ceremony. Heber described the meeting as peculiar, as Sahajanand Swami was accompanied by 200 horsemen, and many of his followers were armed with guns. This security arrangement was provided by the British. Heber, also accompanied by a hundred horsemen, found himself meeting amidst a commotion of shields and war-horses, filling the city with a dramatic scene. William Hodge Mill had briefed Heber on Sahajanand Swami, and upon arriving in Nadiad, Heber also met a prince from Kathiawar who expressed a negative view of the Swaminarayan sect. This prince had attempted to suppress the sect but was prevented by the British. However, since the British praised Sahajanand Swami, Heber met him with respect, as the British had informed Heber that Sahajanand, like Christians, also preached about one true God.

During their meeting, Sahajanand sought Heber's support for some of his local projects and hoped to gain influence with British officials. After their discussion, Sahajanand asked Heber for assistance in securing funds for a Lakshmi-Narayan temple, a residence, and a hospital in Vadtal. Heber declined to support the temple's construction but agreed to forward Sahajanand's request for funding the hospital and residence to the Governor of Bombay, Sir Elphinstone. The main point of contention was their differing concepts of God. Heber did not accept the Hindu conception of a distinct form of God, as promoted by the Swaminarayan sect. Sahajanand explained his beliefs, and in response, Heber recited a well-known Christian phrase: "One God, the Creator of all things in heaven and on earth, who fills all space, supports all things, governs all things, and especially dwells in the hearts of those who diligently seek him." Sahajanand Swami's concept of one God resonated somewhat with this Christian view, although Heber was well-versed in Hindu doctrines. He questioned whether Sahajanand referred to Brahman, to which Sahajanand replied, "The One who exists and is called by many names is known as Brahman by us and other Hindus." Heber interpreted this as a form of monotheism, though distinct from Christian monotheism.

Heber was surprised when Sahajanand clarified that Lord Krishna was one form of God whom they worshiped, and that Sahajanand himself was also considered a form of God. Sahajanand elaborated: "There have been many avatars of God in different countries—one for the Christians, and in the past, another for the Hindus," adding a hint that Krishna or the Sun had another avatar in himself (Sahajanand). Following this, Sahajanand Swami presented Heber with a picture depicting Vasudev, the Lord of Svetadvipa, at the center, with Nar-Narayan sages fanning him from the sides.

Gradually, with the help of British support and connections, Sahajanand Swami's influence and dazzling prominence grew. He established six temples, one after another. Insights from Hebar's account reveal a critical turning point: in 1824, Sahajanand Swami wrote the Shikshapatri, where he declared Lord Krishna as the supreme deity (Purushottam) and advocated the worship of the five primary deities (Panchdev Upasana). However, in later texts such as the Vachanamruts, statements began to emerge claiming that he himself was the supreme Purushottam Ishwar. This shift seems to have occurred after the composition of the Shikshapatri.

Evidence suggests this change may have taken place around the construction of the Lakshmi Narayan Temple in Vadtal in 1825. Hebar perceived Sahajanand Swami's concept of God as a form of monotheism resembling Christianity, though he noted certain differences. Despite this, Hebar refused to grant land for the Vadtal temple but provided financial assistance for a hospital and a residence hall, hinting that if Sahajanand aligned his monotheism more closely with Christian theology, British officials and missionaries might extend greater support.

Possibly for this reason, when the Lakshmi Narayan Temple in Vadtal was completed in 1825, Sahajanand Swami installed a second idol beside that of Lakshmi Narayan, representing himself, and named it Harikrishna Maharaj. Today, Vadtal Swamis often state in their discourses that Sahajanand Swami declared at that time: "When people come to this temple to worship their chosen deity, Lakshmi Narayan, over time their devotion will gradually deepen to recognize Harikrishna Maharaj (i.e., Sahajanand) as the supreme deity."

Thus, the foundation of this distorted sect, which contradicts Sanatan Dharma, can be traced back to that pivotal moment.

Governor John Malcolm, by aligning British officers and Christian bishops behind Sahajanand Swami, helped consolidate Pax Britannica in Gujarat through Sahajanand's influence. As their collaboration reached its peak, John Malcolm visited Sahajanand Swami for the first time in February 1830, just before his retirement, as Sahajanand was seriously ill.

"*Raymond Williams writes in his book: "On February 28, 1830, a meeting took place in Rajkot between Sir John Malcolm and Swaminarayan, which had become inevitable given British control in Gujarat and the growing popularity of Swaminarayan Hinduism under Sahajanand Swami. This meeting was the result of numerous prior meetings between British officers and Christian missionaries with Swaminarayan's religious leaders. It occurred during Sahajanand Swami's final illness and was one of his last meetings. Sir John Malcolm returned to Britain in December of the same year, following Sahajanand Swami's death in June. Their meeting set in motion forces that significantly influenced the political, social, and cultural landscape of India. These forces continue to have an impact, both in Britain and wherever Gujaratis have migrated from Gujarat.""*

"*Williams further notes, "Gujaratis have long recognized the connection between British rule and the ministry of Sahajanand. There is an old Gujarati saying from that time: 'The Topi [the British helmet] and the tilak [the mark worn by followers of Swaminarayan] came together, and they will leave together.' The British came and were the agents of immense change in Gujarat. Their legacy is everywhere, but they have disappeared. Meanwhile, the tilak remains prominent in Gujarat and England, and the religious institution established by Sahajanand remains a central force in the religious life of Gujarat and wherever Gujaratis are found.""*

In understanding the nuances of Gujarati society and the sentiments of Gujaratis, the British writer makes a crucial error. The old saying reflects the deep-seated disarray that the entire society faced, a distortion of faith that our Gujarati ancestors endured two centuries ago. The proverb reveals the discomfort in society due to the collaboration between foreign powers and a sect opposing its own religion. Many in the community found refuge in this saying, holding onto the hope that such times would eventually pass. Yet, as the distortion discussed in the next chapter shows, the reality is different: that time never fully passed. This sect has continued its practice of linking itself to influential powers, just as it did historically—first with Congress post-independence, and now with the BJP. Today, in 2024, the same disarray persists in Gujarat's Sanatani society as it did between 1817 and 1830. The only difference is that in place of British officers and missionaries, it's now the BJP and Hindu organizations involved. For the past several years, modern Gujarati society has repeated that old proverb in new words: "This sect is completely supported by the current government; that's why all this deception continues. When this government is gone, their wrongdoings will come to justice."

Yet neither today's Gujarati society nor the current ruling parties recognize that this sect was founded on such power plays. The BJP and its allied organizations, influenced by the sect's wealth, resources, and offerings, overlook the fact that this sect has switched alliances many times before to take over Sanatan Dharma, and they may be next in line. John Malcolm taught them the European approach to ruling a society through political alliances, and this sect, empowered by that strategy, is now using this alignment to undermine Sanatan Dharma and its deities.

Following interactions with Christian missionaries and British officials, a significant shift occurred within the Swaminarayan sect, wherein Lord Krishna was no longer deemed supreme. Instead, Sahajanand Swami was elevated as the supreme and complete Purushottam Bhagwan. Moreover, all deities of Sanatan Dharma, including Lord Krishna and Vishnu, were demoted to his servants. As the saying goes, "You reap what you sow." After Sahajanand Swami's death, hypocrisy and internal power struggles plagued the sect. These struggles are documented in The History of the Bochasan Revolt, a record of court cases between Vadtal and BAPS, revealing a pattern of Swamis declaring themselves as the supreme God, being expelled, and forming new factions—each introducing further distortions into the religious and spiritual landscape of Sanatana Dharma.

Upon gathering this information, I wrote articles on how Christianity was established in Europe with the support of Roman power. The history of this sect demonstrates its consistent approach to spreading an anti-Sanatan Dharma structure in Gujarat by aligning with whichever power is in place—first the British, then Congress, and now the BJP. This pattern of opportunistic alignment reflects its modus operandi. Consequently, I authored two articles warning people about how this Abrahamic model of establishing a new supreme God led to the decline and destruction of previous civilizations and the atrocities committed during that process.

How Christianity Was Established and Parallels in Gujarat Today

· October 2, 2023 / Facebook

In 33 AD, after Jesus' death, his followers began leaving Nazareth, migrating across regions to spread his message. They reached Rome, attempting to establish Jesus as the one true God. However, for nearly 300 years, Roman emperors persecuted Jesus' followers, crucifying them as Jesus was crucified. During these centuries, the followers of Jesus Christ in the Roman Empire grew to about a thousand. Among them, a Roman queen converted to Christianity and eventually influenced her husband, Emperor Constantine, to do the same. In 312 AD, Constantine convened a council where the community following Jesus' teachings was officially recognized as Christianity. He declared it the Roman state's official religion. During this council, Jesus Christ was elevated to God status; until then, he had been seen as a saint. The Roman Church was founded, forming the rules of Christianity as we know them today, including the decision to celebrate Jesus' birthday on December 25. Many aspects of Jesus' life that had not existed before were created at that council. This is strikingly similar to the events of 1830, when Bombay's Governor John Malcolm, Christian missionaries, and Sahajanand Swami collaborated, transforming the Krishna devotee Sahajanand Swami into the Swaminarayan Bhagwan, with new anti-Sanatan narratives emerging.

In this way, Christianity became reliant on Roman power, enforcing new religious laws on society. Citizens now had to adhere to the combined rules of the state and religion. The doctrine of Jesus Christ as the sole God became central. Christian priests gained increased authority over society. The doctrine of the Virgin Mary rendered women as perceived threats to the Church, leading to an era where over 50,000 free-thinking women were burned at the stake. In extreme cases, the Church even forced queens to marry their sons to keep power centralized. The alliance between the state and Church became so oppressive that the entire 1,400-year period is known as the "Dark Ages," as detailed in A History of the Christian Church.

This book also recounts how scientists like Galileo and Newton faced harassment. Finally, in the 18th century, scientists and thinkers emerged who sought to free society from the grip of both political and religious sectarianism. Thinkers like Voltaire promoted the concept of secularism. Born from the recognition that religion should be a personal matter, free from state interference, this intellectual movement sparked the American and French revolutions in the late 18th century, resulting in the establishment of democratic governments.

In India, the earliest case of religion aligning with state power occurred during Emperor Ashoka's promotion of Buddhism. However, Ashoka's descendant Brihadratha, who embraced Buddhist atheism, was assassinated by his general, Pushyamitra Shunga, a devotee of Shiva, who restored Sanatan-Dharma-aligned kingship. State support for Buddhism waned, setting the stage for Shankaracharya's revival of Sanatan Dharma through debate. Sanatan Dharma does not impose itself on society through state power, whereas foreign sects, in both India and abroad, follow a political path.

The Root of the Muslim-Jewish Conflict and Its Lessons for Hindus

- October 19, 2023 / Facebook

Abraham's wife, Sarah, was initially unable to bear children. Abraham, seeking offspring, asked Sarah's permission to marry Hagar, and their union produced a son named Ishmael. Later, Sarah bore a son, Isaac. Arabs claim their prophet descended from Hagar's son, Ishmael, while Jews assert their lineage from Isaac. Thus, Arabs and Jews—descendants of the same father but different mothers—came into being, with different figures seen as prophets.

Later, Jesus was born among the Jews, advocating belief in one God. Roughly 300 years after his death, Emperor Constantine, under his wife's influence, accepted Christianity and declared it the official religion of the Roman Empire. Jews, now a minority, faced persecution that persisted for 1,600 years, culminating in the Holocaust. This persecution arose because Jews refused to recognize Jesus Christ and his Father as their God.

In the seventh century, Prophet Muhammad rose among the Arabs, establishing Islam. He included Isaac's descendants, previously unrecognized by Arabs, as prophets. When Muslims encountered Jews, they demanded that the Jews include Ishmael'sdescendants and hence,

Muhammad as the final prophet. The Jews refused, aware that such recognition meant accepting the Quran and, thereby, undermining their own beliefs. Their rejection led to the long-standing conflict between Muslims and Jews which continues today.

Lessons for Hindus

1. Quickly rein in any external sects that declare a new supreme God other than Panchdev from within, or you will suffer the same fate as the Jews faced under Christians for 1,600 years.

2. Preserve the structure of the Panchadev (the five deities) Upasana as given in the Puranas, just as the Jews preserved their identity. If anyone tells you to abandon the Panchadev or accept an outsider in their place, recognize them as your enemy. They have come to break down the last fortress around your religious identity. Once that is breached, anyone can claim to be your supreme God. If you preserve your identity, you will be able to rise again, even after centuries, like the Jews. If you abandon your identity, it will be as though you never existed. Your enemies will tear you apart.

Therefore, if you are a Hindu, remain steadfast in these two matters. An identity is formed only when it has a boundary, even if that boundary is vast, and that boundary must not be violated. There can be no compromise regarding this boundary.

I then wrote a satirical piece about the current situation in Gujarat, which in a few words explains a lot about how things work.

Let's Become Supreme Gods... Nothing Is Easier.

· October 20, 2023 / Facebook

Let's write some small or big book and become supreme gods ourselves. I've already written one, and it is far more advanced than what any so-called supreme god of the past hundred or two hundred years has written. If you gather all the articles I've written over the last eight years, it would form a substantial volume, more deep and knowledgeable than the Vachanamrut. Come on, you should do this too. Let's all become supreme gods. Every household should have its own supreme god of the entire universe. It's not that hard. You just need to do one thing. Persist shamelessly in claiming, "Yes, I am supreme." Keep speaking in circles, never give a logical response. Just stay adamant about being supreme. Eventually, the other person will get tired and leave. They might consider us foolish or evil, but we'll just say, "Look, over time, anyone who opposed us has left. We were supreme, are supreme, and will remain supreme."

This is the whole game. The inner leaders of these sects know this. That's why, from time to time, someone breaks away and declares themselves to be God. Their history is filled with such supreme gods, and even today, they are wandering around everywhere. If power is simply asserted, all the self-proclaimed supremes would fall in line within six months. But when it comes to politics and ruling power, there is always uncertainty about where the power needs to be wielded and where it is actually being exerted. So, rather than opposing them, it's easier to create numerous supremes and sects in every household. After all, there are thousands of names of Hari, so stealing Vishnu's name for a thousand supremes won't be an issue. Let's go, it's simple. We just need to cross the final threshold of shamelessness. What do you say?

XI

A Three-stage Conspiracy of the Sect for Hindu Conversion

Let us return to the moment when Bishop Reginald Heber received the hint from Sahajanand Swami that Krishna or Surya had incarnated in him. In his account of this incident, author Raymond Brady Williams writes, "The hint to Heber was actually related to a complex teaching in the Swaminarayan religion about the form of God. The followers of the religious tradition he established worship Sahajanand as Swaminarayan, who is the form of God (though there are disagreements among them about the nature of this expression). This is a regional form of Hinduism, and there are variations in interpretation among its groups."

In his book An Introduction to Swaminarayan Hinduism, Raymond Williams, drawing from the experiences of 19th-century British officials and Christian missionaries as well as his interactions with current followers of the Swaminarayan sect, writes that there are essentially three groups of followers within the Swaminarayan sect. One type of follower holds the view that Sahajanand taught that Krishna is the supreme form of Purushottam or Parabrahman and is the only deity worthy of devotion and meditation. Hence, the Swaminarayan religion is sometimes, though not entirely precisely, recognized as a Krishna sect of Gujarat. There is considerable support for this identification in the literature, temples, and religious practices of the sect.

However, the author explains that the matter does not stop there; two more levels of philosophy emerge, which are increasingly prevalent among the followers of this sect. The second level claims that Swaminarayan was a form of Krishna. In some places, it is stated that Purushottam is the supreme God, with Krishna as his ancient incarnation and Sahajanand Swaminarayan as his modern incarnation. But they do not stop there; they introduce a third philosophy, asserting that Sahajanand Swaminarayan himself is the original supreme God, Purushottam, and that Rama, Krishna, and others are his incarnations.

In reality, this is not a three-tiered philosophy but rather a three-tiered conspiracy. In regions where this sect does not yet have a presence, it begins at the first level, where Krishna is acknowledged as the supreme Purushottam and Sahajanand Swami is presented as a devotee of Krishna. This allows the sect to enter as a Vaishnav tradition. After spending some time establishing itself and gathering regular followers, it moves to the second level, where Swaminarayan (Sahajanand Swami) is said to be a form of Krishna. Then, once the followers are fully committed, an intermediate idea is introduced—that there exists a supreme Purushottam God who first incarnated as Krishna and has now appeared in his latest form as Swaminarayan. Finally, it transitions to the third level, where Swaminarayan is declared to be the supreme Purushottam himself, residing in his divine abode, Akshardham, while Rama and Krishna are reduced to his mere incarnations residing in lower realms.

The Hindu scriptures are manipulated to promote this distorted ideology. Christian missionary William Hodge referred to Sahajanand Swami's alterations of Hindu texts as "purifying Hindu scriptures." Through this gradual, three-tiered process, the sect ultimately reaches a point where Ghanshyam Pandeji (Swaminarayan) is placed above the five primary deities of Sanatan Dharma as the supreme worshipped deity.

To achieve this, Krishna is used as a foundation or stepping stone. This was evident in the early 20th-century court case between BAPS and the original Vadtal seat of the sect, where the Vadtal faction accused BAPS of abandoning Krishna—who was supposed to be the foundation of the sect. However, when they referred to Krishna as their foundation, they were not acknowledging him as their supreme deity. Their scriptures repeatedly emphasize that only and only Swaminarayan Sahajanand is their ultimate deity of worship. In reality, they were using Krishna as a foundation to elevate Sahajanand Swami (Ghanshyam Pandeji), first by portraying him as an incarnation of Purushottam alongside Krishna, and then by declaring him to be Purushottam himself. Without Krishna, there would be no basis for the term "Purushottam," as only Krishna is described as the complete Purushottam in the Bhagavata Purana. Without Krishna as a stepping stone, they could not have elevated Mr. Pande (Sahajanand Swami) to the status of Purushottam. This is their fundamental truth.

So, what changes did BAPS introduce? The Vadtal seat of the sect depicts Neelkanth Varni (Sahajanand Swami's coined name before entering in Ramanand Swami's Udhdhav Sampradaya) worshiping the Sun God in the forests before arriving in Gujarat. Pleased with his penance, the Sun God grants him a boon. The texts also show Neelkanth Varni installing an idol of Lord Vishnu and worshipping him for several days. Meanwhile, Shiva and Parvati, impressed by his devotion, appear before him disguised as an elderly couple and bless him. Recognizing them, Neelkanth Varni praises them with folded hands, and in response, Shiva and Parvati grant him the boon of asceticism. Later, when Neelkanth Varni reaches Gujarat and meets Ramanand Swami, he requests initiation into the Vaishnav tradition and asks for a vision of Krishna. In the original Vadtal tradition, Krishna is first established as the supreme Purushottam, and Sahajanand Swami is presented as his devotee. Over time, through the three-tiered deception described above, Ghanshyam Pandeji is ultimately declared to be Purushottam himself.

However, BAPS and the other factions influenced by it bypass this gradual process and start directly from the claim that Swaminarayan is Purushottam. Even the books of the Kalupur seat of the sect contain similar distortions. BAPS texts claim that the Sun God visited Neelkanth Varni in the forests for his darshan, and Neelkanth Varni, in turn, blessed the Sun God. They further claim that Hanuman, Shiva, and Parvati came to seek Neelkanth Varni's blessings and requested to serve him. This, they say, is why later, as Sahajanand Swami, he installed Shiva and Parvati's idols in his temples—to keep them in his service. In BAPS literature, even Nar-Narayan of Badrikashram is shown bowing to him. Lakshmi herself is depicted as approaching Ghanshyam Pande, addressing him as her husband, and requesting an opportunity to serve him. Mr. Pande then supposedly responds that he will call upon her when he reaches Kathiawar in Gujarat.

This distortion, discussed in Chapter 2, is what separates the original Vadtal seat from the later factions. To put it simply, just as a father engaged in illegal liquor trade may have children who take it a step further into drug and arms smuggling, the difference between the original sect's deception and the later factions' deception is of a similar nature.

Now, let us analyze excerpts from the chapter 3 - 'The Structure of Swaminarayan Theology' of the book 'An Introduction to Swaminarayan Hinduism' to further understand this three-tiered deception of the sect.

Shri Krishna as the Complete Purushottam Bhagwan

Shri Krishna is the divine form of Narayan who manifests himself on Earth. In this form, Sahajanand praised both Ram and Krishna as forms of God and said that devotees should meditate on these forms of God. In a verse from the Shikshapatri written the year after his meeting with Bishop Heber (according to Raymond's book), Sahajanand gave this instruction: "That existence, which is known by various names—such as the radiant Krishna, Parabrahman, Bhagwan, Purushottam—is the cause of all manifestations. He is worshiped by us as our chosen deity." Sahajanand explained that Krishna appears in many forms. When he is with Radha, he is worshiped as Radha-Krishna, the supreme lord; with Rukmini, he is known as Lakshmi-Narayan; when with Arjuna, he is known as Nar-Narayan; and when associated with other divine figures, he is called by other names. Sahajanand told his disciples, "I understand that many avatars are ultimately of God. But I have millions of times more love for the avatar of Shri Krishna. I feel that 'this avatar is greater and more powerful than all others. Moreover, in him, there is no distinction between the avatar and the source of the avatar.'" (Vachanamrut). In the hierarchy of avatars, Krishna is supreme because he manifests the divine nature at the highest level. The different names—Radha-Krishna, Lakshmi-Narayan, Nar-Narayan, Krishna-Balaram—refer to different forms of the same deity. He taught that even though God appeared under different names and with different companions, all were related to Krishna as the supreme God.

At the time of initiation, Sahajanand continued the use of the Krishna mantra: "Shri Krishna, you are my refuge," and this mantra is still used in the religious practices of Ahmedabad and Vadtal. Krishna is the supreme form of God—this teaching closely parallels the position of the Vallabhacharya sect, which emphasizes the primary worship of Krishna. Therefore, there is some justification in identifying this tradition as "Krishnaite." However, this is only one perspective, and the situation is more complex than that.

Swaminarayan as a Form of Krishna

A broader belief holds that Sahajanand was a form of Krishna. Bishop Heber understood Sahajanand as saying that Krishna was the form of God worshiped by his followers and then adding a hint that "the next avatar of Krishna or Surya has occurred within him." It is believed that Krishna has assumed various forms in different worlds and at different times for the benefit of humanity. Some followers believe that Sahajanand, who is referred to as Swaminarayan in his highest role, and Krishna are essentially the same. He manifested himself as Krishna at one point and as Swaminarayan in another form, which is the latest expression of God. Thus, this view separates God as Purushottam, and both Krishna and Sahajanand are seen as his incarnations.

The early poet-singer of the sect, Premanand's poetry reflects the transition from Krishna devotion to Swaminarayan devotion. Yogi Trivedi explores this development: "Premanand carefully draws a line between Krishna devotion and Swaminarayan devotion to preserve Krishna devotion and use it to connect the sect with the Vaishnav tradition, while simultaneously making space for his unique form of writing in Swaminarayan devotion. In doing so, he shapes the vision of the nascent sect." (2016: 198). Trivedi concludes:

> "*"Krishna retains his role as the protagonist in devotional narratives during certain religious rituals, festivals, and pastimes, where Swaminarayan does not play a central role. However, when higher theology (Books of the Sect we saw in chapter 2) is developed, Premanand replaces Krishna devotion with Swaminarayan devotion. Perhaps it is this strategic expression of Krishna devotion through music, bhajans, and other mediums that allows the sect and its followers to walk a fine line where they can develop and propagate their unique vision while also blending in with other Vaishnava sects. It might be this desire that inspired Swaminarayan poets to encourage the singing of bhajans dedicated to both Krishna and Swaminarayan." (213-214)*"

Thus, in these excerpts, Yogi Trivedi and through him, the English author, understand the subtle strategy of the followers of this sect, which many mainstream Sanatan saints and organizations have not yet grasped. The author delves deeper into this point and writes:

During Sahajanand's lifetime, the acceptance of his divinity as Swaminarayan grew steadily. The history of the Swaminarayan sect began with Ramanand Swami, who was a Krishna devotee. Ramanand Swami (b. 1739) was born into a Brahmin family in Bihar. At the age of twelve, he traveled to holy temples to learn from renowned scholars. Eventually, he came to Kathiawar, where he met the ascetic Atmanand, who initiated him into the Advaita tradition following Shankaracharya. Later, he went to Srirangam in South India, where he realized the truth of Ramanuja's modified Advaita (Vishishtadvaita), which developed as an alternative to Shankara's philosophy. According to legend, after about six months in Srirangam, Ramanand meditated on Ramanuja one night and fell asleep. Ramanuja appeared to him in a dream, initiated him, and gave him the marks of Vishnu, which were said to have appeared on his body when he awoke. Thus, he entered the line of acharyas appointed by Ramanuja and received a commission to return to Kathiawar in the north to spread Ramanuja's teachings.

When he returned to Gujarat, Ramanand gathered followers from both ascetics and householders. At this time, it is difficult to determine the size of his movement. In 1799, when he went to Bhuj, Nilkanth Varni came to his ashram. After being convened back from Bhuj to meet the new ascetic, Ramanand accepted Nilkanth into his group and initiated him as a Vaishnav ascetic. Along with the initiation, he gave Nilkanth a new name to reflect his new status: Sahajanand Swami. He remained in Ramanand's ashram for nearly two years (1799-1801) as one of the ascetics. Then, according to the story, Ramanand recognized the young ascetic's spiritual excellence and divinity and, despite the strength of his youth and the maturity of other potential successors like Muktanand, he appointed Sahajanand as the guru and successor in a public assembly in Jetpur. Shortly after this, in December 1802, Ramanand passed away. Thus, in the narrative of the Swaminarayan sect, Ramanand Swami appears as someone who paves the way for a great teacher. The Swaminarayan sect also claims that Ramanand Swami was an incarnation of Uddhava, the cousin and devotee of Krishna, who was to reincarnate and prepare the way for Krishna's new incarnation, Sahajanand Swami. Hence, Ramanand Swami's sect was known as the Uddhava sect. (*This could be a later embellishment, as Uddhava is an important figure in Krishna devotion, much like Radha. In Vaishnava

Puranas, Uddhava is portrayed as a male devotee with intense Krishna devotion, akin to Radha and the gopis. This might explain why any Vaishnava sect could be called 'Uddhava sect,' referring to male devotees of Krishna like Uddhava.)

Sahajanand Swami became the accepted leader of the group, though not without significant opposition. Some members left the group. Two women, Valbai and Harbai, who had long been associates of Ramanand and were leaders and preachers in the group, refused to accept the authority of Sahajanand, who was young enough to be their grandson. They strongly opposed him and were expelled by Sahajanand. A male leader in Ahmedabad took fifteen monks from the group and one of the four temples associated with Ramanand and formed a separate faction. Other temples also seem to have distanced themselves. Fortunately for Sahajanand, Muktanand Swami, the most senior disciple of Ramanand and 22 years older than Sahajanand, accepted his leadership. Despite considerable opposition within the group, many people accepted his leadership and divinity based on his claims of being divine. Muktanand Swami is said to have had a vision in which he realized that Ramanand was just the drumbeater [the one who draws attention and makes announcements], while Sahajanand was the true artist [whose work was being announced]. As a result, Muktanand composed a hymn, which he sang as an aarti to Sahajanand in 1802. This hymn is traditionally sung at regular worship (aarti) times in homes and temples, as well as during special festivals.

Soon after, in 1804, Sahajanand was described as the manifestation of God in a work called Yam-dand, which is of historical importance in the sect as it is the first text written within. Nishkulanand Swami, the author of 24 significant poetic works, including Yam-dand, believed that liberation would come through Sahajanand, who was the perfect teacher and the manifestation of Krishna. Anyone who approached him was promised freedom from suffering. Even at this early point in Sahajanand's career, some followers believed that at the time of death, Swaminarayan would come to take his devoted followers to his residence, where they would dwell as liberated souls. The final chapter of Yam-dand is a song of gratitude for this bringer of liberation. In fact, Ramanand Swami had given him the name "Narayan Muni," but by the time Yam-dand was written in 1804, he was referred to as Swaminarayan. After receiving this name and being equated with God in Yam-dand, he gave his followers a new mantra to recite in their religious practices: Swaminarayan. In a very short time, the messenger of

God (Swaminarayan) himself became God.

Thus, it seems that while there was significant opposition from parts of Gujarati society and some of Ramanand Swami's disciples, the remaining followers of Ramanand Swami worked diligently to exalt and divinize Sahajanand Swami. As the situation changed, so did Swaminarayan's lifestyle. Previously, he had followed strict discipline in renouncing worldly things, severing all contact with family and property. He followed strict rules of celibacy, prohibiting his followers from touching, seeing, or speaking to women. But as the divine leader of the sect, he had to ease some of his personal austerities, at least outwardly, although he continued to demand renunciation from his ascetic followers. His followers showered him with food, clothes, gold, and extraordinary gifts of expensive jewelry. He lived a life befitting a prince, in a land where princes lived very opulently.

At various points during his ministry, followers experienced that Sahajanand was the form of God in human form.

> "As a result, it was said: "Upon hearing this discourse, all the monks and devotees realized that the unmanifest form of Shri Krishna Bhagwan, which Shriji Maharaj spoke of, is none other than Shriji Maharaj himself, the son of Bhakti and Dharma. And there is none other who transcends him. He alone is our chosen deity, and he alone is our guru" (Vachanamrut, Vadtal). (*In other words, the original unmanifest form of Shri Krishna Bhagwan as Parabrahman is none other than this embodied form Swaminarayan, according to the Vachanamrut of Vadtal.)"

The path to spiritual development was to recognize this mystery through inner insight. Some followers were put into a state of samadhi by Sahajanand, where they were able to "see" this truth, and these experiences were regarded as miracles attributed to Sahajanand during that time. Those who had not developed spiritual insight to that level frequently opposed this doctrine. (*Here, Swami Dayanand Saraswati's accusation is relevant, as he claimed that Sahajanand Swami had mastered the art of pressing a nerve in the neck to render people unconscious, which he called putting people into samadhi. This passage suggests that those who did not accept Sahajanand as Parabrahman in such a samadhi continued to oppose him.)

Following this, there has been a merging of images and stories of Swaminarayan and Krishna. Attempts were made to link the stories of

Krishna's foretelling in the Bhagavat and other Puranas with Swaminarayan's birth narrative. One faction of followers identified Ramanand Swami as Uddhava, who called forth Krishna in the form of Sahajanand Swami. Francois Mallison has suggested that the name by which Krishna is worshiped in the temple of Dwarka—Ranchohod Chhogala—was used by Muktanand Swami to refer to Sahajanand, and that Swaminarayan's iconographic dress in temples closely resembles that of Krishna in Dwarka (Mallison). Thus, some followers view Swaminarayan as equivalent to Krishna, and this similarity is displayed in various legends and symbols.

Swaminarayan as the Supreme Purushottam

Meetings with members of various groups show that most followers believe that Swaminarayan is the sole and complete manifestation of the supreme being, Purushottam, and surpasses all other forms of gods, including Ram and Krishna, in power and effectiveness.

The sect's theologians refer to these passages in the Vachanamrut:

- "God has an eternal form. He is the creator, sustainer, and destroyer of countless universes; He is eternally present in His Akshardham; He is the lord of all lords; and He is the same who appears before your eyes in this manifest form (Swaminarayan)" (Vachanamrut Gadhada III 35.12, p. 731).

- "He is the same Guru of that dham – the lord of Akshar and the liberated souls, Parabrahman Purushottam – who is present in this satsang" (Vachanamrut Ahmedabad III 6.9, p. 752). Sahajanand Swami is saying this for himself in Vachanamrut in front of his followers.

Those who hold this belief argue that Swaminarayan was not a form of Krishna, as some believe, but the complete form of Purushottam, the supreme God Himself. Among some followers (like of BAPS), comparing Swaminarayan to other avatars is considered inappropriate. This forms the basis of their understanding of the sect's monotheism. This belief was evident in banners displayed at temples during the bicentennial celebration of Swaminarayan's birth, reading: "God is one and incomparable."

With the emergence of the vision of supreme Swaminarayan, the hierarchy of deities begins to take shape. Deities (gods) are involved in the activities of creating, sustaining, and destroying the universe. They are within the flow of the universe (maya) as they are connected with the activities of creation. Avatars are sent into the world by Purushottam, and they manifest according to his will. In this interpretation, all avatars do not manifest the same level of completeness of Purushottam's fullness. As we have seen, human forms are given precedence, with Ram and Krishna among them. The highest, however, is Swaminarayan, who is considered the complete and full manifestation of Purushottam in his human form on Earth. Some modern interpreters use the language of avatar and suggest that "he is the avatari, not an avatar" (Vachanamrut Loya 18.18, p. 364).

On occasions when Sahajanand revealed this to his early disciples, he faced opposition (Vachanamrut, Loya 18.4, p. 358). He recognized that this was a difficult doctrine, easy to misunderstand, and would cause many to leave the fellowship. Nevertheless, he believed that failure to understand God in his human form would result in failure to attain liberation from the bonds of the world. Therefore, he taught, "The divine form of Purushottam that appears before you here and the divine form that resides in Akshardham are one and the same, and there is absolutely no difference between these two forms" (Vachanamrut Gadhada III 38.3, pp. 337f). The person who meditates on the manifest human form of God on Earth will see the divine radiant form of God in Akshardham and will transcend the flow of the world and rebirth because both Purushottam and Akshar are beyond maya (Vachanamrut Gadhada II 13.9, p. 445).

"*After describing these three types of belief systems in the sect, author Raymond Brady Williams says, "Thus, we see at least three levels of understanding of the relationship between Swaminarayan, Purushottam, and Krishna in the sect's literature and in the responses of devotees to questions on the subject. Those who hold all three views claim to represent an accurate understanding of Sahajanand's teachings.... One theory is that Sahajanand's understanding evolved slightly, so he began as a reformer of asceticism and Krishna worship and came to believe that he was the full form of Purushottam by the end of his career. A similar theory is that, although he had a clear vision of his true nature at all times, there was progressive development in his teachings as his audience became prepared for a more complete understanding of his nature. While it is clear from the literature that he tailored his teachings to match the capacity of his listeners and was reluctant to speak openly about his identity as Purushottam except with his closest disciples, the members of the group argue that from the moment of his birth, Sahajanand was the full form of Purushottam and understood himself as such. They assert that the differences in interpretation found in the literature are not due to development in his understanding or teaching but to differences in the understanding of individual disciples."*

The Structure of the Universes

Raymond says, "As followers imagine the sacred universe, deities and gods are believed to possess separate heavenly abodes or realms. These may be depicted, as in some temples, and referred to as places, but they are states of existence. The supreme abode is Akshar, or in its unmanifest form, Akshardham, and the supreme being, Purushottam, resides there with his devotees. Many believe that Swaminarayan is Purushottam, the lord of Akshardham, and that he manifested as Sahajanand in human form. Some believe that Krishna and Ram are not direct manifestations of the supreme being but belong to another eternal existence. It is said they preside over the lower realms of Goloka and Vaikuntha, respectively. Others believe that Krishna and Ram were indeed forms of the supreme being, though at a level below Akshardham, with Krishna's abode being Goloka and Ram's being Vaikuntha. Other gods preside over lower abodes. Thus, a hierarchical structure of abodes exists, with Akshardham as the primary abode. Akshardham is the supreme realm, and Purushottam, described as the radiant form of God, is believed to reside in Akshardham and be the cause of all avatars."

Thus, English authors have come to understand the inner workings of this sect quite well, yet those in Gujarat, who claim to serve and protect the Hindu religion, have no awareness of the profound alterations made to their scriptures and the nature of their Dharma. The English author Raymond Brady Williams, in his book An Introduction of Swaminarayan Hinduism, attempts to explain the complex and fabricated three-tier philosophy of the sect in practical terms as a foreigner, while also subtly highlighting its disarray and imaginary nature.

So, in any place among Hindus, this sect uses these three successive levels of deception to establish a new supreme deity named Swaminarayan above the Vedic deities of Sanatan Dharma. Following this, all the distortions seen in Gujarat, particularly in Chapter 2 of this book, begin to unfold. This three-tiered deception is their primary tool for converting Hindus. They are attempting to gain a foothold in places like Chhapaiya in Uttar Pradesh, the Ram Temple in Ayodhya, the sacred sites of Uttarakhand, and Jagannath Puri under the guise of a Vaishnav sect at the first level. In Puri, they have been granted a vast area to construct their temple within just five kilometers of the Jagannath Temple. In the newly built corridor of the Mahakal Temple in Ujjain, the symbol of this sect's tilak has been inscribed on the murals as the contract to build that corridor was given to the company affiliated with this sect. In Gujarat, this sect takes contracts to renovate old Sanatan Dharma temples in villages and cities, and during reconstruction, they place their tilak symbols, statues, or photos of their Swamis inside. Eventually, they usurp the entire temple, reducing the presiding deity of that Sanatan temple to a mere servant of their Sahajanand Swami. Many Ram temples, Krishna temples, Shiva temples, and Hanuman temples in Gujarat have already suffered this fate. Now, by influencing the current ruling powers, they are attempting to adopt the same strategy for major temples outside Gujarat, such as Mahakal in Ujjain. Thus, by aligning with political power, this sect is now trying to expand beyond Gujarat and establish itself in other states of India through its same three-tiered deception.

Their biggest deception in this endeavor is the theft of terms from Sanatan Dharma's scriptures, such as "Purushottam" and "Aksharbrahm," which is originally used for Lord Krishna, and the sect is falsely attaching them to their fake Narayan, stolen from Ramanuja's Vishishtadvaita philosophy (refer to Chapter 18). In Vaishnava Puranas, the term "Purushottam" is used exclusively for Lord Krishna and comes directly from him. In the eighth chapter of the Bhagavad Gita, Lord Shri Krishna says, "In this world, there are two kinds of beings: the perishable (Kshara) and the imperishable (Akshara). Bodies of creatures, humans, and plants are perishable, but the soul that sustains these bodies is imperishable. But beyond these two, there is the highest being, who enters all three worlds and sustains the entire creation. This highest being is called the imperishable, supreme lord, and supreme soul. Therefore, I transcend both the perishable and imperishable. This is why I am known in the world and in the Vedas as Purushottam" (8.16-18). Then, Shri Krishna, the manifest form of the unmanifest Parabrahman, says, "O Bharata, the wise person who knows me as this supreme form of Purushottam, knowing everything, worships me constantly as the supreme lord" (8.19).

Since Shri Krishna is the only complete avatar of Vishnu, he is called Purna Purushottam. For this reason, there is no difference between Krishna and the complete form of Lord Vishnu. This is why the Shrimad Bhagavatam was composed as the Purana, where Krishna is placed in the position of Vishnu and worshiped as the supreme Purushottam Parmeshwar through the path of devotion. But in Shrimad Bhagavatam too, it is repeatedly told that Krishna is Vishnu. This is the primary philosophical reason behind the Krishna devotion of all Vaishnava sects, from the path of Ramanujacharya's Vishishtadvaita to ISKCON. This was also the Purushottam-centered Krishna devotion of Ramanand Swami's Uddhav sect, which was given a deceptive and fraudulent twist under the name Swaminarayan after the arrival of Sahajanand Swami. Sahajanand separated the term "Purushottam" from Krishna and "Narayan" from Vishnu, proclaiming himself as Purushottam Narayan and demoting Krishna and Vishnu to much lower deities. This is an attack on the essence of Sanatan Dharma and its scriptures, an internal betrayal perpetrated by this false Narayan's deceitful sect.

Before concluding this chapter, let me leave you with an excerpt from pages 65-66 of the BAPS book Akshar Purushottam Upasana, where Sahajanand Swami himself boasts about how he implemented this three-tiered conspiracy in the Gujarati society of his time. This three-tiered conspiracy is their modus operandi, which has been consistently applied, from the Gujarati society of that time to the Hindus and Gujaratis living abroad today.

> "On pages 65-66 of Akshar Purushottam Upasana, a question is posed: "If Bhagwan Swaminarayan is supreme, why has he been described as Krishna in the Vachanāmrut, in other shastras of the Sampradaya and in the kirtans of the paramhansas?"
>
> The answer given is strikingly similar to how the concept of Allah was introduced in pre-Islamic Arabia, where many gods existed. The answer is: "During the time of Shriji Maharaj, there were many faiths

and cults, some of which expounded irreligious practices, accepted false gurus, believed in superstitions and indulged in black magic. Their influence was widespread. All of these fiercely opposed the new Sampradaya. In such trying times, if any person tried to identify himself as God, people would naturally be reluctant to join the Sampradaya out of sheer dismay. The acceptance of a new idea is always gradual. Shriji Maharaj was therefore identified initially as a Satpurush, then as an avatar and finally as Purushottam – the avatāri of all avatars. As the aspirants' faith in him deepened, the paramhansas depicted Shriji Maharaj in more inspiring and enlightening terms.

.....To attract people, Shriji Maharaj consecrated the murtis of those deities at the places where they were popularly worshiped. Their devotees came for darshan. By subsequent association with the sadhus, they developed unshakeable faith in Shriji Maharaj's supreme and sublime form. Gradually, the true upāsanā began to be widely accepted in the Sampradaya."

XII

Sanatan Dharma Protection Committee

Let us now return to the press conference held on the evening of September 4 at the Shivanand Ashram in Ahmedabad. Swami Paramatmananda Saraswatiji reported to the press about the meeting held between the Sanatani saints and the Swaminarayan sect, mediated by the VHP (Vishva Hindu Parishad). He announced that the controversial murals at the Salangpur temple would be removed by the next morning. He also announced the formation of a committee, which would be chaired by Jagadguru Shankaracharya Shri Sadanand Saraswatiji of Sharada Peeth and Acharya Rakeshprasadji, the head of the Swaminarayan Vadtal Gadi. With their blessings, this committee would attempt to resolve all disputes related to the Swaminarayan sect. It seemed like a promising idea, but the committee never materialized.

Seventeen days later, on September 21, a large assembly of Sanatani saints was held at Shernath Bapu's Gorakhnath Ashram in Junagadh, where it was announced that a committee would be formed to protect Sanatan Dharma. The assembly took place on September 21, 2023, and today, as I write this chapter, it is September 27, 2024. Everything that has transpired over the past year has revolved around and involved this committee. After Swami Paramatmanandji's press conference on September 4, things took a different turn. The committee, which was initially meant to include Swaminarayan sect members and Sanatani saints, ended up consisting solely of Sanatani saints. The reasons for this are not entirely clear, but there was some hushed speculation that the Sanatani saints felt that the VHP was influenced by the money and vote bank of the Swaminarayan sect and was, therefore, not completely impartial. Some even mentioned that RSS leader Ram Madhav attended the September 4 meeting at Shivanand Ashram, and after the decision to remove the murals was made, he went to Vadtal to meet with the Acharya or other prominent Swamis there, but he did not go to meet any Sanatani saint or Shankaracharya. In the press conference that day, Swami Paramatmanand Saraswatiji addressed both the Shankaracharya and Acharya Rakesh Prasadji of Vadtal with equal respect, without preserving the reverence typically associated with the position of the Shankaracharya as the highest sovereignty in Sanatan Dharma.

In the following days, videos surfaced of Hindu saints expressing frustration, asking, "Why does the VHP need to interfere in religious matters to this extent? Will religion and saints function as the VHP dictates?" It became clear that the Swaminarayan sect was under the protection of the RSS and VHP, and that the VHP's stance was influenced by the sect. However, the Sanatani saints viewed this as overreach by the VHP into religious matters. In harsher terms, it appeared that the Swaminarayan sect, the RSS, the VHP, and the BJP were acting as a single unit, holding discussions and making plans behind the scenes before presenting a united front against the Sanatani saints. This prompted the Sanatani saints to proceed with forming their own committee, separate from the VHP.

At that time, I was the coordinator of the research wing of the Sangh. I received calls from Sanatani warriors, saying, "Sir, we are recommending that you be included in the committee, and we want you to be part of it." I was told that I would receive a call from a gentleman named Dr. Vasant Patel, who was also involved with the saints in this endeavor. I did receive a call from Vasantbhai, and thus I came into contact with Dr. Vasant Patel, an Ahmedabad-based physician with whom I would collaborate on this effort over the coming year. Vasantbhai regularly appeared on Gujarati TV news channels as part of panel discussions on various topics and was known for his fearless, impartial views. He had called for the establishment of a Sanatan Protection Board to safeguard the principles and traditions of Sanatan Dharma. Since Gujarati news channels were not watched in my home, I was unaware of this. After speaking on the phone, we became acquainted with each other's work, and he said, "I will put your name forward, and we will form a team of householders to serve as an advisory group." I agreed, and the next day, on the morning of September 21, as the meeting was about to take place, I wrote this post on Facebook:

A humble suggestion to the assembly of saints gathering in Junagadh today.

· September 21, 2023

On this day, I am reminded of the assembly of saints held at Baba Ramdev's Acharyakulam before the 2014 elections, where all the major saints of Sanatan Dharma gave their support and blessings to Narendra Modiji to become the next Prime Minister of India. In that assembly, all the major saints, including Morari Bapu, Baba Ramdev, Rameshbhai Oza, Arya Samaji saints, and saints from other Sanatani institutions, were present. Modiji said, 'This country was not made by kings or leaders. This country was made by saints. And when necessary, it was the saints who saved this country.'

The sect for which today's assembly is convened did not have any members present at that event. That was the scene in 2014, but the events of 2015, 2016, and 2017 completely changed the equation. The Sanatani saints who stood by Modiji in 2014 gradually disappeared, and the Swaminarayan sect's swamis began to appear in their place. The shift that occurred over those three years is the reason for the current state of Gujarat's Sanatani society.

Today, if I had the privilege of meeting Prime Minister Modiji, I would tell him one thing: "Modiji, you have done much and done it excellently. But the cost of all those achievements has been paid in Gujarat. And now, with the time you have left in politics, you must take responsibility for correcting that situation. For this is a situation that will tarnish your legacy long after you are gone, as Gujarat's entire Sanatani society will be pushed into the same kind of servitude that the Sanatani Hindus of Tamil Nadu and the Sanatani Sikhs of Punjab face today. Don't leave without addressing this issue. If you are not fully aware of this situation, know that your contacts have been compromised. Come yourself and speak with Gujarat's true Sanatani saints and society to understand the real situation."

This, in essence, is the root cause of the issue. The insults we have heard, the painful writings we have read, and the distressing images and models we have seen over the past two or three years all stem from this transformation.

My humble suggestion to the saints is this: Whether it was Modiji's mistake or yours, whether a wrong turn was taken by him or by you—reflect on it and make efforts to restore the scene from 2014, where the Sanatani Hindu society stood proudly with its beloved leader and true saints. The satisfaction, pride, and sense of security in that scene have since faded, no matter how much patchwork is done to make it look the same. Some Sanatani friends have been advising me to attend this Junagadh assembly and speak for five minutes, but I have already said most of what I needed to on social media. Today, I am sharing the fundamental diagnosis, which I have not mentioned before. As for the decisions to be made in this saint assembly, I don't need to say much, but addressing this root issue is most crucial and must be done with true intent. Victory to Sanatan Dharma.

✿

But the VHP played its own game in the Junagadh meeting as well. They had already planted their so-called government saints within the Sanatani saints. The atmosphere was charged. The efforts made by Sanatani warriors over the past two years had brought the matter to this point, with the issue now in the spotlight on all Gujarati news channels. A display was set up in the meeting to showcase all the videos, images, and writings that insulted Sanatan Dharma and its deities, which we saw in earlier chapters. But the VHP men, along with their government saints, opposed this and had the display shut down. They were also included in the committee alongside Vasantbhai and me. Later, when it was time for the saints to speak, those same VHP-affiliated government saints delivered speeches praising the Swaminarayan sect, even saying that without this sect, the green color in the tricolor flag would rise to the top. Once again, the fear of Muslims was used to push people to accept a new supreme god. The Hindus in Gujarat were caught between two extremes: They were being told to live in fear of Muslims and to accept a sect that claims its ordinary devotees possess so much brilliance that they need not visit Krishna at Dakor, but Krishna should come to receive their blessings instead. They were also told that the goddess Adya Shakti derives her power from chanting "Jai Swaminarayan," that Lord Shiva can be defeated by an ordinary disciple of Sahajanand Swami, and that even Shiva joins his hands in front of this disciple because his Karmas and status is not so rich that Swaminarayan can give him Darshan. The Sanatani society was being told to accept all this if they wanted to survive against the Muslims!

On that day, the "Sanatan Dharma Protection Committee" was indeed formed, along with various sub-committees. However, the confidence of the Sanatani saints was shaken. The movement that had been building against the anti-Sanatan activities of the Swaminarayan sect was thwarted. Steps were immediately taken to ensure that the committee would never become functional, with everyone being quietly contacted and pacified.

The attempt to form a committee of Sanatani saints was derailed in its very first meeting. A section of the Sanatani saints expressed their frustration against the Hindu organizations, saying, "Who are you to interfere in matters of religion? Why do you feel the need to get involved? We can protect our religion ourselves." On the other hand, the RSS, through the VHP, positioned certain government-aligned saints, who countered by saying, "Without the Swaminarayan sect, there is no salvation for us. It is the future." These individuals did not care to understand what books the Swaminarayan sect's swamis studied, what stories were told to children as they grew up, or how these ideas were being ingrained in Gujaratis at home and abroad. Their focus was solely on instilling fear of Muslims and defending the sect. Meanwhile, the common Sanatani society, with its collective awareness, easily sensed that these people were entangled in the sect's wealth and privileges. They were no longer concerned about religion or the deities; after becoming monks, their only aim was to remain in the "good list" of power and to elevate their status.

Thus, the committee lost its significance. The people from the VHP and the government-aligned saints who had infiltrated the committees led the conversation toward postponement. Once again, our unknown Sanatani warriors became active, returning to meet the Shankaracharya to request further progress. They contacted me, saying, "Sir, last time, we took your letter, and the Guruji said, 'Next time you come, bring the person who wrote the letter.' So this time, please join us and speak on our behalf." Once again, I hesitated initially but eventually decided to accompany them as a member of the committee.

Dwarka and the Shankaracharya:

For years, visiting the Dwarkadhish temple had been an unfulfilled task for me. My spiritual lifestyle was such that I never actively planned visits to temples. I would keep the desire for darshan in my heart and continue to flow along the spiritual path of life. When the flow of life brought me to the gates of a temple, I would gratefully dedicate my mind and soul to the experience. The opportunity to visit Dwarka came at the age of 35, in the context of opposing an attempt to elevate a devotee of Lord Krishna above the Lord Himself, a move that sought to undermine Sanatan Dharma. We were to meet the head of the Sharda Peeth in Dwarka, Jagadguru Shankaracharya, regarding the newly formed committee.

Three days after the formation of the committee, on September 24, we visited Dwarka. That day, we had two discussions with the Shankaracharya—one in the morning and one in the evening. The morning meeting was formal; I presented him with my book, and he offered me his blessings. We discussed the sect and the committee. In the afternoon, I consulted with Vasantbhai Patel over the phone about what we should request in the evening meeting. Vasantbhai suggested, "We should ask Guruji to send a notice to all the temples and factions of the sect on behalf of Sanatan Dharma, addressing the anti-Sanatan writings and insults found in their literature. They should be given a week to respond. Let's start this way." I agreed with the idea. In the evening meeting, we had a long discussion with the Shankaracharya, delving into the teachings of the scriptures and the sect's false arguments and lies. He also said, "The idea of sending a notice is good, but give them a month to respond. We should give them that much time. But the notice must go out on the committee's letterhead. For that, the committee needs to be registered as a trust." He added, "In Junagadh, they requested that I become the president of the committee, but I have not accepted it yet. I will consider it when someone from the committee comes to meet me. So far, no one has come to see me except for you."

Our meeting ended at 7:30 PM, and we left feeling positive because the path had been laid out. All that remained was for the committee to be registered as a trust. However, there was no structural coherence among the saints. Who would approach whom? Who would take the initiative to ask the Shankaracharya to assume the presidency? Those who were active were intent on keeping the matter dormant. Meanwhile, the Swaminarayan sect was focused on restoring its lost reputation. After being forced to remove the controversial murals from the Vadtal temple, they had suffered a loss of face, especially after being called out for spreading lies about Hindu scriptures. To regain their standing, the Vadtal temple was planning a grand festival. Their followers on social media became more active, mocking the Sanatani saints and the committee. Some were still repeating the same radical Islamic-like statements. One would write, "Sanatanis, accept it now.

Swaminarayan is the source of all incarnations. Now that He has come, there is no need to worship any of the previous deities. Only Swaminarayan, the original Parabrahman, should be worshiped." Another would mock the ascetics of Girnar, accusing them of smoking cannabis and asking, "Are they the ones who will form a committee?" Some would say, "All of the Sangh, BJP, and VHP's programs are held in Swaminarayan temples. That is the future. It is said to us that the name of Swaminarayan will be on every leaf."

In response to all of this, I announced a new initiative to keep the spirits of the Sanatani warriors alive until the committee was registered. The announcement was that "The Sanatan Dharma Protection Committee will register temples of Sanatan Dharma across Gujarat, listing the names and contact details of their presiding deities and priests. A website will be created, and a whole network of Sanatan temples will be formed. Only temples dedicated to the Vedic and Puranic deities, those aligned with the Panchdev form and YogiGuru tradition of Sanatan Dharma will be included. Temples associated with sects like Swaminarayan, Sai Baba, and Brahma Kumaris will not be included. The center of this network will be the Sharda Peeth in Dwarka."

This announcement came just six days after the Junagadh meeting, yet as soon as it was made, reports began circulating in the Sanatani community and local newspapers that the committee was now active. This showed how eager the entire Sanatani society was to respond to the internal betrayal that had insulted their deities and attempted to destroy their Sanatan Dharma. This awakening was the hallmark of Hindu consciousness, something the Sangh and VHP had failed to grasp in this matter. Vasantbhai, Harshad Bharati Bapu, and I each made a video for social media, requesting priests from every temple to assist the volunteers who would come to register their temples. Within five days, we had assembled around 40 volunteers from various parts of Gujarat and registered about 150 temples.

This was also the time when blind followers of the sect began leaving one-star ratings and negative reviews on the Google pages of my clinic and Vasantbhai's clinic. This was a form of counterattack on social media. Vasantbhai faced no major issue, as his clinic had been established for 25 years and had around 400 positive reviews, making the 15 or so negative ones insignificant. However, I had only created my clinic's Google page two years earlier, and since people in my city were not yet in the habit of checking online reviews before visiting a clinic, no patients had left reviews. Consequently, my Google page was flooded with one-star ratings and negative comments like "bad doctor," "clinic was dirty," "treatment was terrible," and many more false claims. They did not stop there. They also went to Amazon and gave one-star ratings to my English novel, leaving negative comments. This novel, which had received four-and-a-half stars from India's no. 1 book review agency and was ranked among the top 10 legal thrillers of 2023, was now being attacked. I know that this will likely happen with this book as well, and by the time you are reading this, it may have already started. But do you know who these reviewers were? Brainwashed blind devotees from Vadodara and Surat, 300 to 400 kilometers away from my place, some of whom were doctors themselves.

When the Sanatani warriors learned of this, they tried to improve my clinic's rating by leaving positive reviews. Even today, my Google page still contains those conflicting reviews, and none of them are true. Of the thousands of patients I have treated, not a single one has left a review on Google. Today, when I look at those reviews, I read the negative words calmly. I find solace in knowing that by speaking the truth, I caused pain to some genuine people trapped in this sect, and in a way, I take my retribution there.

But this malicious behavior of the blind followers had no effect on us. We continued working with even more determination to register temples on a large scale and to obtain video messages from the saints and the Shankaracharya. We asked the saints on the committee to create videos for the temple registration initiative and relayed the request to the Shankaracharya's disciples as well. As soon as this happened, curiosity was rekindled among both the Sanatani and government-aligned saints: "Who is running this committee?" Once again, they became active, negotiating and exchanging messages behind the scenes. Finally, they realized the need to act quickly and provide a platform for the committee. We had asked for videos from the saints, but instead, we received news that "Stop everything for now. On the 27th of October, a grand religious assembly will be held at Kailashdham in Pethapur, Gandhinagar, presided over by Sri Muktanand Bapu. On that day, the 'Sri Sanatan Dharma Culture Protection Trust' will be announced, and Jagadguru Shankaracharya will assume the presidency of the committee and the trust. He has sent an invitation to all the Sanatan Dharma saints, and they will all be attending."

The arrow had hit the target. On October 27th, Vasantbhai, another Sanatani warrior, and I arrived at Kailashdham in Pethapur. We met several saints who were genuinely concerned about this issue and were working toward a solution. One of them was Gaurangasharanji, a Ramanandi saint from the Himatnagar area. I saw a sincere saint in him. Upon seeing the politics involved in the committee, he had distanced himself from it. He was not driven by the desire for fame or followers, nor did he crave political significance. Another such saint was from Gorakhanath sect named Dr. Jyotirnath Maharaj, who had always been seen eager to do someting for this issue and always remained active in the media as well. However, we also observed that Muktanand Bapu, the head of the ashram, was pacifying the other saints, saying, "Look, don't escalate this issue too much. We must concentrate on the fight against Muslims and Christians." Once again, the same rhetoric.

At around 6 PM, the saints took to the stage, and more speeches followed. However, this time the atmosphere was somewhat balanced. The Junagadh meeting had been almost a direct confrontation between the VHP and the Sanatani saints. The same government-aligned saints were present here, as they had been in Junagadh, and they delivered the same speeches that were contrary to the committee's objectives, but this time with more restraint. On the other hand, Kankeshwari Mata, Acharya Gaurangasharanji, a young saint from Kutch, and a few other Saints spoke fearlessly and accurately in defense of Sanatan Dharma. But it was Shankaracharya's half-hour speech that not only rekindled a sense of hope within us but also increased our respect for them. Without hiding anything or showing any fear, he said what needed to be said.

The main focus of the event, however, was the central role played by Muktanand Bapu in the entire movement. It was announced that one building in his ashram would serve as the office for the newly formed committee and trust. Shankaracharya was appointed as the president of the committee and trust, and Muktanand Bapu was appointed as the executive president. After listening to Muktanand Bapu's speech, that was before the speech of Shankaracharyaji, we, as his guests, almost fully understood what this was all about. This was exactly what A.O. Hume, a British civil servant, had done so in 1885 when he founded the Indian National Congress to prevent another rebellion like the one in 1857. The Congress Party was created to give Indians a platform to gather, hold meetings once every few months, and make speeches. This committee was going to be a Congress of sorts, with Muktanand Bapu as the BJP and RSS's A.O. Hume.

With this final conclusion, Vasantbhai, another Sanatani warrior, and I left the venue. In our hearts, we found some solace in the fact that the

Shankaracharyaji remained firm in his stance, and despite all the political maneuvering around the committee, his approach had not changed. He was a beacon of hope. But aside from that, we had almost removed any major expectations from the committee that day, understanding that from now on, things would move at a slow pace, with Muktanand Bapu only doing as much as the Sangh allowed. The Shankaracharya would remain entangled among empty formalities, and whatever had been told to A.O. Hume would eventually be done.

After this conclusion, Vasantbhai and I changed our course. The idea was, if everything is going to happen through the Sangh, then let's meet the saints of the All India Saints Committee, which operates as an organization of the Sangh. Surely, there would be saints concerned about Sanatan Dharma there. Accordingly, we tried to enter the atmosphere of the Sangh's Saints Committee. We will discuss that in the upcoming chapter. But I will conclude this chapter with an article I wrote the day after attending the religious assembly in Pethapur, where one of the VHP's government-aligned saints made a controversial statement. The saint said on stage, "Look at history. If you study history, you'll understand that those who separated from Sanatan Dharma have progressed. Just look at how Buddhism, after separating from Sanatan, spread to so many countries! Therefore, do not divide people away from Sanatan." The comment was mainly aimed at defending the Swaminarayan sect, and I responded to it in the article below, which I also sent to the same saint.

What Happened to the Sects That Separated from Sanatan Dharma?

Did They Progress, Shrink, or Burst Like a Bubble? A Logical Analysis

• 28th October 2023 / Facebook

The sects that emerged from Sanatan Dharma but are still considered part of Hinduism, such as Buddhism, Jainism, and Sikhism, were never originally created to separate from Sanatan Dharma. Two Kshatriya princes, Siddhartha Gautama and Vardhamana, left the material world in search of truth, heading into the forest. Both had received Vedic education in Gurukuls. However, during their search for truth, they did not follow an established Vedic guru but instead began their own meditative journeys. Truth is singular and not monopolized by anyone. According to Sanatan Dharma, all paths ultimately lead to the same truth. Thus, both princes found the truth, which was the same as what they had been taught in the Gurukul through the Upanishads. The only difference was in the words they used to describe it and the unique paths they presented to the world for its discovery. This is how the Jain and Buddhist sects emerged, with slightly different ways of searching for and explaining truth from the Vedic tradition. Similarly, in the face of Muslim invasions, Khatri Gurus founded the Khalsa sect, a militant force that fought for the protection of the Vedic Om as the supreme divinity. One child from a Hindu family remained Hindu, while another adopted the turban and sword to become Sikh. Thus, none of these sects were created to separate from Hinduism, but were paths discovered by Hindus to fulfill their duty toward truth. Over time, these paths began to diverge from their Vedic roots.

Now, let's examine the current state of these sects, which separated from Sanatan Dharma, in relation to Sanatan Dharma today.

At one time, more than half of the world was Buddhist, but today, Buddhism survives only in small countries like Japan and Myanmar. The total Buddhist population in these small countries is significantly less than the population of Sanatanis in India alone. China, once a major Buddhist nation, has become communist and atheist. The same China has displaced Buddhists from Tibet, the largest Buddhist region between China and India, and those displaced Buddhists are now living in exile in India. Afghanistan, once a Buddhist nation, is now under the control of the Taliban, where Buddhists have either been killed or converted to Islam. Indonesia, once Buddhist, has now become the world's largest Muslim country. In Sri Lanka, most people have converted to Christianity.

Sikhs have remained in India's Punjab, but they have been wiped out from Pakistani Punjab and Kashmir. Those who moved to Canada are losing their Indian identity and are being brainwashed in the name of Khalistan. In India's Punjab, the situation resembles that of abandoned and backward villages from where educated people flee. The poor Sikh community in Punjab has also converted to Christianity.

The Jain sect, which exists in India, has fragmented into various branches but still survives, albeit as a minority. The reason the Jains have not met the same fate as the Buddhists or Sikhs is due to two clear reasons. First, they never sought power like the Buddhists did. They have preserved their existence by adhering to the ascetic path of their Tirthankaras even today. While some may consider this overly rigid, it is this very asceticism that has helped the Jains maintain their existence. Second, the Jains have never completely separated from their Vedic roots like the Buddhists and Sikhs. Their first Tirthankara, Rishabhdev, is considered an avatar of Vishnu in some places in the Puranas, and in others, an incarnation of Shiva. Even subsequent Tirthankaras, and the Jain community as a whole, have remained culturally and socially close to the Sanatanis. They have not become as socially and culturally distant as the Buddhists and Sikhs. This has protected them.

This suggests that those who remain close to the form of Sanatan Dharma—often called the seed of truth and immortality—survive, while those who stray far away eventually burst like a bubble. Sanatan Dharma recognizes Nirakar Parabrahman and OM as the supreme divinity, and only those who do not recognize anyone other than the Panchadev as the manifest form of the formless God are truly part of Sanatan Dharma. Anyone who speaks of a manifest complete God outside the Panchadev or a formless God other than OM is not part of Sanatan. And those who try to elevate any form of deity beyond OM or the Panchadev as the supreme God are not just sectarians but invaders attacking Sanatan Dharma.

XIII

Traditionalist Saints and Sangh-Aligned Saints

Now we will dive into the political game being played between the Sangh and the saints. For that, we need to go back in time a little. I mentioned earlier that when the Sanatani warriors wanted me to meet Shankaracharyaji, I was initially hesitant. The first time, I wrote a letter, and that sufficed, but the second time, after some initial reluctance, I agreed to meet him. My hesitation stemmed from the fact that the Shankaracharya of Puri, Jagadguru Shri Nishchalanand Saraswatiji, had, for the past few years, been promoting the idea that Varna and jati (caste) are predetermined, meaning everything is decided by birth. He would even interpret that verse from the Bhagavad Gita, where Lord Krishna says, "I have divided this creation into four varnas based on people's qualities and actions," in a way that suggested that based on the qualities and actions in a person's previous life, they are born accordingly in this life. Essentially, he claimed that everything is determined by birth. Brahmin is pure and higher by birth and Sudra is lower due to his birth. I feared that if I heard the same from the Shankaracharya of Sharada Peeth, Shri Sadanand Saraswatiji, I might lose respect for the position of Shankaracharya and the revered peeths (seats of spiritual authority). I worried that I would end up opposing them too. Nevertheless, the time had come, and I had to meet him and face whatever came.

When I arrived at Dwarka's Sharada Math on September 24th, before meeting the Shankaracharya, I met some of his disciples and peers. They had all heard about me, and our conversation primarily focused on scriptures and the opposition to the Swaminarayan sect. At one point, I stopped them and asked, "Before I meet Guruji (Shankaracharyaji), I have a question. The views that the Shankaracharya of Puri, Nishchalanandji, is promoting, that caste is based on birth—are these his personal opinions, or do they reflect the views of our Shankaracharyaji as well?" They responded kindly and lovingly, "Not just our Shankaracharya or the four Shankaracharyas, Kaushik Bhai, but all six schools of philosophy's acharyas hold the same view. We have distanced ourselves from this under the pressure of leftists, but we have a whole varna ashram system." What followed was a long discussion between us where I argued, using common sense and scriptures, that varna is based on qualities, actions, and nature, and how this aligns with the societal framework of the scriptures. The learned Brahmins, however, presented different interpretations of the scriptures to defend their stance.

In the end, we concluded the conversation on friendly terms, laughing, and shifted our focus to the current issues when it was time to meet Guruji. However, that day, both I and the Sanatani warriors who accompanied me realized that the cold war between the Sangh and the Shankaracharya peeths, or Brahminical acharyas, is largely due to this issue. In response to this, the Sangh has aligned itself more closely with independent babas, sects, and institutions to balance the power of the acharyas. The Swaminarayan sect has taken full advantage of this, especially in Gujarat and abroad, by influencing the Sangh and set up a new supreme God over Sanatan Dharma.

After returning from Dwarka, I reached out to Sanjay Dixit Ji, founder of Jaipur Dialogues. Sanjay Dixit Ji, originally from Uttar Pradesh, was a retired IAS officer, having mostly served in Rajasthan. He had also been a member and director of the Rajasthan Cricket Association, with extensive contacts in India's bureaucracy. After retiring, Sanjay Ji founded a YouTube channel called Jaipur Dialogues, where he invited pro-Hindu thinkers and researchers from India and around the world to discuss various topics in podcast format. His channel had become very popular and inspirational, spreading a great deal of knowledge. I was connected with him, and we would often discuss issues related to Hindu civilization through WhatsApp chats. Jaipur Dialogues had offered a challenge, stating that if anyone could prove that Varna and jati in Hindu scriptures are based on birth, they would be awarded 2 million rupees (the prize amount might vary). I told him about my discussions at the Dwarka Sharda Peeth and asked, "Are we really ready for this challenge?" He responded, "Yes, we are. But let's review everything again for a month."

We re-examined all the scriptures, arguments, and logic. As we became more confident in our understanding, I continued to write articles on Facebook in Hindi. Some of our Sanatani warriors were not happy about this. They said, "Sir, why are you bringing up this issue now? Don't we already have enough obstacles in this movement? Why should we bring up the issue of whether Varna and Jatis are based on birth or actions right now?" I responded, "You don't understand the bigger game. This issue is just waiting to surface. Initially, attempts were made to portray the movement against the Swaminarayan sect as a Congress political conspiracy, but nothing came of it. All the Sanatanis leading the movement were anti-Congress, and pro-Sangh, pro-BJP. Now, as Shankaracharya becomes more active, a new narrative will be spun that this is all being done by Brahminical forces trying to restore their dominance and bring back Brahminism. What I am doing will prevent that weapon from being used against us because I am countering it with accurate logic and scriptural evidence that they have never considered. Meanwhile, the Swaminarayan sect is fundamentally caste-based. I am simply assuring the Sangh that this movement has nothing to do with Brahminical caste-based ideas. In fact, we are opposed to those too. I know exactly what I'm doing."

Finally, when I wrote an article on the science of varna based on qualities and actions in the Prasthānatrayi (Upanishads, Bhagavad Gita, Brahma Sutras), the response was overwhelming. People started asking, "Who is your guru? Who are you associated with?" A few days later, some scholars connected to the Shankaracharya visited my home—people who had become friends during these discussions. We had another four-hour debate. My conclusion was that Sanatan Dharma is based on attaining self-knowledge and liberation. All the scriptures containing knowledge were written by those who had attained self-realization or were written based on their teachings. Therefore, the acharya traditions are essential for maintaining the structure of Dharma, but they should not try to bind the conscious nature of Dharma. The Brahmin friends' main demand was that the authority to perform rituals and sacrifices should remain exclusively with those born as Brahmins, and this authority should not be given to people of other castes, as is done in Arya Samaj, Gayatri Parivar, and other places.

However, they did not claim that they had a monopoly on knowledge just because they were born Brahmins. In fact, they even said that the word Brahmin does not mean "knower of Brahman," as is often claimed. Just as someone who knows everything is called 'Sarvagya' and someone who knows Dharma is called 'Dharmagna', the correct term for one who knows Brahman is 'Brahmgna'. From this comes the term Brahmgnani. Therefore, a Brahmin is not necessarily a knower of Brahman; rather, they are someone who performs rituals and sacrifices for the invocation and worship of Brahman, and this role should be birth-based. I told them I had no major objection to accepting that ritualistic roles should remain with those born as Brahmins, as long as it is not claimed that this is God's creation but rather understood as a cultural and social arrangement.

But even for that exception, I raised a possible threat that the self-realized awakened people will continue to come forth time by time, and they will not be connected to any specific caste. When they project some rituals with their enlightenment, they will be more effective and result-driven. This will cause new rituals to be born and with that new and new tradition and sects like Jains and Buddhism will be born. Their followers will object to the ineffective and stagnant invocations of Brahmins. This is all that has happened to date in the history of Hindu society so far.

Later, I wrote a book on the subject that provides my final conclusion. It is available worldwide in both English and Hindi. The English title is The Science of Varna & Jati, and the Hindi title is Varn aur Jati ka Vigyan. Sanjay Dixit Ji contributed a highly useful foreword for the book. In just 90 pages, the book explains the concepts of varna and jati according to the four means of knowledge in Indian philosophy, including the Vedas, Upanishads, and the Gita, and proves that they are based on a person's qualities, actions, nature, and abilities.

In this way, I saved myself and the movement against the Swaminarayan sect from the accusation of being Brahminical. However, the term Brahminism (Brahmanvad) is actually a very misleading term coined by leftists in the 20th century. The first attempt to clarify this was made by Ambedkar, who said, "We are not against Brahmins; we are against Brahmanism." By this, he meant that Brahmins are knowledgeable and scientific, and we are not against that. We are against the unscientific idea that such knowledge and ability can only come from being born in a particular caste, while those born in another caste are automatically foolish and inferior. But even after this clarification, the problem persisted. If

Brahmin means knowledgeable and scientific, then what is the debate about? Do we create terms like physicsism or scienceism and say that a physicist or scientist is born into a specific family? Of course not. So why should we do that with the word Brahmin? With this logic, people began to refer to those who claim that Varna and Jatis are based on birth as traditionalists, because they don't see Brahmins as scientists but as ritualistic priests whose roles are to be maintained as a tradition. They also want to maintain the roles of other castes based on birth which is highly objectionable.

Akhil Bharatiya Sant Samiti (All India Saint Committee):

Gradually, the Sangh also adopted the views of various Hindu thinkers and began to form new organizations for Hindu leaders and saints, separate from traditionalist acharyas. One of these organizations was the Akhil Bharatiya Sant Samiti, whose formation we have discussed earlier. The national president of this Sant Samiti is Guru Shri Avichaldas Maharaj, the head of the Satkeval sect. The Gujarat president of the Samiti was initially Vadtal's Nautam Swami, but after he was removed, the new Gujarat president became the chief priest of Ahmedabad's Jagannath Temple, Dilipdas Ji Maharaj. After the Sant Sabha held at Kailashdham in Pethapur on October 27, 2023, when we realized that the Sangh had also brought this new Sanatan Dharma Protection Committee under its influence through Muktanand Bapu, we turned toward the Sangh's Sant Samiti. I cannot reveal who we met there because this is a government-backed Samiti, and revealing someone's name and opinions could jeopardize their position. In truth, the saints in this Sangh-backed Samiti impressed us against our expectations, and their names, if disclosed, could elevate their respect in the Sanatani society, but they could lose their positions in the Samiti. Vasantbhai Patel and others contacted the Sant Samiti, and I was informed of the conclusions of their meetings.

According to those conclusions, the saints of this Sant Samiti were well aware of the Swaminarayan sect. They fully understood the sect's books, the writings within them, and their anti-Sanatani nature. They were angered by this and had developed a clear sense of animosity towards the sect as an anti-Sanatan group. However, they were bound by the strings of the Sangh. They had to act and speak as per the directives of the Sangh and the government. One saint even expressed this frustration, saying, "Now, even in matters of religion, we have to do what these people say. This is how everything will run now." This was the same time when Champat Rai from the Ram Mandir Trust was regularly addressing the media, and allegations were emerging that the proper scriptural rituals were not being followed during the pran-pratishtha (consecration) of Lord Ram's idol. When we asked the members of the Sant Samiti what the Sangh and the government thought about the Swaminarayan sect, they said, "Right now, they are on both sides. The 2024 elections are coming, and the Swaminarayan temple was chosen to represent the Hindu temple built in Abu Dhabi, so Modi Saheb will also have to go for its inauguration. Until then, nothing will happen."

Within a month of removing the controversial wall murals from Sarangpur, around the beginning of October, more disappointing news reached us through images. These were photos of murals from the Mahakal Corridor in Ujjain, which was built last year, and they showed the Swaminarayan sect's tilak symbol painted over images related to Lord Shiva. Visitors from outside Gujarat posted these pictures on websites like Quora, questioning why the Swaminarayan tilak symbol was present in the Mahakal Temple dedicated to Shiva. As these images surfaced, a wave of disappointment spread through the Sanatani community. The corridor was inaugurated by Prime Minister Narendra Modi, and people were left wondering, "Has everything been sold out?"

Murals at Ujjain's Mahakal Temple Corridor featuring Swaminarayan
Sect's Tilak Symbol

At that moment, I made the final decision to leave my position within
the Sangh. When I posted these pictures in our Shodh Aayam (Research
wing) group, everyone was stunned. However, one of our Padadhikari (post

holder) friends tried to calm me by sharing an online pamphlet with an absurd definition of Hindutva, suggesting that "this is how things work openly and freely in Hindutva." But another friend immediately pointed out, "Rahul Gandhi posted this pamphlet on Twitter today, saying Hindutva means accepting all including Muslims and Christians." The office-bearer friend seemed a bit embarrassed, and I angrily told him, "Yes, this is the truth now. In your appeasement of this sect, there is no difference between your actions and Rahul Gandhi's appeasement of Muslims." However, I was not surprised or angry at them. I knew they were part of a bureaucratic structure where they had to defend their superiors' stance until a new directive came from above. Despite my ideological opposition, I continued to feel genuine love for the true volunteers of the RSS.

But one member of the group was a Patel from Surat, a very sweet man who fully embodied the Sangh. Once, I even asked the post-bearer, "Is this brother from the Swaminarayan sect?" He denied it, saying, "No, there's no one from that sect in our group." But when I posted the pictures from the Mahakal Corridor, while most friends were shocked and silent for a few minutes, the Patel brother revealed his true colors. He commented under the photos with two saffron flag clip arts, meaning only one thing—his faith was spreading. A few days later, this brother started posting pictures of himself wearing the Swaminarayan tilak on Facebook. This was the day I decided that I would fight for Sanatan Dharma against this sect with the other warriors, instead of being in the compromised atmosphere of Sangh in this matter.

When we showed these pictures of the Ujjain Corridor to the saints of the Sant Samiti of the Sangh, the fear and seriousness on their faces were evident. They assured us, "We will investigate how this happened," and a few days later, they gave us their report. They said, "The quarries and factories that supply the red stones used in these temples are in Jaipur, and since the Swaminarayan sect has built many temples using those stones, they have infiltrated the entire company, from the owners and managers to the laborers. In other words, the sect has bought the company. The company that was contracted to build the Mahakal Corridor was linked to the Swaminarayan sect, and without anyone's permission, they insidiously placed their tilak symbols there." After learning this, both Vasantbhai and I, as well as the saints of the Sant Samiti, felt a deep sense of fear: "What if this happens on the walls of the Ram Mandir?" It was in the news that the stones for the Ram Mandir had also been sourced from Jaipur. Within three days,

I prepared a PDF in Hindi with five chapters exposing the truth about this sect. Consider it a shorter version of this book, containing the facts about the sect, supported by evidence and website links.

We gave this PDF to the saints of the Sangh's Sant Samiti, urging them to distribute it wherever necessary, from Kashi to Uttarakhand, to raise awareness among the people. We warned them, "This sect is trying to establish a major center in Ghanshyam Pandey Ji's village near Ayodhya in Chhapaiya. Tomorrow, they might erect a large statue of their fake Narayan there, making Chapaiya bigger than Ayodhya itself. They are also building a big temple in Jagannath Puri. Wherever there are major Vishnu and Shiva pilgrimage sites, they are attempting to issue a challenge. It may not be apparent now, but over the next decade, when the opportunity presents itself, they will unleash their ambition for supremacy, much like Islam did. While you may be fighting alongside them elsewhere, their real agenda will always be working in the background." According to the information we received, the saints of the Sant Samiti and some loyal saints from Shankaracharya Ji's committee spread this message across UP and Delhi, even bringing it to the attention of Yogi Adityanath Ji in a direct meeting.

Thus, the anger and resentment we felt towards the government-aligned saints who had infiltrated Shankaracharyai's committee never arose when meeting the saints of the Sangh's Sant Samiti. Meeting them filled us with joy and pride, knowing that despite being bound by the reins of the Sangh, they had not let their inner loyalty to Sanatan Dharma die. The government-backed saints of the Shankaracharya lead Samiti on the other hand, seemed desperate to curry favor with the government, salivating at the thought of becoming something in the government's eyes. Besides this, another organization was playing its part in this issue—the Hindu Dharma Acharya Sabha. We will discuss this in the next chapter when our journey with Shankaracharyaji's committee leads us there.

Before going into the next chapter, I am sharing the article I wrote to inform and guide the Sangh on the subject discussed in this chapter. This article offers a beautiful conclusion and direction on the matter.

Sangh, Society, and Traditionalist Acharyas: Where is the Harmony Between Them?

· September 22, 2024 / On Facebook

I have often raised questions about the Sangh's methods, which lack a deep understanding of the Hindu scriptures. Today, let's look at the other side of the coin to understand what the Sangh is actually doing and the right path it needs to follow.

Part 1: An Enlightened Acharya vs. a Traditionalist Acharya

Even today, a bitter reality in Hindu society is that the Acharyas of our various sects and the entire system associated with them still believe that Varna and Jatis are determined by birth. They believe that all the rules mentioned in the Smritis (Hindu texts for social and personal rules dependent on time) are true, which grant religious authority to Brahmins by birth and impose various restrictions on other Varnas based on their birth. When contradictions arise between the Smritis and the Prasthanatrayi (the three foundational texts of Upanishads, Bhagavad Gita, and Brahmasutras), the rules set forth in the Smritis for that era are given precedence over the eternal knowledge of the Prasthanatrayi. It doesn't stop there. In this system, knowledge is not attained through self-realization. Instead, one is expected to remain in the lineage of a guru, and only the knowledge given by that guru is considered valid. Just as the Mullahs claim that only they can interpret the Quran and Hadith for the common Muslim, so too is it believed that a person cannot directly attain knowledge of God.

This also reflects in their opposition to enlightened individuals like Mahavir and Buddha, who achieved self-realization and established different paths. They oppose not only them but also modern enlightened beings who, without creating new sects, merge their wisdom with Hindu scripture and offer it to society. The people surrounding them criticize figures like Swami Vivekananda, Sadhguru, Jiddu Krishnamurti, Sri Sri Ravi Shankar, and many others, spreading baseless negative views against them because, in their minds, these enlightened individuals are a threat to their authority. Whenever such enlightened beings emerge in society, they offer a clearer and more accessible understanding of the truth through their personal experience, and as a result, people follow them instead of traditional Acharyas. And why not? There is a vast difference in the way an enlightened person and a traditionalist Acharya convey the same truth. Let's understand this through three examples:

· A traditionalist Acharya might explain the reason for not touching their feet like this: "You might have gone to the bathroom or touched something else, and we don't know if you've washed your hands afterward. We must remain pure while performing various rituals, so we ask you not to touch us but to touch the sandals instead." According to ritualistic rules, this explanation is not wrong.

· However, an enlightened being might explain the same thing with this wisdom: "Every touch carries a karmic bond. An enlightened being, having touched the consciousness of the Divine, accepts as few external bonds as possible to stay aligned with that realization. Therefore, there is no benefit in touching the Guru. A heartfelt inner surrender before him is enough for your spiritual well-being. If it will be necessary, the Guru will touch you on the right spot."

· Another example: An Acharya might say, "The Vedas are self-evident. It is said that they were born from the breath of Brahma, which is why they are considered apaurusheya (not of human origin)."

· An enlightened being might explain, "Our soul is Brahman. When we achieve self-realization, we become one with Brahman. As a result, knowledge of how the cosmos functions naturally unfolds within us, because we are Brahman. With each breath, new layers of understanding open up, and this is how the Vedas were revealed to the enlightened seers, as if with every breath, new knowledge was born. The mythological representation of Brahman as Brahma suggests that the Vedas emerged from his breath. This knowledge is not born from the mind or intellect of any person, which is why the Vedas are called apaurusheya and self-evident, as they come directly from Brahman, the formless cosmic force."

· One more example: An Acharya might say, "Rishi Yajnavalkya saw the Vedic hymns written in the Akasha (sky), and he read those hymns and imparted that knowledge in the Upanishads."

· An enlightened being might explain, "When one attains self-realization, the soul merges with Brahman, and knowledge begins to unfold with every breath. That knowledge is expressed through words in the human mind. The Nyaya philosophy and other scriptures say that space (Akasha) is the element where sound is produced. Akasha is associated with the fifth chakra in humans. The words that describe self-realization are formed in the Akasha element, meaning in the part of the brain associated with it. Therefore, it is said that Rishi Yajnavalkya saw the Vedic hymns in the sky, referring to the Akasha element in his brain."

Thus, there is a significant difference between an enlightened being and a traditionalist Acharya, and this difference can be traced back to the debate between Adi Shankaracharya and Mandana Mishra. Their debate revolved around the Vedanta philosophy, which teaches that liberation is attained through self-knowledge, and the Mimamsa philosophy, which teaches that liberation is achieved only through rituals. Shankaracharya represented Vedanta, while Mandana Mishra advocated for the importance of rituals. The condition of the debate was that the loser would accept the winner's path. If Shankaracharya lost, he would renounce his monastic life and live as a householder following Mandana Mishra's teachings. If Mandana Mishra lost, he would take up sannyasa and follow Shankaracharya's path. Mandana Mishra lost the debate, and it was proven that self-knowledge, not rituals, leads to liberation. Mandana Mishra then became the first Shankaracharya of Kanchi Math.

Thus, although the debate was won by the enlightened Shankaracharya, the one who assumed the throne was the traditionalist Mandana Mishra, who believed in rituals. Since Mandana Mishra was not in a state of self-realization, the tradition of Shankaracharya's Maths became more focused on ritualistic practices, which Mandana Mishra believed in. These Maths, established by an enlightened person, gradually became structured institutions that deviated from the original self-realized wisdom. Whenever new enlightened beings like Shankaracharya emerged, the traditionalist system viewed them as threats and often opposed them, while those who upheld ritualistic traditions as born Brahmins were recognized as new Acharyas and allowed to generate new philosophies and sects. The problem lies in the fact that self-realized consciousness cannot be bound by structured institutions. Institutions can only be created by scholars of scriptures and rigid rules. If an institution is flexible and promotes self-realization, enlightened beings may occasionally emerge within it. However, most of the time, deeply enlightened beings come from free, unstructured environments, just like Adi Shankaracharya had come out in his childhood.

Part 2: The Role of the Sangh

The Sangh's role is to create an atmosphere of mutual respect and acceptance between the enlightened yogis who emerge unexpectedly for the welfare of Hindu society and the traditionalist Acharyas. If I put myself in the place of an enlightened yogi, meeting a traditional Acharya would bring me joy. I would prefer to remain in their presence, as they are scholars of scriptures written by self-realized seers. Through these scriptures, an enlightened person connects with the wisdom of enlightened beings from centuries ago. Therefore, an enlightened yogi will not harbor resentment or jealousy toward the Acharyas. He will even find joy in serving them, as he has no interest in positions of power. There is no conflict of interest between an enlightened yogi and an Acharya. However, as demonstrated before, the ability to understand the knowledge expressed in the scriptures varies between the two. The enlightened yogi's understanding comes from direct experience, while the Acharya's understanding comes from memory, intellect, and imagination. If there is a debate on the meaning of the scriptures, there will naturally be differences of opinion. An Acharya may resent the knowledge of an enlightened being because the yogi's clearly realized wisdom challenges the authority of the Acharya, who is said by the tradition that only what he says is true. Therefore, we need to encourage traditionalist Acharyas to be a bit more humble for the welfare of Hindu society. They need to develop the capacity to accept the self-realization that emerges in young individuals living amidst society due to their past life's spiritual practice.

We cannot ignore the impact of the environment and upbringing that a Brahmin, Kshatriya, or Vaishya child receives in their household from an early age. However, this does not mean that their qualifications are determined solely by their birth. Ravana, born into a Brahmin family, learned the Vedic hymns and Sanskrit verses, yet he was not a Brahmin. He was a Kshatriya. I am a Chaudhary, a caste associated with the role of village leaders like Sarpanch or Mukhi. It is possible that I have some inherent qualities to become a Sarpanch due to my DNA and upbringing, but that does not mean these qualities cannot be found in other Kshatriyas or even in Brahmin, Vaishya, or Shudra children. We cannot say that only Chaudhary caste members can become Sarpanch, and no one else can hold that position. Even if seven out of ten Chaudharis naturally become Sarpanch due to their inherent traits and upbringing, if three times someone more qualified than any Chaudhary emerges, that person should be made Sarpanch. Thus, while the influence of birth and upbringing is acceptable, giving anyone a birthright to any position in society is inhumane injustice. Even if all the Acharyas of a tradition happen to be born into Brahmin families, there's no issue with that, as it can be seen as a part of tradition. However, to secure their religious authority, they should not try to establish a scripturally opposed system of birthright in any position or duty. And they must stop harboring resentment toward independent enlightened yogis.

The Sangh's fundamental task is to create a situation where a Sadguru and a Shankaracharya can accept each other and work together. Where Vivekananda and Shankaracharya can accept one another and work together to awaken spirituality in society. The Sangh must move in this direction. To do so, it must avoid appeasing anti-Sanatani sects like the Swaminarayan sect, which has turned anti-Sanatani due to its Christian-influenced interference. This sect elevates an ordinary Vaishnava devotee of Krishna to a position higher than Krishna himself, disrespects the established gods of Sanatan Dharma, and seeks to replace the Vedic deities with a new supreme god. If the Sangh empowers such corrupt and perverted sects to balance the power of traditional Acharyas, it is not only ignorant and foolish but also compromised. If you send your government-made saints, who have been trained in your workshops and aligned with your ideology, into society, it will appear as though you are trying to seize religious authority from the traditional Acharyas and bind society in your rigid mindset. These are all wrong paths, which will not only provoke dissatisfaction but may eventually lead to outrage.

The Sangh needs to immerse itself in the scriptures of Sanatan Dharma to unite enlightened beings like Vivekananda and Sadhguru with traditional Acharyas and establish mutual respect and acceptance between them. Only then can you truly create a Sanatan Dharma Raksha Board, where Hindu society will be ideologically harmonious and united. If an enlightened person were to rise to the top position of the Sangh, before taking any action against Muslim and Christian activities, he would first strive to strengthen Sanatan Dharma and society from within through self-realization. The victory over the outside world will naturally follow. If we want to fight for global establishment, not just survival, we must first accomplish this.

XIV

Swamis of the Sect and Swamis of Sanatan

The Sanatan Dharma Protection Committee, chaired by Shankaracharya, met once again in Surat in March 2024 after a gap of four or five months. However, this time, a new turn of events surprised everyone. Around 2003, under the leadership of Nautam Swami and supported by other descendants of the Acharyas, a group of Swamis from the Vadtal Gadi staged a rebellion against sitting Acharya Ajendraprasadji. The issue dated back to 1996, where it was said that Acharya Ajendraprasad was imposing stricter rules on the initiation of monks due to cases of corruption, immorality, and even murder within the sect. In protest, the opposing group filed a case, and under orders from the Gujarat High Court, Ajendraprasad was removed from his position as Acharya and replaced by the current Acharya, Rakeshprasadji, with Nautam Swami becoming the chief saint. Meanwhile, the ousted Ajendraprasadji, along with his chief Swami, SP Swami, took refuge in Gadhada, continuing their opposition. Currently, Ajendraprasadji's son, Lalji Maharaj, has become the leading voice of this opposition.

When I met Shankaracharyaji in Dwarka, he hinted that the Acharya who had been ousted from Gadhada was not as wrong as some thought. Those who took control of the Gadi in 2003 were involved in these various corrupt activities, including forming new scriptures. This explains why the committee announced on the evening of September 4th in Sivananda Ashram, which was supposed to consist of both the Swamis from the sect and those from Sanatan, was never formed. The committee was to be led by both Shankaracharya and the current Acharya of Vadtal, Rakeshprasadji, placed on an equal footing. The press note used these words: "With the blessings of the Dwarka Peethadheeshwar Jagadguru Shankaracharya Param Pujya Shri Sadanand Saraswatiji Maharaj and Vadtal Gadi Acharya Param Pujya Acharyashri Rakeshprasadji Maharaj…" This clearly indicated the establishment of equal status between an Acharya of one of the various sections of a sect and the head position of Shankaracharya within Sanatan Dharma. Additionally, Shankaracharyaji did not consider Rakeshprasadji and the chief saint, Nautam Swami, as deserving figures. They did not say anything explicitly, but in a way, the image of Rakeshprasadji and Nautam Swami among the followers of the sect remains tied to the events and controversies that occurred and came to light between 1996 and 2003. Recently, in a TV news channel interview, a follower of the sect openly mentioned something similar about Nautam Swami. The video link is provided below:

- (Video Link: https://drive.google.com/file/d/ 11KiwAHCbpPdZhFH0BZ70a-TB2fxY3Men/view?usp=drivesdk)

Now, the vision of Shankaracharyaji was being implemented in the Sanatan Dharma Protection Committee. In the meeting held in Surat, Ajendraprasadji's son, Lalji Maharaj, and SP Swami were included in the committee. Both publicly declared that they had accepted the six points of the committee and had returned to Sanatan Dharma. They claimed that there was nothing in the original sect that opposed Sanatan Dharma or its gods and goddesses. They stated that all the deities of Sanatan Dharma were accepted in the original sect and that the deviations occurred later in factions that split from the main sect. They further claimed that when these deviations began in Vadtal, Ajendraprasadji had opposed them, which led to his removal from the Gadi. However, during their speeches, SP Swami and Lalji Maharaj consistently referred to "Bhagwan Swaminarayan," without ever stating that they were devotees of Bhagwan Krishna. They called both Krishna and Swaminarayan "Bhagwan." The committee's anchor tried to clarify on their behalf, saying, "We also refer to the Guru as Bhagwan, so it's acceptable to call Sahajanand Swami Bhagwan as well," but the two guests had not said this themselves.

Two months later, in June 2024, the committee met again in Tramba, Rajkot, where the same two guests were present, continuing to speak in the name of "Bhagwan Swaminarayan." Among the Sanatan warriors, there were many questions and doubts about what was happening. I and Vasantbhai were continuously receiving phone calls, but we had no clear information. Due to this confusion, I wrote this article on Facebook two days later to seek clarification and shared it with the committee members. However, no clear response was received.

A Message from Sanatani Society to the Saints Who Gathered in Tramba

• June 13, 2024 / On Facebook

A severe doubt has arisen in Sanatan society about whether our saints who gathered in Tramba are fully aware of the anti-Sanatan agenda of that sect. In both the Surat and Tramba meetings, the Acharya from Gadhada and his SP Swami repeatedly claimed, "In our original sect, there is no opposition to any deities of Sanatan Dharma, and all are accepted." This statement is echoed by every branch of that sect, which has degraded the deities of Sanatan Dharma in the most perverse ways. Their stance is that "We accept all the gods and deities of Sanatan Dharma because they are all servants of Sahajanand Swami. We do not oppose any deity of Sanatan Dharma; we only state that they all originated from Sahajanand Swami, now called Swaminarayan, and derive their power from him. Swaminarayan is the supreme incarnation of all incarnations."

In other words, they accept your deities and gods because their new god needs some deities as servants to demonstrate his superiority. If they do not accept the God of Sanatan Dharma, how can their solitary god be considered supreme above all? This is the truth of the matter. Now, even the Acharya and Swami from Gadhada are saying, 'We accept everyone and oppose no one,' carefully adding that Swaminarayan is supreme and the gods of Sanatan Dharma are his servants – a point they are not openly stating for now. However, they also do not clarify that 'The gods described in the Vedas and Puranas of Sanatan Dharma are the original gods of us all, and Sahajanand Swami is merely a devotee of Lord Krishna, whom we revere as a true devotee of Krishna and hence, we call him 'Bhagwan' in our reverence.' And until they make this statement, it remains unclear why Sanatan saints are so delighted and organizing these frequent meetings.

When Prophet Mohammed founded Islam, he said the same thing about the earlier prophets of Arabia. He said, 'We accept all those prophets before me, they are all true. But I am the last, and I have brought the final message of God. No one else will come after me. So from now on, you must follow what I say.' This sect is telling the same thing to Sanatan Dharma, that Sahajanand Swami has come, and all the gods before him, who are his avatars and servants, no longer need to be worshipped. Just worship this new supreme god and do as he says. This is an attempt to establish Islam within Sanatan Dharma from within – only with a different name for God, and the sect's structure is Christian. The Swaminarayan sect is like borrowing Hindu attire to establish an Islamic soul within a Christian body in India. Hindu symbols, Hindu names, and Hindu scriptures are used, but the body is Christian and the soul is Islamic. This is the fundamental truth. Ask the original members of the sect for clarification on this, and let us know what they say.

✵

However, after these two committee meetings and the arrival of the Acharya from Gadhada and SP Swami, several interesting events unfolded. Scandals began to surface from Vadtal and some of its splinter groups and Gurukuls that left us shocked. One Swami kept a young woman captive for months and repeatedly raped her, and later took her to a doctor to have her pregnancy terminated. Another video surfaced showing a Swami committing unnatural acts while bathing a boy from his Gurukul. Yet another video showed a Swami fondling the genitals of another Swami. Scandals also emerged where Swamis were involved in land grabbing under the pretense of temple construction. This spread across newspapers and TV news channels everywhere. Every day brought a new scandal linked to some faction of this sect. To avoid breaking the narrative's flow by writing about all of them here, I have compiled links to the relevant news articles and TV news channels into one PDF, and here is the link to it:

- Pdf link: https://drive.google.com/file/d/1Hoxxfm0UTptRC0b80St982WPnNgJY1H5/view?usp=sharing

✵

At this time, I made a post on Facebook explaining how this entire scenario resembles what was happening with the Catholic Church priests in Europe.

The corruption seen in Vadtal is not of Sanatan Dharma; it belongs to the Christian sects of Europe.

• June 16, 2024 / On Facebook.

Never make the mistake of understanding the sexual exploitation cases involving these Swamis and children or women as part of Hindu Dharma. This is the same Christian form that this sect has adopted while only borrowing Hindu names and attire. After the establishment of the Christian sect by Roman Emperor Constantine in the 3rd century, this continued for about 1500 years in Europe and later in America. In Christian sects, where sex is considered the original sin, the mentality of priests and bishops remained the same as that of the Swamis of this sect. Outwardly, they disrespect women, while internally, they sexually exploit the same women. The corruption of these scandals grew to such an extent that in the 12th-13th centuries, around 50,000 women were burned alive across Europe, as they were considered the greatest obstacle to the path of God.

It was the same mixture of power and sectarianism between the Catholic Church and Roman rulers that led to the birth of modern democratic thinkers and scientists like Galileo and Newton in opposition. Even today, scandals involving priests and bishops are continually being exposed in Europe and America. If you watch films like the Oscar-winning Spotlight or Primal Fear, you will see the same picture that is now emerging in our media about these Swamis. The structure of BAPS mirrors that of the Roman Catholic Church, where their institution's head is seen as the representative of God sitting in the Akshardham, just like the Pope. The other factions are modeled on the Orthodox Christian structure. While Europe and America have struggled and emerged from such evils, here in Gujarat, we are being engulfed in the same wickedness. Therefore, power must now dissociate itself from this corruption and see it as its duty to eradicate it in time. We are not here to destroy people, but to eliminate the corruption and distortion, which begins with the twisted writings in their books. The root cause is there, and foreign poison has been poured into that root.

An example of what was said above can be found in Spain where an independent commission's report reveals how over 200,000 children have been sexually abused in a church in Spain since 1940.

With the exposure of these scandals, information also surfaced that similar scandals had come to light after Ajendraprasadji was removed in 2003. What was happening now was a repetition of those events, connected to Lalji Maharaj, the son of Ajendraprasadji, after his alignment with Shankaracharyaji's committee.

And then came the Chaturmas period – a 106 to 108-day period when Shankaracharyaji halts his travels and stays in one ashram, and people come to see him there. But this time, the news was different. It was reported that during this Chaturmas, Shankaracharyaji would stay at the Shivanand Ashram in Ahmedabad, the same ashram of Swami Parmatmananda Saraswatiji, where the meeting to resolve the Salangpur dispute was held.

Hindu Dharma Acharya Sabha:

Swami Dayanand Saraswati, a prominent disciple of Swami Chinmayanandji, the founder of Chinmaya Mission, was a famous saint from South India. This Swami Dayanand Saraswati was different from the founder of the Arya Samaj, sharing only the same name. A thinker of Advaita Vedanta, born in Tamil Nadu, he worked for many years in the Chinmaya Mission before independently establishing Arsha Vidya Gurukuls across India. One of his centers is in Ahmedabad, known as Shivanand Ashram, currently managed by his disciple Swami Parmatmanand Saraswati. In 2015, Swami Dayanand Saraswati attained samadhi at his ashram in Rishikesh. It was he who founded the Hindu Dharma Acharya Sabha in 2003 in Chennai. But today, its main center is effectively the Shivanand Ashram in Ahmedabad. The press note resolving the Salangpur dispute on September 4th was issued on the letterhead of the Hindu Dharma Acharya Sabha.

Swami Dayanand Saraswati's idea behind founding the Hindu Dharma Acharya Sabha was to create a spiritual parliament that included all sects and beliefs of Sanatan Dharma. However, due to connections with Shivanand Ashram in Gujarat at that time, the Swaminarayan sect was also included in this parliament. Today, looking at the truth in this sect's books, we can understand that this decision was likely made under social and political influence rather than based on study or knowledge. Because the nature of this sect's books has been the same for many decades. A Swami of BAPS named 'Dr. Swami' had attained and given a speech on the founding day of the Acharya Sabha.

Today, the Hindu Dharma Acharya Sabha operates under the presidency of Swami Avdheshanand Giri Maharaj, with Swami Parmatmanand Saraswati as the general secretary of the institution. When these truths about the sect started to surface, and the Sangh was not supporting it, and no one had yet shown the path to reach Shankaracharyaji, I happened to listen to an interview with Swami Parmatmanand Saraswati on Vedanta. He explained how the philosophy of Hindu Dharma is broader compared to Abrahamic sects. As a follower of Advaita Vedanta, I liked his knowledge, and I showed his photo to the Sanatan warriors, saying, 'I am thinking of meeting him. We should fight this battle with the support of such a knowledgeable person.' As soon as they saw his photo, the Sanatan warriors started laughing at me, saying, 'Sir, how naive are you? Since you are new to this subject, you don't know. This Swamiji is a government saint, he does whatever the Sangh tells him. He is especially close to Madhavpriyadas Swami of Vadtal, and they keep elevating him in the Acharya Sabha.'

Later, everything became clearer when Ram Madhav came, and the meeting to resolve the Salangpur dispute was held in his Shivanand Ashram. When the BAPS temple was inaugurated in America, and no BJP minister or Sangh official attended due to massive opposition to the sect in Gujarat, Swami Parmatmanand Saraswati and Govindgiri Maharaj, the treasurer of the Ram Janmabhoomi Trust, had attended the function as representatives of the Acharya Sabha. Seeing their photos, the Sanatanis in Gujarat were outraged. Moreover, after the Salangpur dispute was settled and a grand festival was organized in Vadtal to improve the sect's image, Nautam Swami invited Avichaldas Maharaj, the national president of the Akhil Bhartiya Sant Samiti, to attend. But Avichaldasji refused to go. When no saint from Gujarat was willing to attend the festival, Govindgiri Maharaj, treasurer of the Ram Janmabhoomi Trust, and Acharya Chinna Jeeyar Swami from Telangana's Vaishnav Ramanuj tradition were the ones who attended. Both were saints from the Hindu Dharma Acharya Sabha, and it became clear that it was Parmatmanandji who arranged their visit, which may be due to the connection with Madhavpriyadas Swami from the Swaminarayan sect in the Acharya Sabha.

In this way, I had never had the chance to meet Paramatmanandji. But now, hearing that Shankaracharyaji was staying in Ahmedabad at his ashram for Chaturmas, I couldn't pass up the opportunity to meet both of them. Despite trying for a long time, it was only as Chaturmas was nearing its end that I finally visited Sivananda Ashram on a Sunday. Since I had already met Shankaracharyaji two or three times, my priority was to meet Paramatmanandji. I took with me my English book explaining the Vedantic model of creation for modern science, which I had also been discussing with several scientists. In the evening, I met Paramatmanandji in his meeting room among five or six other people, presented my book, and explained its purpose. To be honest, I liked him at first sight. Yes, there was an impression of RSS workshops (Karyashalas) in his talk with a base of a Vedantin saint. Some duties associated with the Sangh seemed to reflect a certain pride or self-importance on his face. But in that first meeting, we met with mutual affection and respect, as if we were long-lost friends. Vedanta was the bond between us. If there was any unease, it was on my part—due to the rumors I had heard about his inclination towards the sect. If those were true, I didn't want to suffer the heartache of disillusionment with a Vedantic saint.

After his devotees and other visitors had left, he asked me to stay, and we engaged in a few discussions. During the conversation, I casually mentioned, 'The entire campaign that exposed the Swaminarayan sect's perversion— I was the one who led it on the grounds of logic and knowledge. In a way, I'm the one who brought all this out.'

He replied, 'What did you uncover? There's an upcoming meeting with the VHP's national leaders about this. Send me whatever you have. I was the one who mediated the Salangpur controversy.'

'Yes, I know,' I said. 'I'll send you all the PDFs and related literature. If someone genuinely takes responsibility to address this crisis and earns my trust, I want to withdraw and focus on other work.' By 'other work,' I meant what I wanted to accomplish with my book. Swamiji said, 'You came at the right time. I'm organizing a conference here on Saturday on science and spirituality. Scientists from ISRO and other institutions will attend, along with our Vedantic saints. Please join us. I'll send you an invitation on WhatsApp.'

So, our meeting ended somewhat like the reunion of old companions. I happily drove the 150 kilometers back home that day. The next day, I sent him all the PDFs on WhatsApp, some of which are linked in this book, along with Hindi and English PDFs we were circulating in India and abroad. He sent me an invitation card for the conference, and I returned on Saturday. But as soon as I entered the conference hall, I was struck with a profound shock. Swamiji was seated on the stage next to that very Madhavpriyadas Swami from Vadtal, engaged in conversation with him. I kept wondering, what were these people doing at a conference on science and spirituality when they had no connection to science, spirituality, or even the Sanatan cosmos? My concern proved justified, as Madhavpriyadas mostly indulged in comedy, trying to draw attention to himself in front of scientists and spiritual scholars like Paramatmanandji by saying things like, 'What's the point of all these discussions? Everything is Advaita. I am Brahman, and that encompasses everything.'

When he gave his lecture, he played the same trick his sect always plays. He would speak about the Vedas and Upanishads, but whenever the subject turned to God, he would only mention Narayana. For example, he once said, 'In the Upanishads, Lord Narayana says...,' but what he said afterward had no connection to the Upanishads. To mislead people, he would hide the fact that in the Vedas and Upanishads, the name Narayana refers to Lord Vishnu. In his sect, the name Narayana is linked to Sahajanand Swami, placing him above all the Panchadev, including Vishnu. The narrative would subtly imply that the Vedas and Upanishads speak only of Lord Narayana, and for them, that Narayana is none other than Swaminarayan Sahajanand Swami. But this deceptive portrayal was left unchecked by saints like Paramatmanandji, who, out of friendship, maintained the illusion that 'Look, it's all part of our tradition. Where's the harm?' It was like a betraying lover who has done much behind your back but still tries to keep you deceived, and you, choosing to remain in that deception, showing your weakness that you can't live without them. This is the state of Sanatan saints in front of the sect's swamis.

The greatest falsehood was consistently presented by Madhavpriyadas Swami when he tried to link Akshardham with Advaita, the Vedas, and the Upanishads. In his sect, the supreme formless Parabrahman (OM) of the Vedas is replaced by the tangible Sahajanand Swami, who is given the title Parabrahman. To reach Akshardham, one must accept Sahajanand Swami as the supreme god and rank the rest of Sanatan Dharma's deities below him. Just as Christians aim for heaven where Jesus resides, here salvation is only for those who acknowledge this swami as the highest deity. So where does Advaita even enter this picture? And all of this was happening with Paramatmanandji sitting on the stage, giggling and chatting with

Madhavpriyadas afterward in the spirit of friendship. The scene felt like a Duryodhana trapping Karna in the web of friendship, with Paramatmanandji as Karna. It also seemed that perhaps Paramatmanandji was still unaware of the full reality of the sect, or maybe his friendship kept him away from fully acknowledging and accepting it. Or maybe he was so deeply involved with the Sangh's work and this sect that he couldn't see the closer and more significant danger beyond the Muslim and Christian opposition.

Somehow, the Sangh and its affiliates still seemed to operate from the same mindset I had when I responded to two Sanatan warriors from Rajkot who had come to inform me about this sect two years ago. But within two months, I realized the gravity of the threat, whereas even after two years and such a significant movement from the saints, the slow-moving Sangh has failed to grasp its seriousness. I hope that this shortfall is due to the limitations in their ideology and approach, not due to any internal politics or corrupt compulsion.

About fifteen days after that scientific conference at Sivananda Ashram, there was news that Madhavpriyadas Swami was sent by the Hindu Dharma Acharya Sabha to Banaras Hindu University to deliver a lecture on the Vedas and science. Once again, it was not only laughable but also repulsive. When the Patel brothers, aware of the true nature of this sect, learned of this, they commented, 'This Madhavpriyadas Swami is a Patel. If you put our Patels to sell anything in a shop, they can convince the customer of anything to make the sale. If you dress him in saffron and make him a swami, he could even turn Ghanshyam Pandeji into the father of Sanatan Dharma in the name of the Vedas and Narayana. That's what it is. There's a saying in business, "A business without lies is impossible." Now, if you send these businessmen to preach religion, they'll turn it into their business with clever hypocrisy. Listen to these swamis who indulge in luxury day and night, and they'll talk about renunciation and charity. That charity funds their pleasures and lavish lifestyles. From Pramukh Swami to Madhavpriyadas Swami, this is the true reality of this sect.'

Thus, my journey on this topic reaches to the present day with this conclusion. It's not that I don't understand the practicality of the situation—if this sect is removed from all places, there would be no bridge for dialogue, and as I write, the Acharya Sabha is the only platform where someone from this sect still holds a place in Sanatan Dharma. The Sangh, VHP, and BJP still have people from this sect among their ranks. The Sangh has become somewhat aware of this issue, as seen in its pro-Sanatan expression. But all of this is due to our campaign led by society, not self-initiative. So, as soon as Sanatan warriors become absorbed in their worldly responsibilities and the campaign quiets down, a new appeasement move emerges from Hindu organizations. And it's this appeasement that creates more anxiety and fear among society than the sect itself.

When it comes to Sanatan Dharma's religious institutions, at present, it's only Madhavpriyadas in the Hindu Dharma Acharya Sabha who represents this sect. And as far as I've understood, Paramatmanandji is dedicated to slowly reforming the sect from within by maintaining a friendly dialogue with swamis like Madhavpriyadas. This is also the vision of the Sangh, and I saw Paramatmanand Saraswati trying to fulfill it.

It is possible that efforts were made to facilitate discussions between Shankaracharyaji and the swamis of the Vadtal Gadi during Shankaracharyaji's Chaturmas stay at Sivananda Ashram. This is because Madhavpriyadasji of Vadtal was associated with Paramatmanandji and visited there frequently. During this Chaturmas, a meeting of other Sanatani saints with Shankaracharyaji was held to condemn the atrocities committed against Hindus in Bangladesh and express outrage to the media about the attacks on Hindus. Swaminarayan sect swamis who tried to attend the program were not allowed to participate, and this incident was reported in newspapers the next day.

Thus, it is likely that Shankaracharyaji avoided meeting Madhavpriyadasji of Vadtal or any other swami during the Chaturmas and refrained from further discussions. If this was the case, it is justified. Engaging in dialogue with Pakistan while it continues its terrorism is akin to legitimizing its power. A sincere and virtuous person needs only one indication to correct their mistakes. They will recognize their error and reform themselves. However, for those who refuse to change even after extensive efforts, scriptural truths, and movements, and instead use flawed arguments to justify their adharma, maintaining relations with them holds no meaning. The Congress government acted similarly with Pakistan—continuing engagement despite terrorism. The current government's approach was correct: "Stop terrorism first, and then friendship or harmony can follow." Strangely, the views and actions of the Sangh and BJP regarding this sect are strikingly similar to Congress's approach toward Muslims and Pakistan over the past few decades.

Before fostering goodwill among beings, one must first uphold Dharma, and to uphold Dharma, one must first destroy Adharma. As long as the corrupted teachings and views exist in the texts of that sect, Adharma is alive. As long as that false 'Narayana' placed above the Panchadev remains in those texts, how can Dharma be prevailed? What is the point of dialogue and harmony without that? Therefore, showing friendship where only Adharma and hypocrisy prevail makes one a Karna, and history shows us through experience that Karna could not influence Duryodhana in friendship; rather, it was Duryodhana who used Karna under the guise of friendship. Where there is a Duryodhana, one must challenge him, warning him to uphold Dharma. That makes one a Rama or a Krishna, a trait of Vishnu, the establisher of Dharma. The Hindu society as a whole contains this expectation from the Hindu Dharma Acharya Sabha and the Sangh that they should embody this characteristic of Lord Vishnu in this subject.

But, every time, the opposite happens. Two months later, another festival was organized at Vadtal—celebrating 200 years of the Lakshmi-Narayan Temple. Saints from the Akhil Bharatiya Sant Samiti attended the inauguration under the guidance of the Sangh, but they didn't issue any significant statements. However, during the final days of the event, all the Acharya Sabha saints were seen there alongside Madhavpriyadasji, and the Acharya Sabha president, Swami Avadheshanand Giri Maharaj, delivered a speech that sought to clear the tarnished image of the past year.

In his discourse, the sect was praised profusely as part of Sanatan Dharma. He justified referring to Sahajanand Swami as Bhagwan (God) by saying, "We even consider stones, water, and trees as forms of God in Sanatan Dharma, so why should there be hesitation in calling a guru God?" He further elevated Sahajanand Swami as a high expression of the divine and welcomed his significance as a guest. However, the distortion of depicting Sahajanand Swami above all other Sanatan deities, portraying Sanatan gods as servants of Swaminarayan, and exclusively worshiping Swaminarayan as the supreme deity while rejecting others—all of this was left unaddressed. Neither was there any acknowledgment of the issue nor any effort to rectify it, nor was there explicit support for it. Instead, the sect's contributions to Hindu culture through festivals, education, and service were highlighted, ignoring the fact that these activities are akin to the Church's social work, designed to convert Hindus into believers of a singular supreme deity.

These statements by the saints left Sanatanis disheartened and angry.

The "makeup" applied at this event also upset me. I sent Paramatmanandaji a video of a discourse by Vadtal Swami (link below). In it, the Swami states, "We do not believe that Swaminarayan resides in Golok (Krishna's abode) or Vaikuntha (Ram's abode). We believe he is above all, the supreme Purushottam Narayan, the ruler of the highest Akshardham." He elaborated that in the Vadtal temple, their deity's idol, Harikrishna Maharaj, was installed alongside Lakshmi-Narayan and declared, "Today, we have established ourselves in accordance with the Vedic tradition, so that those with indirect faith in the Vedas will come to the temple. Our saints will then instill exclusive devotion to our supreme deity in them..."

- (Video link : https://drive.google.com/file/d/ 11oFph4ZaYDWN8hfQK-18C7revM2rjbyM/view?usp=drivesdk)

After this, I wrote one final article giving a conclusive statement on this subject, expressing the sentiments of hurt Sanatanis and highlighting the roles of the Sangh, saints, and government in this matter.

Should we call them saints or makeup artists?

- November 14, 2024 / Facebook

An aware Sanatani works hard to support their family, yet when Sanatan Dharma and its deities face threats, they step forward to fight. They meet people everywhere, raise awareness, and plead with others to take a stand for Dharma. Despite family opposition, limited financial resources, and caring for ill parents, they still find time and spend money to raise their voice against internal conspiracies. It is because of such unknown, ordinary Sanatanis—without names, wealth, or faces—that the dangers posed by this sect have come to light.

Two years ago, I met similar ordinary householders who awakened people like me, exposed the conspiracy and its history, and brought it to the attention of society and saints. These ordinary Hindus, with their dedication and awakened Sanatan consciousness, have emerged as a ray of hope. Who else but them?

Most saints awakened by these Sanatanis, barring a few like Shankaracharya Jagadguru of Sharadapeeth and some devoted saints, appeared like agents bowing before power and organizations. Some prominent saints even lamented, saying, "Now, even in matters of Dharma, we must do and say what these organizations dictate. Everything has changed."

Now that the sins have been exposed and the potential future crises are clear, these saints are being used to cover up the sinners' schemes and apply makeup to make them appear as before. The foundation of this sect was laid by British officials and their representatives, Christian missionaries, and it continues to operate on the same model today—only the faces and attire have changed.

We've seen the makeup artists called to Vadtal to spray perfume over these schemes. Next, which makeup artists will be invited to the BAPS events? Even with yearly festivals and constant touch-ups by government-backed saints, the truth felt by people's hearts and the distortions engraved in their records cannot be concealed. This makeup won't cover the truth; the spray will wash away people's respect and trust in these saints.

In a way, while fighting Islam without self-awareness, we are conforming to their Caliphate system—a central Caliph as the custodian of religion, with regional rulers waging wars and playing politics under his command, and clerics defining religion and engaging in politics to spread it. No one is independent; everything is handled by the Caliph and his inner circle. The Caliph is just a face; the real force is the ideology, which remains unchanged even if the Caliphs change.

In our pursuit of building an ecosystem, we are heading down this path because we lack the divinity and spirituality to re-establish the independent, conscious systems of our Brahmajnani rishis. Instead of kings seeking guidance from enlightened rishis, today's saints are being ordered by rulers and Caliph-like representatives to "go here and say this."

Wake up in time. True enlightened rishis, wherever they sit, will speak the truth to your face. Whether you choose to understand or ignore it is up to you. Power has its intoxication, and very few awaken before it wears off.

XV
What's the Solution?

The solution is straightforward and simple. It has always been that way. However, certain people, filled with arrogance and the belief that they have taken responsibility for Hindu society and religion, and that no one else has the right to think or act on these matters, have complicated this simple solution with their ignorance, selfishness, and ego. And they are still trying to do so.

Let's start with something Muktanand Bapu said during a gathering of Shankaracharya-led Samiti in June 2024 at Tramba in Rajkot. Bapu said, 'We will resolve this issue through understanding. If they don't understand and we have to go to court, we will resolve it in court as well. And if the court doesn't provide a solution, we will have to leave it to society to decide. Let society believe whatever it chooses.' Someone, either a great fool or a traitor to Sanatan civilization, has advised Bapu on this matter. In that last line, the desire to impose the deceased sect's so-called supreme god over the entirety of Sanatan Dharma is hidden, and Bapu has been made to speak in such a way to gradually prepare Hindu society to accept this. I ask, what if tomorrow your neighbor starts saying and writing in books, 'Your father is my father's servant, your ancestors are all my father's servants, and they worship him. Not only that, your mother is not your father's wife, but my father's wife.' Wouldn't you file a defamation case, forcing them to apologize and destroy such writings? Does the judicial system of this country not grant you the dignity of living with respect, free from having to hear such things about your parents, ancestors, and deities? What kind of ignorance would produce such statements from a person who has become a sadhu?

Can I declare my father to be a god tomorrow, and claim that Ram, Krishna, Shiva, and Goddess Amba are all his servants? I could gather a small following of family and community members, and they might say, 'Why only your father? Our father is also the boss of Vishnu and Shiva, and even the Panchadev bow down to him.' They would start their own narrative, forming a close-knit group around their new supreme god. This is exactly what has been happening in this sect for the past one hundred and fifty years in this Sect, and you don't have the strength, either in yourselves or in the judicial system, to stop this? Are our Panchadev, from the Vedas to the Puranas, mere footballs lying in the street for anyone to play with and insult as they wish? You have no idea what you're saying, and it's painful for the Sanatani community to hear such things from the mouth of a sadhu.

In Sanatan Dharma, everyone has the freedom to consider anyone a god, but not at the expense of insulting others' deities. I have the right to consider my father a god, but I do not have the right to call everyone else's father a servant of mine. You don't need to reach the principles of Sanatan Dharma to understand this; it's a matter of basic human decency and constitutional rights. The Panchadev, accepted as gods in Sanatan Dharma, are not subordinate to any other deity or human. They are manifestations of the formless Parabrahman OM. No one is above them. If you cannot defend even this basic understanding of Sanatan Dharma, why are you standing there wearing saffron? If you cannot, then step aside. Gujarat's Sanatani society is not so weak that it cannot protect the dignity of its deities. This society will fight, and it will obtain orders from the courts. All we ask is for the Sangh and its associated institutions to step aside. Don't bring any excuses to protect this sect.

If the Sangh had stood firmly with us for the defense of Sanatan Dharma, this issue would have been resolved by now. But much of our energy has been spent fighting the Sangh's politics rather than the sect itself. The Sangh and the BJP have stood against us, like Bhishma and Drona defending Duryodhana. To them, we say: 'Either correct Duryodhana yourselves or step aside. Our only concern is avoiding a fight with you; we do not care about Duryodhana.'

The actions of government-backed saints associated with the Sangh and the Modi government are so controversial about this sect that they seem to have no limits. At the 2025 Mahakumbh, on one hand, the Sri Vaishnava Acharyas of the Vishishtadvaita tradition are organizing a program to refute the Akshar Purushottam Darshan authored by Bhadreshdas of BAPS, exposing it as an insult to Sanatan Dharma and the Vedic deities. On the other hand, saints from the same Hindu Dharma Acharya Sabha, who are affiliated with the Sangh, are legitimizing that very doctrine by meeting with Bhadreshdas. Meanwhile, saints on both sides are showing their weakness by trying to accommodate the Vadtal faction.

As if this were not enough, the same Kashi Vidvat Parishad, which had earlier issued a public letter against this sect during the Salangpur controversy, is now granting recognition to BAPS's most distorted writings and making arrangements for them to be taught at the Sampurnanand Sanskrit University in Varanasi.

Seeing all this, the helpless Sanatani society of Gujarat is left sighing in despair, realizing that when saints and Acharyas themselves are being sold in the market of power and wealth, then there is nothing left of spirituality and morality in civilization. What remains is merely the politics of power in the name of religion. These so-called saints should be reminded that with the advent of Google, the knowledge of Sanatan Dharma's scriptures has already reached everyone, and in the age of AI (Artificial Intelligence), even AI models will begin imparting this pure wisdom with a sweet tone that they are using while saying the scriptural stuff. The only place where these people are truly needed is in raising the voice of the ultimate truth without any greed for power, prestige, or material gain. They are needed to become the voice of the people who know the truth and feel its pain. If they do not fulfill this role, then their saffron robes are merely costumes, and their seemingly profound religious discourses are nothing but artificial intelligence. Where there is no fearless character filled with self-realization, where there is cowardice in compromising religious principles just for a few photos with politicians, chief ministers, and prime ministers, there, all talk of scriptures and religion is pure hypocrisy.

Meanwhile, the head of the Sangh is delivering speeches about Hindu unity, which in Gujarat and within the Sangh is being used as a justification to protect this sect. However, there is not even basic common sense in considering how those who convert Hindus and separate them from their Vedic deities can still be called Hindus. The only clear distinction between being Hindu and being anti-Hindu is precisely this. Muslim and Christian sects convert Hindus and sever them from their Vedic gods and Om, which is why they are our enemies. The Jews, on the other hand, have a similar philosophy and culture but do not engage in conversion, so we do not consider them enemies. But this sect, like Muslims and Christians, is separating Hindus from their Vedic Panchadev and Om, instead connecting them to a single supreme deity—a man who died just two hundred years ago and was a companion of British and Christian missionaries. The method is exactly the same as that of the British: using trade and politics to establish religious and political dominance over society.

From 1757 to 1764, the British had barely established a foothold in Bengal by overthrowing the rule of the Muslim Nawab, and at first, the Hindu population even rejoiced at this. But soon after, the British took complete control over Bengal and then extended their grip over all of India. This sect is following the same strategy—starting from Gujarat and now, with the support of the BJP government and Sangh institutions, working to uproot Sanatan Dharma across India. In essence, the British are still operating in disguise through them. When the British defeated the Peshwas in 1818, they gained control over India's politics. And as we saw in Chapter 10, the first thing they did after defeating the Peshwas was to summon Sahajanand Swami to Ahmedabad and build his first temple. Thus, the foundation of this sect was laid alongside the establishment of British rule in India. We drove out the British, but we kept this sect alive. Today, the same sect, carrying forward the plan of the British and Christian missionaries to erase the worship of Sanatan Dharma's deities, is executing it from within. And Hindu organizations, instead of realizing this betrayal, are shamefully defending them under hollow calls for Hindu unity.

As early copies of this book's Gujarati version spread, an old RSS volunteer from Saurashtra responded after reading it. In reply, I wrote this article, exposing the dangerous flaws in RSS thinking.

Is Gujarat's Sangh affiliated Organizations an Accomplice of Ravan Waiting to Abduct Sita?

· December 29, 2024 / Facebook Post

Today, I watched a video of RSS chief Mohan Bhagwat, where he was advising Hindus to take an activist approach in encouraging people around them to quit addictions and work on social reforms. The idea is thought-provoking because it is rooted in the ideals of Hindu spiritual traditions, where yogis believe that whatever happens in the world, you are responsible for it, as you are fundamentally connected to the universe. This means that wherever you can raise your voice or take action, you should do so selflessly, without considering personal gain or loss. That is the duty of a yogi.

However, this very statement also raises a valid criticism of the RSS, which I feel responsible to express. The RSS chief gives a message about fulfilling one's duty by intervening in small matters like addiction recovery in people's lives. But when an entire conspiracy is being carried out by a perverted group of Hindus to destroy Sanatan Dharma and the Vedic deities, the RSS does not ask its volunteers to take responsibility and stand against it. In other words, the RSS is interested in making people quit chewing tobacco and smoking, but it has no interest in stopping those who are forcing Hindus to abandon their Vedic deities and accept the slavery of an unknown, supreme God similar to Christian Jesus and Islam's Allah. The RSS does not openly speak against this, and worse, it has bound its own volunteers from speaking up.

A former RSS volunteer from a region in Saurashtra, where this sect has significant influence, shared his thoughts after reading my book. He told a Sanatani who was fighting against this sect, "Yes, this sect is indeed a problem, and we Hindus must act in time, but expecting the RSS to do anything about it is too much." He also recounted how, in his childhood, he was physically removed from this sect's temple with the words, "He is the child of a Kusangi (someone with bad company)." Why? Because he and his family was a devotee of Shiva. He further mentioned that in parts of Amreli, Sanatanis who worship Shiva are not allowed to buy or even rent homes. We have already heard on VTV News how a folk singer was stopped from invoking Mataji during a performance in a village because the entire village followed this sect. They told him, "Here, we do not chant for Mataji or any other deity. We only chant for the supreme God, Swaminarayan."

The pattern is clear: just as increasing Muslim populations in an area lead to Hindu gods being abandoned and temples turning into mosques, in places where this sect gains influence, Hindu deities stop being worshipped, Hindus can no longer find homes, and Hindu temples are converted into sect temples. Already, from Surat to Ahmedabad, business and real estate circles have reached a point where you can only progress if you are associated with this sect. When I asked that RSS volunteer's friend, "So isn't it the RSS's responsibility to awaken Hindus about this sect and protect Sanatan Dharma?" the response was: "Hindutva is the RSS's concern, but devotion and spirituality are not. Anyone who arrives to accompany RSS in its work, the RSS believes him its associate."

I then asked, "It means a demon who is destroying truth and Vedic religion also can be yours, if he aligns with you in your work! And because spirituality and devotion is not your subject, you will not utter word against that evil, you will keep him as an ally! Can you explain what Hindutva even means without Hindu spirituality and Panchdev worship? You have reduced Hindutva to external symbols like saffron robes, tilaks, and temple architecture while ignoring its deeper meaning. You are making yourself in a group which can accept even Ravan, when he disguised himself as a sage to abduct Sita. If you had been there at that time, you would have silently stood by and let Ravan take Sita. And when Lord Ram and Lakshman asked you, 'Why did you help Ravan abduct Sita?' you would have replied: 'O Lord, we are like artificial intelligence robots. Our programming says that anyone who wears saffron, tilak, and a saintly appearance is a Hindu. So, according to our logic, Ravan is more Hindu than you at this moment with those cloths and cosmetics. Moreover, our programming also states that whoever supports our work must be considered a Hindu. Ravan has built grand temples of the demon kings like Hiranyakashipu and Paundraka, he has also built temples of Daitya Guru Shukracharya across the world, which strengthens Hindutva and even provides us with venues for events. So now that he has abducted Sita (i.e., the Vedic deities), that is your personal issue. The RSS will not interfere. The RSS's job is only to keep Hindus united.'"

This is precisely the RSS's logic. And even in this, it is not honest. When Lord Ram gathers the Vanar Sena to build the bridge and rescue Sita, the RSS, through the VHP, infiltrates his army to weaken it from within, ensuring it never reaches Lanka. It sings praises of Ravan's power, demoralizes Ram's warriors, creates internal conflicts, and secretly turns key fighters into Ravan's supporters. The VHP and other Hindu organizations have done exactly this—sabotaging the movements against this sect, led by Sanatani saints through the Sanatan Dharma Protection Committee. They obstructed it at every step, and while approaching for help, they said, "This is not our issue." If it wasn't their issue, why didn't they stay out of it? Why did they act as brokers? These ignorant and foolish people, in the name of Hindutva, are silently handing over Gujarat's Hindu society—Sita—to a sectarian Ravan.

There are also different kinds of RSS volunteers. Those who were true Sanatanis and had a living conscience have distanced themselves from the

RSS and are now fighting to save Sanatan Dharma from this sect. Some of them were those who had played a major role in removing illegal encroachments from Bet Dwarka. Many RSS volunteers have reached out to us via phone, messages, and personal meetings, lamenting, "We don't understand why our own people are supporting such a massive crisis. Our Guruji always said that an RSS volunteer can do anything, but now why are we being told not to interfere? And why is it that anyone who speaks up against this issue has to stay out of the RSS?" Something is deeply wrong, and they are beginning to realize it.

Then there are RSS volunteers who, being more loyal to the RSS than to Sanatan Dharma, say things like the Saurashtra volunteer: "Yes, something must be done, but the RSS won't do anything." And when asked, "Fine, if not the RSS, will you individually act?" they fall silent—because they cannot speak or act without RSS approval. Others remain in the RSS purely for personal gain—whether it is social prestige, a BJP position, or a government role in the future. This is how the RSS has bound a large section of Hindus under the guise of loyalty.

And if their response is, "But we never stopped you from acting. You go ahead and do it," then they should reflect on their actions over the past two years. The RSS has done nothing but obstruct Sanatanis from rescuing Hindus from this sect's grip. They make wise superficial speeches, but their only real job is to secure BJP's vote bank and hold onto power, even if the entire society falls into the hands of a Ravan-like sect. Even if Sanatan Dharma's principles and Vedic deities disappear, as long as BJP remains in power, they call it Hindutva. That is their absurd and unclear definition of Hindutva.

Below is a link to a video, revealing the harsh truth:
Video Link: https://drive.google.com/file/d/1--ZFUV5Mggfra2wcd8sAY_VlOpGtoAV1/view?usp=drivesdk

The Solution:

The solution is as clear and simple as this. There are two options for this sect:

1. They have to re-establish Sahajanand Swami as a devotee of Lord Krishna, turn all their temples into Krishna temples, and revert to the sect's original Vaishnav tradition. At most, they may worship Sahajanand Swami as a partial incarnation of Lord Krishna, where Krishna remains the central

deity in their teachings, scriptures, idols, and worship. Just as Chaitanya Mahaprabhu is considered an aspect of Krishna, but the temples and idols focus on Lord Krishna, the same should be done here. It is unfortunate that we even have to explain such basic things to people who come from Hindus, but this is necessary. They must also revise their books, hold press conferences, and publicly announce these changes to the Hindu society.

2. If they do not choose the first option and wish to continue declaring Sahajanand Swami as a god or supreme deity, they should stop using the names of Sanatan Dharma's scriptures and gods. They should remove all idols of Sanatan deities from their temples. Their books should not contain any mention of Sanatan Dharma's scriptures, its terminology, or its gods. Worship your god like Jesus, Allah, or Ahura Mazda, and give your Swamis the power you wish to. But you should not use the names Narayana, Hari, Madhava, or Shreeji—any names of Sanatan gods—in your sect. In Sanatan Dharma, the Panchadev are the manifestations of the formless Parabrahman, and no one is above them. Changing the structure of the scriptures and inserting a new god is an attack on Sanatan Dharma. It is a violation of Hindus' religious rights, a constitutional offense. Insulting the deities of Sanatan Dharma in such vulgar ways is an infringement on the basic right to live with dignity. That is a legal crime.

The matter is as simple as that. If the Sangh and VHP want to convince their Duryodhana-like friend, they should guide them to the first option; otherwise, they should accept the second option. If this sect chooses to declare itself a separate religion with its own god, it will not harm Sanatan Dharma. In fact, Sanatan Dharma will become clearer and stronger as a result. The Hindus abroad who are trapped in ignorance of this Sect will also become aware of the reality that this sect is not Sanatan Dharma. It's a Christian-like sect in Hindu clothes, trying to convert Hindus. The only ones who will suffer are them, and they know it. That's why they remain inside like a snake, gaining nourishment and waiting to strike. So, don't be afraid without reason. Your fear is as imaginary as Congress's reluctance to respond to Pakistan's terrorist attacks, fearing nuclear war. Just as that fear was unfounded, so is your fear of this sect. I have already written about this in an article as follows.

Can Sanatan Dharma, Which Is Eternal, Be Broken? So Why Shield Corruption and Hypocrisy to Save It?

• October 19, 2023 / On Facebook

The biggest lie and delusion being spread is the idea that if we strongly oppose this sect that betrays Sanatan Dharma, the Dharma will break! You fools, why flaunt the intellect corrupted by dishonesty and greed? First, Sanatan Dharma means upholding your duty towards the truth. It is not a sect that can be broken; it is the eternal truth. Second, correcting or removing a rotten fish from the pond purifies the pond; the pond does not break. Some may lose votes, others may lose money from their temple, or their luxurious lives may be disrupted, but the Sanatan Dharma will survive and purify. That is why debate is the core of Dharma. A sect of Swamis, who avoid debate, send brainwashed sheep to waste people's time with meaningless talks, while continuing their propaganda with the force of power. So, the selfish fear you feel is Adharma. Don't associate it with Dharma and society.

When we say, 'May Dharma be victorious, may Adharma be destroyed, may goodwill prevail among beings, may the world be blessed,' these are not just slogans. Each sentence is a condition for the next. Only when the truth is established—when Dharma is victorious—can Adharma be destroyed. Only when Adharma is destroyed can goodwill prevail among beings. Supporting Duryodhanas and Dushasanas will never lead to peace and goodwill. Only when Dharma is established, Adharma is destroyed, and goodwill prevails, can the world be blessed. So, awaken your soul, uphold your duty towards the truth, and fulfill your Dharma. Don't spread delusions by imposing your selfishness on society.

Christians were originally Jews until they declared Jesus Christ and his Father as the supreme God, above the deities worshiped by the Jews. Similarly, Muslims were originally Arabs until they proclaimed Allah as superior to all Arabian deities. Now, for the first time, we witness an Indian version of this phenomenon. In the past, individuals who left Hinduism, like Gautama Buddha and Mahavira, offered alternate paths to realizing God, slightly diverging from the Vedic approach. Their spiritual teachings expressed the same truths found in the Upanishads, albeit in different words. For this reason, they are still considered part of Sanatan Dharma, even though their paths are called Nastik, or non-Vedic, sects. Unlike these paths, which did not establish a new supreme god over the deities of Sanatan Dharma, we now encounter individuals in India attempting to do what Christians and Muslims once did in their societies.

Whenever individuals emerged from a civilization with a singular, supreme god, they often attempted to dismantle their previous culture, branding it as backward, dispensable, or unworthy of adherence. They criticized it while enslaving humanity in the name of that one god through priests, mullahs, and Swamis. This is the typical pattern with the concept of a supreme god; without such actions, they cannot assert their unique existence or significance.

So, if this sect refuses to choose one of these two options, the Sangh should not delay fulfilling its duty to Sanatan Dharma and society.

1. Dispel the mistaken belief that all Patels are members of the Swaminarayan sect and that opposing this sect would result in political losses. Many Patels are silent warriors for Sanatan Dharma, actively challenging this sect. They have created various PDFs and reached out to individuals like me for involvement. In America, a group of over 100 Sanatani Patels and another group of over 80 in Australia work to raise awareness against this sect. Only about 20-30% of Patels belong to this sect, many of whom are involved for business, possibly for laundering black money. Some insiders provide us with information on the inner corruption of this sect. Therefore, initiate opposition against this sect, just as there is opposition to the Muslim community's superiority complex. Stand firmly against their disrespect for Sanatan Dharma's deities, and you will see people speak up and leave the sect. Many have joined this sect due to the Sangh's endorsement and alignment with it. Engage with Patel leaders of Umiyadham and Khodaldham, encouraging Sanatani Patels to lead the way. Make it known that Patels are not betrayers of Sanatan Dharma by supporting this sect.

2. Support Shankaracharyaji and his committee in filing a legal case, and offer them legal assistance. Collaborate with Sanatani Acharyas to launch a campaign, similar to the one removing Sai Baba's idols from temples, to eliminate false idols of Hindu gods from this sect's temples and Christian churches. Run a campaign to remove all references to Sanatan Dharma's gods and scriptures from the sect's distorted literature.

The solution is straightforward, my friends from the Sangh and affiliated organizations! The entire Sanatani community understands it. Yet, when you hesitate to follow this path, frustrated outbursts like Mukhtanand Bapu's arise. You cannot grasp the amount of doubt, anger, and loss of respect this generates. By appeasing this sect, you are rewriting history much like Gandhi did by supporting the Khilafat movement, strengthening the Muslim cause. In Gujarat, you are repeating the mistakes of Nehru with Sheikh Abdullah in Kashmir and Indira-Sanjay Gandhi with Bhindranwale in Punjab. Just as those leaders had no foresight of their actions' repercussions, you too are blind to the consequences.

So, be mindful, friends. The fundamental error you are committing can be understood through this simple story:

In a household, a father has five sons. Three are good, one is of average intelligence, and one is a troublesome son who disrespects his father, claiming he will one day enslave his father and brothers, making the world know them as his servants. Meanwhile, a thug lives across the street, who also wants to claim the house as his own, threatening the family by shaking the gate. The unruly son inside insults his father daily, declaring he will enslave the family.

Now, tell me, can this father protect his home from the thug by indulging the unruly son? Or will he secure his family by disciplining the son so effectively that the thug becomes fearful? The thug will then understand: 'If they can treat one of their own so sternly in the name of truth and honor, imagine how they will deal with an outsider.'

This is the reality. You are choosing the former when the situation calls for the latter.

With this, I conclude this journey, leaving the choice of next steps to Sanatani society in India and worldwide. Even as I write this, the sect's efforts to spread its three-layered deception are seeping into other Indian states. Recently, they organized a major event near Ayodhya, in Chhapaiya, the birthplace of Sahajanand Swami, attempting to sway the local Hindu community. Yet, the event was a complete failure, with empty seats throughout the hall. The sect is attempting to infiltrate Uttar Pradesh through business and real estate, likely aiming to establish connections with Yogi Adityanath, similar to their influence with Narendra Modi and Amit Shah. In Jagannath Puri, Odisha, they reportedly plan to build a temple, positioning the Swaminarayan idol as the incarnation of Krishna as part of their deceptive agenda.

They actively pursue celebrities, inviting them to their temples or reaching out through their figurehead. For instance, they invited Akshay Kumar and Tiger Shroff to their Abu Dhabi temple and visited Anupam Kher. Anupam Kher, likely aware of their reality through Bhaishree Rameshbhai Oza, ended his video with chants of 'Om Namah Shivaya' and 'Har Har Mahadev,' which went viral in Gujarat. This made people appreciate his stance. Their influence isn't limited to film celebrities; they also target prominent Hinduist YouTubers, known for their stance against Muslims, using facilities, events, and funds, similar to RSS, VHP, and BJP tactics. Much like Duryodhana sought Karna, they keep you focused on anti-Muslim rhetoric, using your support to erase your own Sanatani deities. This book serves as a warning to Sanatani Hindus that this sect, with its three-layered deception, is coming for you. Those unfamiliar with its true nature must remember that your adversaries are not only Muslims and Christians but also sects cloaked in Hindu attire, ready to separate you from Sanatan Dharma faster than any foreign faith. Be prepared to resist them with knowledge and reason.

However, I do not intend to leave you alone against this deceptive sect. In the second volume of this book, I provide an authentic, scriptural understanding of Narayan, along with the essence of the five cosmic deities. Throughout this struggle, Sanatani warriors have emphasized the need for such understanding. Around this time, I was invited to write a column in Loksatta-JanSatta, a well-known newspaper published from Vadodara. I accepted and began explaining Sanatan Dharma's scriptural teachings, from the Vedas to Darshans and Puranas, through a weekly column. These columns are being compiled into a new book titled Sanatan: Dharma, Philosophy, Society, and Life. In Volume 2, selected weekly columns are included. Let us conclude this book with this Prasad of scriptural wisdom.

The real Swami of the Samsara in Sanatan Dharma & Scripturally Defined Narayana Lord Vishnu

XVI

Why are there Panchdevs in Sanatan Dharma? Why isn't there only one personal God?

"*Following is the article written on 6 September, 2024 / On Facebook and 24*[th] *December, 2024 in Newsdaily Loksatta Jansatta.*"

One question raised in defense of this sect is, "Sir, we have too many gods and deities, and that's why we are in this situation. It would be better if we also had only one God to fight for." When I heard this, I felt that those who have no knowledge of their scriptures, no understanding of their religion's principles, and who are eager to become like their enemies in every way—what are these fools fighting for? Their religion is being destroyed by them, and no one else is needed. So, let's answer this question.

What is Dharma? Why is it Sanatan (eternal)?

This entire cosmos ('Srishti' in Hindu texts), made of countless universes, operates according to a certain order, which in the Vedas is called 'Rit.' The word 'Rit' is the root of our word 'Ritu' (season). Just as seasons change one after another in an automatic, regular, and balanced system, so too, within the entire cosmos, there is an order that ensures balance among stars, planets, galaxies, and other celestial bodies, as well as between the sentient and insentient nature, according to the principle of Karma. This balance-maintaining system is called 'Rit.' This term is repeatedly mentioned in the Rigveda, and it is said to follow this 'Rit.' Following this system of 'Rit,' which regulates the entire creation, is called 'Dharma.' You can act against this system, but in doing so, you will lose your balance, and because you are going against the entire cosmos, you will not progress. You will face resistance and destruction. Therefore, the ideal was given that living according to 'Rit' is the only path to progress in this Srishti. Hence, the word 'Dharma' emerged, meaning to hold onto, not deviate from, this cosmic order - Rit.

This system of 'Rit' is born out of the consciousness of Brahman, the cause and creator of this entire existence. As such, it has existed since the beginning of creation. It existed before creation and will continue to exist after. Whatever has happened, is happening, and will happen is due to this system called 'Rit,' meaning it has neither a beginning nor an end. This system always exists, which is why it is eternal. Therefore, the Dharma that adheres to this system is also called eternal, or Sanatan. It too has no beginning or end. In one sense, Dharma in this entire creation means to follow 'Rit.' It has no other meaning. This is why it is said that Dharma is Sanatan (eternal); there is no other Dharma in the world. Everything else is just a sect. Sanatan Dharma is 'ours'—saying so is not appropriate. We are the people who follow Sanatan Dharma—that is the correct statement. This is why Shankaracharyaji, in his discourses, doesn't use the word 'Sanatanis.' He says, 'Sanatan Dharmavalanbi,' which means those who have accepted the fellowship of Sanatan Dharma.

Now, this system of 'Rit' that governs the creation is projected from the fundamental divine element called Brahman. This divine element is inherently formless (Nirakar), without attributes (Nirgun), and unmanifested (Avyakta). But gradually, it creates various manifestations and takes on forms, revealing itself in various qualities, and ultimately, it expresses itself even in the state that transcends all qualities. In the Vedas, Upanishads, and the six Darshanas, this divine element, known as Brahman, remains formless, but from its attribute-less state (Nirgun), it transforms into a state with attributes (Saguna), and from an unmanifested state (Avyakta), it becomes manifested (Vyakta). The thirty-three deities mentioned in the Vedas express the various qualities and powers of Brahman. But they are all formless. So, the deities of the Vedas are formless, but not without attributes. They possess attributes. They are invoked through Vedic mantras, as formless powers. However, as the Vedas progress toward their conclusion, a path for the worship of a personal, embodied God (Sakara) emerges through yantras.

Thus, when Vyasa, who compiled the Vedas and authored the supreme Darshana, Vedanta (Brahma Sutra), composed the Mahabharata and the eighteen Puranas, he presented that same formless God in a personal form. At this point, the realized sage, who has experienced Brahman, uses his wisdom to ensure that the formless divine element governing this creation does not become confined to just one personal form. From the deities mentioned in the Vedas, he highlights five deities as supreme gods, known as Panchadev: Vishnu, Shiva, Shakti (as Devi), Surya/Brahma, and Ganesha. Separate Puranas are written for each, showcasing their individual significance as the supreme forms of Brahman.

Through the Panchadev, the various powers and characteristics of the formless God are expressed separately, so that no one person imagines God in only one form and becomes enslaved to it. When one considers a single form as the supreme God, they must also remember the greatness of the other forms described in different Puranas, preventing them from becoming fanatical about just one form. Ultimately, they should realize that the fullness of the formless God is expressed through these five deities. There were two disadvantages of consolidating all forms into just one. First, the significance of the different powers could not be effectively conveyed, and all these powers would remain as mere words, while the form would take central importance. Second, a person would project their ego onto that single form, becoming fanatical about it. God would be sidelined, and the person's ego, associated with one name and form of God, would seek to exert dominance over the world—just as we observe in non-Sanatan sects, both native and foreign.

This is why, in Sanatan Dharma, the worship of Panchadev (five deities) was given central importance. Out of these Panchadev, one can choose the supreme form according to their own state and nature, while considering the other four as its aspects. This constantly reminds us that no single form is complete. All these forms represent the formless divine energy, which is the fundamental divine element, and it is omnipresent. It also exists within our souls. Therefore, we are not to see these forms as figures in creation, but rather to realize their divinity within our own souls, develop to their level, and ultimately merge into the formless Brahman and become unmanifest. This is Moksha. From the Vedas to Upanishads, and the six Darshanas to the Brahma Sutra, this conclusion and teaching emerge. This same teaching is also provided in the Puranas in the form of Panchadev worship.

The powers and significance of the Panchadev are as follows:

- Vishnu: The all-pervasive deity who maintains and protects the cosmic order (Rit) in the world. In other words, he upholds Dharma.

- Shiva: The yogi Rudra who teaches a person to experience their soul through yoga and to renounce the visible world. At the end of creation, the formless Brahman assumes this form for the destruction of creation.

- Shakti: The dormant power within humans, which, when awakened through yoga, connects a person to the powers of the formless Brahman. This is the power that makes a human into a god. It is the same power that makes Vishnu, Vishnu, and Rudra, Shiva.

- Surya/Brahma: He utilizes the formless divine power in such a way that creation can take place in theithin the formless Brahman. He bestows grace and blessings upon you, smoothing your path and removing obstacles as you ascend the steps toward the truth. He takes care of you on the journey to your development.

- Ganesha: He is a form of the formless Brahman, embodying an essence of compassion. He bestows his grace upon you, casting a benevolent gaze in your direction. As you progress on your journey toward ultimate truth, with each step you take, he strives to make your path smoother and free of obstacles. His role is to guide and nurture you, ensuring your well-being as you advance along the path of spiritual growth.

These five forms represent the formless divine power working in us, and we are meant to become one with it, for we are that very same power. This body is merely a temporary garment that we must shed from time to time until we dissolve once again in our formless, unmanifest Brahman state. This is the true form of Sanatan Dharma.

ॐ

Supreme Dharma Parliament's Religious Decree

To revive the understanding of Panchadev Upasana (worship of the five deities) within the Hindu Sanatani society, the Supreme Dharma Parliament (Param Dharm-Sansad) of Sanatan Dharma issued a religious decree on January 16 - 2025, during the Mahakumbh held in Prayagraj. The decree is given below:

The Religious Decree Issued by the Supreme Dharma Parliament

Sanatan - Vedic - Hindu - Arya

Supreme Dharma Parliament 1008

From Paush Shukla Ekadashi to Magh Shukla Chaturdashi, corresponding to January 10 to February 11, 2025, in Prayagraj, considering the resolutions passed in the Avarsadan (Lower House), the opinions of the Pravarsadan (Middle House), and the written recommendations of the Parmasadan (Higher Houser), the Parama-dharmadhesh has passed the following:

Supreme Religious Decree

Subject: Decision on the Worshipable Deities of Hindus

The scriptures state:

"Where the unworthy are worshipped and the worthy are neglected, there arise famine, death, and fear."

Unfortunately, this disorder has spread rapidly among Hindus, and now, even in temples dedicated to worshipable deities, the practice of worshipping unworthy entities has begun. Hence, in today's session of Supreme Dharma Parliament 1008, deliberations were held regarding the worshipable deities of Hindus. After thorough discussion, the Supreme Religious Decree is hereby issued as follows:

According to our Vedas, there is only one ultimate Upasya Devata (worshipable deity), who is Sachchidanand Parabrahman. This Parabrahman manifests in countless forms. In divine play, five cosmic functions—creation, sustenance, dissolution, restriction, and grace—are performed by Parabrahman. Corresponding to these five acts, five divine names, forms, pastimes, and abodes manifest as follows:

"आदत्यिं गणनाथश्च देवीं रुद्रश्च केशवम्।
पञ्चदैवतमत्यिुक्तं सर्वकर्मसु पूज्यते।।"

The scriptures declare that all religious rituals should be performed while worshipping these five deities.

This worship takes place through Navadha Bhakti (nine forms of devotion): Shravan (listening), Kirtan (chanting), Smaran (remembrance), Padasevan (service at the feet), Archan (ritual worship), Vandan (prayer), Dasya (servitude), Sakhya (friendship), and Atmanivedan (self-surrender).

Even when 33 Koti (categories) of deities are mentioned, they primarily fall under these five groups of deities:

12 Adityas (Sun gods as creators),

8 Vasus (Vishnu as the sustainer),

11 Rudras (Shiva as the dissolver),

Ashwini Kumaras (divine twins responsible for restriction and grace).

Thus, these five deities, in their countless names, forms, pastimes, and abodes, are truly worshipable, and our worship ultimately reaches the One Upasya Devata (Supreme Worshipable Deity).

Therefore, the worship of the one Parabrahman Sachchidanand Paramatma can be performed through its five representations as the Panchayatana Deities—Ganesh, Surya, Vishnu, Shiva, and Shakti—who are the divine rulers of Earth, Water, Fire, Air, and Space, respectively.

The worship of lifeless entities or unworthy beings is strictly prohibited. The Panchayatana Puja should be performed by placing one's chosen deity (Ishta Devata) in the center and the other four deities in the four directions, following proper scriptural guidelines.

Samvat 2081 V.S., Magh Krishna Tritiya (January 16, 2025 A.D.)

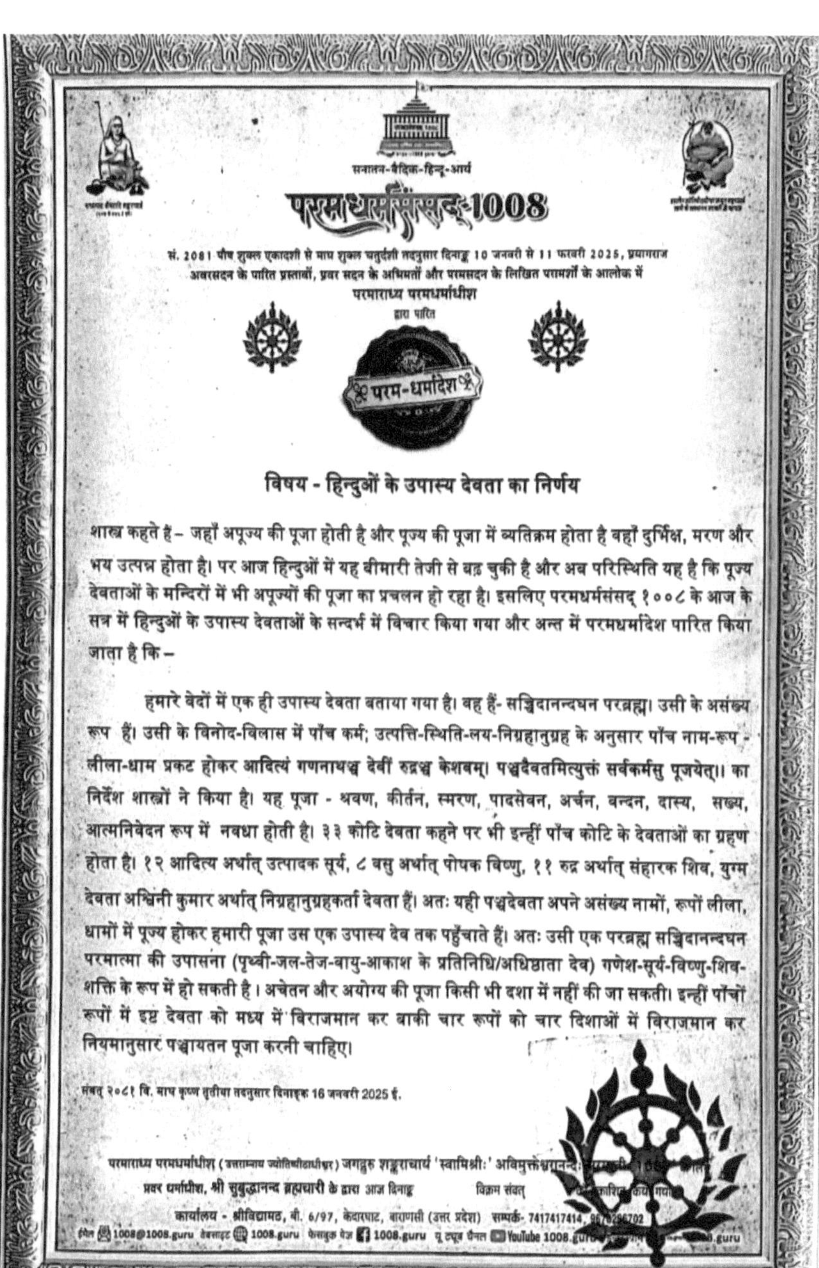

सनातन-वैदिक-हिन्दू-आर्य

परमधर्मसंसद् 1008

सं. 2081 पौष शुक्ल एकादशी से माघ शुक्ल चतुर्दशी तदनुसार दिनाङ्क 10 जनवरी से 11 फरवरी 2025, प्रयागराज अवरसदन के पारित प्रस्तावों, प्रवर सदन के अधिमतों और परमसदन के लिखित परामर्शों के आलोक में
परमाराध्य परमधर्माधीश
द्वारा पारित

परम-धर्मादेश

विषय - हिन्दुओं के उपास्य देवता का निर्णय

शास्त्र कहते हैं – जहाँ अपूज्य की पूजा होती है और पूज्य की पूजा में व्यतिक्रम होता है वहाँ दुर्भिक्ष, मरण और भय उत्पन्न होता है। पर आज हिन्दुओं में यह बीमारी तेजी से बढ़ चुकी है और अब परिस्थिति यह है कि पूज्य देवताओं के मन्दिरों में भी अपूज्यों की पूजा का प्रचलन हो रहा है। इसलिए परमधर्मसंसद् १००८ के आज के सत्र में हिन्दुओं के उपास्य देवताओं के सन्दर्भ में विचार किया गया और अन्त में परमधर्मादेश पारित किया जाता है कि –

हमारे वेदों में एक ही उपास्य देवता बताया गया है। वह हैं- सच्चिदानन्दघन परब्रह्म। उसी के असंख्य रूप हैं। उसी के विनोद-विलास में पाँच कर्म; उत्पत्ति-स्थिति-लय-निग्रहानुग्रह के अनुसार पाँच नाम-रूप - लीला-धाम प्रकट होकर आदित्यं गणनाथञ्च देवीं रुद्रञ्च केशवम्। पञ्चदैवतमित्युक्तं सर्वकर्मसु पूजयेत्॥ का निर्देश शास्त्रों ने किया है। यह पूजा - श्रवण, कीर्तन, स्मरण, पादसेवन, अर्चन, वन्दन, दास्य, सख्य, आत्मनिवेदन रूप में नवधा होती है। ३३ कोटि देवता कहने पर भी इन्हीं पाँच कोटि के देवताओं का ग्रहण होता है। १२ आदित्य अर्थात् उत्पादक सूर्य, ८ वसु अर्थात् पोषक विष्णु, ११ रुद्र अर्थात् संहारक शिव, युग्म देवता अश्विनी कुमार अर्थात् निग्रहानुग्रहकर्ता देवता हैं। अतः यही पञ्चदेवता अपने असंख्य नामों, रूपों लीला, धामों में पूज्य होकर हमारी पूजा उस एक उपास्य देव तक पहुँचाते हैं। अतः उसी एक परब्रह्म सच्चिदानन्दघन परमात्मा की उपासना (पृथ्वी-जल-तेज-वायु-आकाश के प्रतिनिधि/अधिष्ठाता देव) गणेश-सूर्य-विष्णु-शिव-शक्ति के रूप में हो सकती है। अचेतन और अयोग्य की पूजा किसी भी दशा में नहीं की जा सकती। इन्हीं पाँचों रूपों में इष्ट देवता को मध्य में विराजमान कर बाकी चार रूपों को चार दिशाओं में विराजमान कर नियमानुसार पञ्चायतन पूजा करनी चाहिए।

संवत् २०८१ वि. माघ कृष्ण तृतीया तदनुसार दिनाङ्क 16 जनवरी 2025 ई.

परमाराध्य परमधर्माधीश (उत्तराम्नाय ज्योतिष्पीठाधीश्वर) जगद्गुरु शङ्कराचार्य 'स्वामिश्रीः' अविमुक्तेश्वरानन्द ...
प्रवर धर्माधीश, श्री सुबुद्धानन्द ब्रह्मचारी के द्वारा आज दिनाङ्क ... विक्रम संवत् ...

कार्यालय - श्रीविद्यामठ, बी. 6/97, केदारघाट, बाराणसी (उत्तर प्रदेश) सम्पर्क- 7417417414, 9670296702
हिण 1008@1008.guru वेबसाइट 1008.guru फेसबुक पेज 1008.guru यू ट्यूब चैनल YouTube 1008.guru

XVII
The Form of Panchadev in the Vedas

When the Vedas, the earliest scriptures of Sanatan Dharma, were written, let's explore in what forms the Panchadev of the Puranas were present in them.

Vishnu's Emergence in The Vedas as The Supreme God

What are the 33 Koti (types) of Deities and the 12 Adityas in the Rigveda?

• Date: 16-05-2024 / Loksatta Jansatta

Sanatan Dharma begins with the four Vedas, written in a specific order: Rigveda, Yajurveda, Samaveda, and Atharvaveda. Each Veda is a collection of four types of texts: Samhita, Brahmana texts, Aranyaka, and Upanishads, which together form a Veda. The first and most ancient text is the Rigveda, and its Samhita part is the largest. It is the oldest scripture on Earth and marks the beginning of Indian Sanatan civilization. The worship and invocation of 33 types of deities through sacrifices (Yajnas) form the foundation of Indian religion. These 33 deities include 12 Adityas, deities associated with the Sun, 8 Vasus, 11 Rudras, 2 Ashwini Kumaras, and 1 Devi.

Since the Sun is included in both Adityas and Vasus, there are a total of 33 deities along with one Devi. The Rigveda consists of 10 different Mandalas (books), with each Mandala containing a varying number of Suktas (hymns), and each Sukta composed of several mantras. Each Sukta is created by a specific Rishi in a particular meter for the invocation of a certain deity. The names of the Rishi, the deity, and the meter are mentioned at the beginning of each Sukta.

The first Sukta of the first Mandala of the Rigveda begins with a mantra invoking Agni (fire). The deities of the Panchamahabhutas (five great elements)—Earth, Air, Water (Varuna), Space, along with the Sun, Moon, and Stars—are the 8 Vasus, each having their own Suktas for invocation. Similarly, there are Suktas for the 12 Adityas, including Vivasvan, Aryaman, Tvashta, Savitr, Bhaga, Dhata, Mitra, Varuna, Amsa, Pushan, Indra, and lastly Vishnu. There are misconceptions that the 12 Adityas are just 12 names of the Sun, but in reality, Aditya refers to those luminous beings who lead to the source of light beyond the Sun. For instance, Vivasvan is the current name of the Sun, while Indra is the deity associated with lightning and rain, directly connected with human life and frequently invoked for protection in the Rigveda. Hence, most Suktas in the Rigveda are dedicated to Indra, as he is very important for agriculture society. Aryaman represents the deity traveling across the entire galaxy, radiant between dawn and noon, protector of horses, and presiding over rituals like marriages. Bhaga grants fortune, while Dhata is the Aditya who bestows health. Savitr represents the primal energy of the Sun before sunrise, Mitra governs the dawn and is the deity of principles, treaties, rules, and truth, while Varuna governs the dusk. Pushan is the Aditya who protects travelers.

But the most expansive of the Adityas is Vishnu, the last Aditya. Vishnu is first mentioned in the 22nd Sukta of the first Mandala of the Rigveda, from the 16th to the 21st verses, where his definition is given. Vishnu is the one who is all-pervading. Among the 33 deities, Vishnu is the only one described as being as pervasive as the Sun's light, upholding all the worlds. He is Indra's best friend in helping mankind, and his three strides measure the Earth, the heavens, and the space between. Even though there are more Suktas dedicated to Indra and other deities in the Rigveda, Vishnu stands out as the all-pervading deity with fundamental power, just as in the Mahabharata, Krishna's presence is not as much as Pandava and Kauravas have, but yet, Krishna is the highest and most significant character of the scripture.

Further on in the first Mandala, the 153rd Sukta, known as the Vishnu Sukta, praises Vishnu's glory, continuing through Suktas 155 and 156. In the seventh Mandala, the 99th and 100th Suktas once again sing the praises of Vishnu as the all-pervading deity. After this, the Samhita portion of the Rigveda concludes, and the Aitareya Brahmana, the first Brahmana text of the Rigveda, opens with the very first verse stating, "Agni is the lowest of the gods, and Vishnu is the highest. All other gods are between them" (Aitareya Brahmana 1.1.1).

Thus, while Vishnu is assigned only five Suktas in the Samhita portion of the Rigveda, he is subtly presented throughout as the all-pervading deity among the 33 deities. In the Brahmana portion, Vishnu is firmly established as the highest deity. In the subsequent Yajurveda, Vishnu is referred to as Narayana, the one who creates water (Nara) with a full Narayana Sukta dedicated to him. The first famous verse of the Narayana Sukta, "Om Sahanavavatu Sahanau Bhunaktu..." is well known. This Sukta glorifies Narayana as the primal creator of the universe: "Narayana is the eternal, auspicious one, immutable and unchanging. Narayana is the most worthy of knowledge, the supreme being within all. Narayana is the supreme object and the ultimate goal of attainment. Narayana is the supreme Brahman, the highest reality, the supreme light, and the supreme self." After this, the Narayana Sukta concludes with the famous Vishnu Gayatri mantra:

"*Om Narayanaya Vidmahe Vasudevaya Dhimahi*
Tanno Vishnuh Prachodayat.
Meaning:
We meditate on Narayan, who is the same as Vasudev, and also
Vishnu. May that Vishnu inspire us."

Vasudeva means the deity who dwells everywhere, revered by the eight Vasus. This verse is called the Vishnu Gayatri mantra and appears multiple times (around 25-30 times) in the Yajurveda and other Vedas, continuously glorifying Vishnu as Narayana and Vasudeva, identifying him with the Vishnu of the Rigveda. Then we come across the Purusha Sukta of the 90th Sukta in the 10th Mandala of the Rigveda, which describes the supreme creator of the universe as Purusha or Virat Purusha, encompassing the entire cosmos. The invoked deity in the Purusha Sukta is Narayana, though the name Narayana does not appear anywhere else among the 33 deities invoked throughout the Rigveda, first emerging in the Yajurveda. Therefore, it is believed that the Purusha Sukta was later added to the Rigveda.

Thus, it is a misconception that the Vishnu of the Puranas is a minor deity in the Vedas and that Indra is a greater deity. Indra is more frequently mentioned in the Rigveda because he is more accessible and directly useful for agricultural activities. However, the Rigveda is the first text to reveal Vishnu as the all-pervading deity, and the Brahmana portion establishes him as the supreme deity. It is also important to note that the sage who compiled all four Vedas, Ved Vyasa, or the rishis in his tradition known as Ved Vyasa, also wrote the eighteen Puranas. Therefore, the Puranas expand and popularize what was already present in the Vedas. The Vedas already present the formless and embodied aspects of God, and the Puranas merely give them bodily forms and stories to make them more devotional and accessible to the masses.

The Emergence of Shiva, Shakti, and Ganesha, including the Sun God in the Vedas

- 23/05/2024, Loksatta Jansatta

We have seen that the compilation of the Samhita, Brahmana texts, Aranyakas, and Upanishads of the four Vedas, as well as the writing of the eighteen Puranas, was done by the sage Ved Vyasa. Therefore, the same concepts expanded in the Puranas were already present in the Vedas. Lord Vishnu of the Puranas is revealed as the twelfth Aditya, the all-pervading deity (Vishnu) in the Rigveda, and in the Brahmana texts of the Rigveda, he is established as the supreme deity. In the Yajurveda, Vishnu is presented as Narayana and Vasudeva, and established as the primal supreme God. Similarly, today we explore in what form Shiva and Shakti of the Puranas were revealed in the Vedas.

Shiva/Rudra:

The Rigveda contains six Suktas (1.43, 1.114, 2.33, 6.74, 7.46, 8.63) dedicated to the invocation of Rudra. In the Rigveda, Rudra is the god of war, who protects people and warriors. He is depicted as having matted hair and is known as the god of stories. Additionally, he is considered a deity with great intellect, high knowledge, and profound thoughts, and people pray to him for better intellect and thoughts. His diet is always pure and healthy, so people also ask for health from him. Being the fierce god responsible for the destruction of the world, people pray to him not to bring harm to their loved ones, warriors, or their own bodies. Thus, while the Rudra of the Rigveda is fierce and associated with high intellect and knowledge, in the Yajurveda, through knowledge, he becomes calmer and more worshipful.

In the fourth and seventh sections of the Krishna Yajurveda's Taittiriya Samhita, there is the famous Shri Rudram Stotra, also called the Rudra Prashna, spread over several verses. In this Stotra, Rudra is often referred to with the attribute "Shiva," where "Shiva" means "the supremely peaceful" or "the supreme revered." It is in this Stotra that we first see the phrase "Namah Shivaya" in the Vedas, and the Mahamrityunjaya Mantra, "Om Tryambakam Yajamahe..." also comes from this Rudra Prashna. Thus, Rudra is established as Shiva in the Yajurveda, and the characteristics of Rudra in the Rigveda are the same as those of Shiva in the Puranas. Therefore, the claim that Lord Shiva is not present in the Vedas is a gross misrepresentation. Rudra's character, appearing in the form of Shiva, is first revealed in the Vedas, and the Puranas simply personify that character with a physical form and stories.

Devi:

The same applies to Shakti. In the Devi Bhagavatam or the Shakta Purana, we know the form of Bhagavati Devi as Shakti, where Bhagavati in her Shakti form causes each atom to vibrate and grants power to each god. It is she who makes Rudra into Shiva and Vishnu into divine Vishnu. This very concept is found in the 125th Sukta of the 10th Mandala of the Rigveda, known as the "Devi Sukta." It is based on this Devi Sukta that Ved Vyasa composed the Devi Bhagavatam or Shakta Purana. Here are some of the verses from the Devi Sukta:

"I pervade and roam within Rudras, Vasus, Adityas, and the Vishwadevas. I uphold Mitra, Varuna, Indra, Agni, and the Ashwini Kumaras. (1) I uphold the Moon and the Sun to provide light, and I rule over the entire universe with my power. I am the knower of all knowledge, and I reside in various forms as the most glorious and foremost to be worshiped. The gods and enlightened beings perceive me in various forms and experience me. (2, 3) It is through my power that people eat food, it is through my power that they see, hear, and breathe. Whomever I desire, I make radiant and powerful. I place arrows on Rudra's bow and wage war to strike down those who oppose Brahman and oppress others. I have established the Sun as the ruler of the sky, as the head of the world. The entire universe is encompassed within me. I am beyond the touch of this universe, and I encompass all within me. I create all beings and then flow through them like subtle air." (4-8)

Ganesha:

The word Ganapati is used in the 23rd Sukta of the second Mandala of the Rigveda as a term for the lord of knowledge, called Brahmanaspati. This lord of knowledge, Ganapati, is referred to in the Yajurveda's Taittiriya Aranyaka as Vakratunda (one with a curved trunk) and Danti (one with a tusk). The verse is, "We meditate upon that supreme being in the form of Ishvara, who has a curved trunk. That Danti guides us on the right path." (Yajurveda, Taittiriya Aranyaka 10.1.15) This lord of knowledge, Ganapati, was later depicted in the Puranas by Maharishi Ved Vyasa as the son of Shiva and Shakti and a personified form of the supreme Brahman.

Surya/Brahma:

As for the Sun God, who is another of the Panchadev, he is represented in both the Adityas and the Vasus as the protector of the universe in the Rigveda. Therefore, when Maharishi Ved Vyasa describes Surya as the supreme Brahman in the Surya Purana, he uses the all-pervading Aditya Vishnu as an aspect of the Sun. Furthermore, Brahma, who represents the Purusha principle of Lord Vishnu, is shown as a portion of the Sun God. In this way, the Surya Purana also serves as Brahma Purana. Thus, in the Vedas, the formless Ishvara is presented with Saguna (with qualities) names, and in the Puranas, these names are given a body and stories, presenting them as the Panchadev.

XVIII

The Form of Lord Vishnu as Narayana in the Puranas

Now, let's explore how the Panchadev of the Vedas are portrayed in their embodied forms across different Puranas. First, we'll examine Lord Vishnu, who is established as the supreme deity in the Rigveda and takes on the names Narayana and Vasudeva in the Yajurveda. In the Vishnu Purana, we encounter terms like Pradhan, Purusha, Vyakta, and Kala, which have been misinterpreted and used in various charts by the sect of the fake Narayan, leading to the erroneous placement of Lord Vishnu below these entities. After understanding the correct context of these terms in the Vishnu Purana, the absurdity of such interpretations becomes clear.

The Story of Creation in the Vishnu Purana

Part 1: Who are Pradhan, Purusha, Vyakta, and Kala that originate from Vishnu?

· Date: 11/04/2024, Loksatta Jansatta

In the Vishnu Purana, Lord Vishnu is described as the supreme and ultimate deity among the Panchadev of Sanatan Dharma. He is the one through whom creation comes into being, and he is known as Vasudeva, meaning "the one who is everywhere and in whom the entire universe resides." This eternal, supreme, imperishable, unmanifest, pure, and attribute-less Paramatma (supreme soul) is the Parbrahman (Great Brahman), Mahavishnu. This Mahavishnu manifests itself in four primary forms: (1) the manifest universe (Vyakta), (2) the subtle nature behind this manifest universe (Pradhan), (3) Purusha, who is the witness of both the manifest universe and unmanifest Pradhan, and (4) Kala (time), which encompasses and governs all three. Among these, Purusha is the primary form of Mahavishnu, and Kala is his expanded form. The entire creation is brought into being and governed by Mahavishnu through these four forms. Let's explore what each of these forms represents.

The primal energy that exists as formless Parbrahman (Mahavishnu in Vishnu Puran) first creates a formless, imperishable form similar to itself, called Purusha. This Purusha is the representative of the supreme Parbrahman, appointed as the witness of the entire universe. After assigning Purusha as the witness, Parbrahman in the form of Vishnu appoints his second form, Pradhan. This Pradhan is the form from which all nature (Prakriti) and the visible universes emerge. The manifest creation is called Vyakta, the third form of Parbrahman. Above these three forms, the vast form of Brahman is Kala (pronounced as 'Kaal'), which is the covering of energy that encompasses Purusha, Pradhan, and the manifest universe. From the expansion of Kala, time and space are created, and from its contraction, time and space dissolve. In this way, Parbrahman creates the manifest universe through Pradhan, remains present as a witness through Purusha, and binds all three together with Kala.

Now, let's see how the manifest universe emerges from Pradhan. Pradhan is nothing but the Prakriti (nature) described in the Sankhya Darshana (philosophy). Thus, what is explained as Prakriti and Purusha in the Sankhya Darshana is similarly described as Pradhan and Purusha in the Vishnu Purana. Pradhan is the subtle nature from which the entire manifest creation is produced. Pradhan first generates a principle at its center called Mahat, just as a seed exists at the center of a fruit. This central Mahat is of three types: Sattvik, Rajsik, and Tamsik. The surrounding Pradhan element merges with these three types of Mahat and begins the process of manifestation. Once Pradhan merges with the three qualities of Mahat, the first thing produced is Ahamkara (ego), which exists in three forms—Tamsik, Rajsik, and Sattvik—representing the distinct identities of these three qualities of Mahat. This marks the beginning of the creation of nature. From Tamsik Ahamkara (dark, inert ego) arises the subtle consciousness called Tanmatras, which successively generates the five great elements (Mahabhutas)—Akasha (space), Vayu (air), Agni (fire), Jala (water), and Prithvi (earth). These five Mahabhutas are created by five Tanmatras, which correspond to sound, touch, form, taste, and smell. The smell Tanmatra creates the earth element, taste creates water, the form creates fire, touch creates air, and sound creates space.

Thus, the external nature of living beings is created from Tamsik Ahamkara. Next, Rajsik Ahamkara becomes active and creates the ten senses (Indriyas) of living beings. These include the five knowledge senses—eyes, ears, nose, skin, and tongue—and the five action senses—anus, genitals, hands, feet, and speech. However, the senses are merely entry points for sensations, and the action senses are only tools. It is the brain centers connected to these senses that process the sensations and direct the action senses to perform actions. These brain centers are called the presiding deities of the senses. These presiding deities of the senses, along with the intellect (mind), are created by Sattvik Ahamkara. In this way, the outer nature is formed by Tamasik Ahamkara, the body and mind of beings are created through Rajsik and Sattvik Ahamkara, and within this body resides the soul (Atma) as a representative and witness of Parbrahman, known as Purusha. Purusha, as the witness of Brahman, resides in the body made of the Tamsik, Rajsik, and Sattvik Mahat elements, giving it life. Thus, the entire manifest world is created through the combination of Pradhan and Purusha. Mahavishnu, the supreme Brahman, keeps all three (manifest nature as Vyakta, Pradhan, and Purusha) connected to himself through the covering of Kala. This is the true meaning of Pradhan, Purusha, Vyakta, and Kala as described in the Vaishnava scriptures.

The Story of Creation in the Vishnu Purana

Part 2: The Birth and Function of Brahma, Narayana, and Shiva Forms of Lord Vishnu

- Date: 18/04/2024, Jansatta Loksatta

In the previous article, we understood the concepts of Pradhan, Purusha, Vyakta, and Kala from the second chapter of the first section of the Vishnu Purana. Pradhan is the subtle seed of nature, from which the Mahat principle, composed of the three qualities (Sattva, Rajas, and Tamas), is created. This Mahat then gives rise to Ahamkara (ego) in its three forms. Through this Triguni (threefold) Ahamkara, the five great elements (Akasha, Vayu, Agni, Jala, and Prithvi), their associated qualities (sound, form, smell, etc.), the senses of living beings, their brain centers, and the mind are created. The Pancha Mahabhutas (five great elements) become the subjects of the senses of living beings, and the soul resides in them as the witness (Purusha), representing the supreme Brahman.

The Pancha Mahabhutas possess their own powers, but without interaction and without the Purusha merging into them, further creation could not proceed. Thus, Purusha pervades the entire nature formed by Pradhan, and together they create an egg (Andam), which becomes the mortal base for creation, where Brahma, Vishnu, and Shiva manifest from within to perform the creation, preservation, and dissolution of the world. Mortal things ("Prakrit objects") are those that will eventually be destroyed, while their opposite in scripture is "Purusha objects," which are eternal.

In this egg-like base of creation, the unmanifest Lord Vishnu resides as Hiranyagarbha, the golden embryo from which everything will emerge. From here, Lord Vishnu manifests the processes of creation (Brahma), preservation (Narayana), and dissolution (Shiva). First, he takes on the form of Brahma, the one who creates the world, as a Rajas guna (quality) state. Then he remains in the Sattva guna as Vishnu to preserve the world throughout the ages. At the end of the cycle (Kalpa), he takes on the Tamasic form of Shiva, the destroyer, and covers all living beings and the five great elements with the water of dissolution. After this, he lies down on the serpent bed (Shesha) on those waters. When the next cycle begins, Vishnu awakens from his sleep on Shesha and begins creation in the form of Brahma once more (Vishnu Purana 1.2.61-70).

Because he sleeps on the waters during the dissolution, Vishnu is called Narayana (Nara meaning water, and Ayana meaning resting place). Thus, the term "Narayana" first appears in the fourth chapter of the first section of the Vishnu Purana. Contrary to common understanding, it is stated that as soon as Vishnu awakens from sleep as Narayana, his state as Brahma begins. It is said, "The Lord in the form of Narayana, as Brahma, awoke from his sleep on the serpent bed and observed the empty worlds through the influence of Sattva guna." Here, Vishnu is referred to as Brahma in his Narayana form. This description continues to the extent that when Narayana, as Brahma, saw the Earth submerged in water, he took on the form of Varaha (boar) to rescue it. The description of Varaha is similar to that of Vishnu with four arms. Thus, chapter four of the first section consistently maintains that Vishnu, in his Narayana form, is also Brahma, and the term "Narayana" refers to the form of Vishnu lying on the water of dissolution.

After rescuing the Earth from the waters, Narayana, in his form as Brahma, leveled the land and began creation. He created the nine creations (Sargas), beginning with the Pancha Mahabhutas (five great elements). Next came ignorance (Avidya) in the forms of delusion, great delusion, and anger, followed by the creation of gods, demons, and other human beings in the sixth and seventh Sargas. Afterward, Brahma (Vishnu in the form of Brahma) created the four varnas based on the three gunas (qualities), along with progenitors like Marichi, and then the first humans, Manu and Shatarupa, along with their offspring. Following this came the famous churning of the ocean, where Brahma as Vishnu gave permission for the gods and demons to churn the ocean, marking the first time the Brahma state of Vishnu collaborated with his preserver (Vishnu) state to allow the churning. From here onward, the stories of Vishnu's avatars, including Mohini and Vamana, begin. From here they are narrated as Vishnu's forms.

At the end of all the avatar stories, the third and fourth chapters of the sixth section of the Vishnu Purana describe the dissolution of the entire universe at the end of a thousand cycles of four Yugas. At this time, Vishnu takes on his Rudra form, scorching the Earth with the heat of the Sun and drying up the rivers and oceans. Then, in his Rudra form, Vishnu creates a great fire from the mouth of the serpent Shesha, destroying everything. Afterward, he produces clouds that cover all three worlds with water. This tamasic form of Vishnu, with the qualities of destruction, is called Shiva. After the dissolution, Vishnu again lies down on the serpent bed on the waters of the submerged world, in his Avyakta (unmanifest) form as Vasudeva, entering yogic sleep.

Thus, throughout the Vishnu Purana, the one formless, unmanifest supreme Parbrahman, known as Mahavishnu, creates Pradhan, Purusha, Kala, and Vyakta, and takes on the forms of Brahma, Narayana (Vishnu), and

Shiva to perform the creation, preservation, and dissolution of the universe.

ॐ

Now, let's understand the two chapters of the Bhagavad Gita known as Aksharbrahma Yoga and Purnapurushottam Yoga. These two terms have been heavily misused in the BAPS branch of the Swaminarayan sect.

Aksharbrahma Yoga and Purushottam Yoga in the Bhagavad Gita: Announcing Lord Krishna's Supreme Brahman Status

- Jansatta Loksatta, Date: 04/04/2024

The seventh chapter of the Bhagavad Gita, Jnana-Vijnana Yoga, concludes with these two verses spoken by Lord Krishna: "Those who take refuge in me and strive to free themselves from old age and death, they come to know Brahman, the entirety of Adhyatma (the entirety of spiritual knowledge), and the complete Karma (the nature of all actions)." (7.29) "Those who know me as the soul behind all beings including the Adhibhuta, Adhidaiva, and Adhiyajna even at the time of death, their minds fixed on me, reach me alone." (7.30) These statements lead to the eighth chapter, Aksharbrahma Yoga, which begins with Arjuna's questions to understand the terms used by Krishna.

Arjuna asks, "What is Brahman? What is Adhyatma? What is Karma? What is Adhibhuta and Adhidaiva? What is Adhiyajna, and how is it in this body? And those whose minds are fixed on you recognize you in which form at the time of death?" (8.1, 8.2). In response, Lord Krishna explains Aksharbrahma Yoga.

Shri Krishna says, "The supreme, indestructible element is Brahman. The soul of a person, or the individual soul, is called 'Adhyatma,' meaning that which is primordial and fundamental, is the soul itself. The act of creation as immersion or sacrifice of the true form of Parbrahman, which leads to the birth of all beings, is referred to as karma. The Brahman, in the form of God, expands itself, dispersing its essence to create this world, and thus, the primary karma is the sacrifice of its original, unmanifest form. It is called the 'original' or 'primordial' karma. Everything subject to creation and destruction is dominated by this principle. The form of Brahman that creates the visible universe is referred to as 'Adhidaiva,' and above all of this is the supreme Brahman, which is also Lord Krishna himself, known as 'Adhiyajna.' Thus, presenting himself as Adhiyajna, Lord Krishna explains what he truly is and how one can attain him.

Shri Krishna states that the one who, at the moment of death, remembers this supreme element attains it in the end. Whatever one remembers and contemplates at the final moment of life, that is what they achieve. Thus, he advises Arjuna, 'Always remember me and fight for righteousness.' He also explains how one should remain absorbed in this supreme element. By closing all the senses, focusing the mind in the heart, and directing the breath to the head, one should chant OM, the imperishable sound of Brahman, and meditate on the formless, indestructible Brahman in the form of Lord Krishna. In doing so, they attain him in the end. In the chapter of Akshara Brahma Yoga, as in the Upanishads, the formless, unmanifest, and indestructible Brahman is called Aksara Brahman. The sound OM, used to remember this indestructible Brahman, is also referred to as Aksara Brahman, meaning OM itself is the imperishable Brahman.

Shri Krishna further says, 'The unmanifest power known as Akshara (imperishable) is the ultimate path to liberation. This eternal unmanifest form, upon reaching which humans do not return, is my supreme abode where I dwell.' (8.21) Thus, in the chapter of Akshara Brahma Yoga, Lord Krishna describes himself as the unmanifest Brahman, known as the supreme Akshara Brahman due to its indestructibility. He refers to this unmanifest state as his original state, his original place, and for humans, this is the ultimate goal, after attaining which they do not return to the cycle of rebirth. Lord Krishna guides humans to move from his manifest form to his unmanifest, indestructible Brahman form and understand that his true form and place is this unmanifest, supreme Brahman. In simple terms, he says that although he stands there in a bodily form, he is, at his core, the unmanifest, indestructible Brahman.

The concept of Purushottam Yoga is then introduced in the fifteenth chapter of the Gita. Here, Krishna describes the world as akin to an upside-down Ashvattha (Peepal) tree, whose roots are upwards. The unmanifest Brahman is the root of this tree, its branches are the three gunas (qualities) of the manifest Brahman, and the leaves are the verses of the Vedas. From these branches, which are nourished by the three qualities, arise the buds of sensory objects, spreading out in all directions. There are also roots that extend downward, causing worldly activities to take place. However, understanding the nature of this tree is not easy, as it has neither a beginning nor an end. Therefore, Krishna says that the person who cuts down the trunk of this tree with the axe of detachment from sensory pleasures can see and realize the unmanifest Brahman as the root. Such a person has destroyed their pride and delusion, conquered the defects of attachment, and is constantly established in the nature of the supreme soul. Such a person alone can know the supreme position of Brahman (15.1-5).

Then, Krishna reveals his supreme nature. He says that the eternal soul residing in the bodies of all beings is a fragment of himself (the supreme Brahman). This soul is the master of the body and the mind. Similarly, the light in the Sun, Moon, and fire is also his light. As the soul, he supports all living beings and nourishes all vegetation through the light of the Moon. Krishna says, "In this world, there are two types of beings: the perishable (Kshara) and the imperishable (Akshara). The bodies of living beings, humans, and plants are perishable, while the soul that inhabits these bodies is imperishable. But beyond both the perishable and imperishable beings, there is the supreme being who enters and sustains the entire cosmos. This supreme being is called the imperishable, the supreme lord, and the supreme self. Thus, I transcend the perishable and am higher than the imperishable soul. Therefore, I am celebrated in both the world and the Vedas as Purushottam" (15.16-18). Finally, Krishna, who is manifest as the formless, unmanifest Brahman, says, "O Bharata! The wise person who knows me as this Purushottam (the supreme being) knows everything and constantly worships me, the supreme Parbrahman, in all ways" (15.19).

This chapter underscores that Krishna, though present in a form, is actually the formless, unmanifest Brahman, and those who understand him as such attain the supreme knowledge and devotion to him as Purushottam, the supreme unmenifest formless being.

XIX

The Forms of Panchdev apart from Lord Vishnu in the Puranas

Let's explore how Lord Shiva, Maa Shakti, Lord Ganesha, and Lord Surya or Brahma are explained through their respective Puranas.

The Understanding of Creation in the Shiva Mahapurana

- Loksatta Jansatta, Date: 25-04-2024

The Shiva Purana begins with Sage Narada asking his beloved Lord Vishnu for his Hari form. Lord Vishnu, recognizing the worldly desire that had arisen in Narada, transforms him into a monkey because the word "Hari" can also mean monkey. Unaware of his transformation, Narada goes to another place, where he is mocked. Upon realizing the truth, Narada is filled with anger and returns to Vaikuntha, where he curses Lord Vishnu. However, when he regains his senses, he falls at Vishnu's feet, asking for forgiveness. Lord Vishnu tells him that if a sage of Devas like him, who has wandered off, needs correction, only the Lord of Devas, Mahadev (Shiva), can help. Thus, Narada embarks on a pilgrimage to various Shiva lingas on Earth and, while meditating on Shiva, reaches Brahmaloka and requests Brahma to narrate the story of Lord Shiva as the Supreme Brahman.

Brahma explains that only Lord Shiva is worshiped in the form of a linga, unlike other deities. This is because only Lord Shiva represents the formless Brahman, from whom all other deities are born, and the Shiva linga is the symbol of his formless aspect. The Shiva linga represents the union of the lingam (symbolizing Shiva) and the yoni (symbolizing Shakti), depicting the energy of creation formed through the union of Shiva and Shakti. Before the creation of the current cycle of the universe, during the period of great dissolution (Mahapralaya), only the formless Brahman existed. In this state of darkness, the formless Shiva linga desired to create a new universe. Thus, from the formless Brahman emerged the embodied form of Lord Shiva, called Sadashiva. Sadashiva was Ardhanarishvara, meaning half of his body was female. From this Ardhanarishvara form, the female aspect, Shakti, manifested as Goddess Ambika. She became the mother of all creation, and her role was to act on Shiva's will.

After this, Lord Shiva, in his supreme form, created the realm of Shiva, which is known today as Kashi, a place of ultimate liberation (Moksha). Kashi, also called Anandavana (the forest of bliss), is where Shiva and Shakti reside in eternal joy. Even during the great dissolution, they do not abandon this sacred place, hence its name 'Avimukta' (never forsaken). While wandering in Anandavana, Shiva desired to create another being who would take on the responsibility of managing creation, so that neither his meditative state nor the union with Shakti would be disturbed. Thus, from his right shoulder, Shiva projected a male figure who pervaded the entire universe and took on the task of managing it. This being was named Vishnu, as he became omnipresent and responsible for the maintenance of the cosmos.

From Vishnu's body emerged water, which covered the world, and this water became known as Brahmajala, as it purified everything it touched. Vishnu lay on this water, and thus he became known as Narayana (the one who rests on water). The rest of the creation story follows what is mentioned in the Vishnu Purana and the Bhagavata Purana: Vishnu created the principles of Pradhan, Purusha, Vyakta, and Kala, from which Mahat (the great principle) and the threefold Ahamkara (ego) emerged, producing the Panchamahabhutas (five great elements), their associated qualities, and the bodies and senses of living beings. From Vishnu's navel arose a lotus, from which Brahma was born, and Brahma sat upon the lotus. Brahma and Vishnu then argued over who had created whom.

To resolve their dispute, a bright Jyotirlinga (pillar of light) appeared before them, with no beginning or end, stretching from the heavens to the underworld. Unable to find the origin or end of this light, both Vishnu and Brahma stood before it with folded hands. From within this Jyotirlinga, they heard the sacred sound of "OM." Filled with devotion, Vishnu and Brahma bowed before the formless Brahman, and at that moment, Lord Shiva and Goddess Uma appeared in their embodied forms. Shiva explained that both Vishnu and Brahma were his manifestations, created for the purposes of creation and maintenance, while he himself would later take on the Rudra form for the dissolution of the universe.

Thus, Lord Shiva clarified the unity of Shiva, Vishnu, and Brahma as different aspects of the same supreme formless Brahman. After this, Brahma created the Prajapatis, Manus, and other beings, starting human life on Earth. In this way, the Shiva Purana depicts Lord Shiva as the supreme formless Brahman, who is also involved in the creation of the universe, a theme consistent with the Vedas and other Puranas.

ॐ

What is the Relationship of Brahma, Vishnu, and Mahesh with Shakti in the Shakta Bhagavata?

- Jansatta Loksatta, Date: 02/05/2024

In the Devi Bhagavata or the Shakta Bhagavata, which is dedicated to the worship of Shakti, Goddess Ambika is portrayed as the embodied form of the supreme Brahman. However, rather than contradicting the descriptions in the Vishnu Purana and Shiva Purana, it complements them. The Devi Bhagavata illustrates the energy aspect of the formless Brahman, not presenting the supreme as a female embodied deity, but rather emphasizing the energy (Shakti) of the formless Brahman.

The narrative begins with Brahma telling Sage Narada about the creation of the universe. Brahma says, "When I first opened my eyes upon the lotus flower, I saw water all around, but I could not see the Earth on which the lotus stem rested. I descended the stem to find its base, but after searching for years, I returned to the lotus. Then, two demons, Madhu and Kaitabha, appeared. Terrified, I sought refuge in the lotus stem. It was at this moment that I first beheld the divine form of Mahavishnu, who had four arms and held a conch, lotus, mace, and discus. However, Vishnu was deep in yogic sleep. I was filled with anxiety about what to do next. So, I prayed to the divine Yogamaya (the power behind Yogic sleep), who I recognized as Bhagavati, and she awakened Vishnu from his slumber. Vishnu then destroyed the demons, and soon after, Lord Shiva also appeared."

Bhagavati, now stationed in the sky, instructed Brahma, Vishnu, and Shiva to carry out the creation, maintenance, and destruction of the universe. The Trimurti (Brahma, Vishnu, and Shiva) expressed their powerlessness and asked how they could fulfill these duties without Shakti. Smiling, the Goddess summoned a celestial chariot and took the Trimurti to another universe, where they saw creation already in progress, with other Brahmas, Vishnus, and Shivas performing their respective duties. Awestruck, the Trimurti realized that this supreme Goddess was the origin of all creation. They praised her and asked her to reveal her true form.

The Goddess responded, "I am one with Brahman. I am the energy (Shakti) of the formless, attributeless, unmanifest Brahman. The universe moves and functions because of me. Where I am not present, there is no vibration, no activity. Those without energy are not called 'without Vishnu' or 'without Rudra'—they are called 'without Shakti.' I am the Shakti that makes Shiva, the Shiva, and Vishnu, the Vishnu, and sustains the universe." The Goddess goes on to explain that she is the Kundalini Shakti, which resides dormant in every being and, when awakened, turns individuals into enlightened beings (Brahmajñanis) and yogis. This awakened Kundalini is what gives Shiva his Shiva-nature and Vishnu his Vishnu-nature. The Trimurti (Brahma, Vishnu, and Shiva) all have different roles according to their characteristics, but their ability to perform these roles comes from Shakti, which emanates from Brahman.

Thus, the Shakta Bhagavata portrays the Goddess as the energy (Shakti) of the supreme Brahman, and she further explains that Brahma requires Shakti for creation, Vishnu requires Shakti to generate Mahat from Pradhan, and Shiva requires Shakti for the destruction of the universe. All deities perform their duties through her.

After explaining her energy form, the supreme Brahman (in the form of the Goddess) manifested three female deities: Maha-Saraswati for Brahma, Maha-Lakshmi for Mahavishnu, and Mahakali Gauri for Lord Shiva. Through these three goddesses, the Trimurti got the necessary energy to perform their respective roles. After empowering them with her Shakti, the

Goddess Shakti reminded them of their tasks of creation, preservation, and destruction.

Thus, the Devi Bhagavata explains the supreme Brahman's energy form, emphasizing the role of Shakti in enabling the Purusha aspect to carry out their functions. The Goddess is the source of all actions and creation.

This forms the foundation of the Shakta path of worship, which emphasizes the adoration of Shakti. Shakti worship is believed to be effective for both attaining worldly success and spiritual liberation (Moksha). Swami Vivekananda, who played a significant role in reviving true Sanatan Dharma in the modern world, often told his disciples: "If you wish to realize the truth of Yoga, the worship of Shiva is appropriate. But if you wish to work in the world with Yogic power, the worship of Shakti is the path that will lead you to success."

The Concept of Embodied Brahman in the Brahma Purana or Saur Purana, and Ganesha Purana

- Jansatta Loksatta, Date: 09/05/2024

In previous articles, we learned that the formless, attributeless Brahman of the Vedas is depicted in the Puranas as having five embodied forms, which are useful for the paths of devotion (Bhakti) and Yoga. These five forms are known as the Panchadev. We have already discussed the Puranas that present Lord Vishnu, Shiva, and Maa Shakti as supreme embodied forms. Here, we will discuss the Brahma Purana, which focuses on Lord Brahma and Lord Surya, and the Ganesha Purana, which presents Lord Ganesha as the supreme deity.

In the Brahma Purana, Lord Vishnu is praised as the original formless Parabrahman, and it is said by Sage Lomaharshana that just as the Pradhana element emerges as Shakti from Vishnu, the first portion of Vishnu manifests as the Purusha, who creates the universe from Pradhana. This Purusha is Brahma. Brahma is born from the cosmic egg that emerges from Lord Vishnu in the Vishnu Purana, and from him come the five great elements, the ten directions, the Saptarishis, the Prajapatis, the Sanat Kumaras, Manu, and his wife Shatarupa. This marks the beginning of life on Earth, and the lineages of Suryavanshi Ikshvaku and Yayati of the Chandravansh begin. Later, the gods, sages, and seers approach Brahma and ask him where the karmic land (Karmabhumi) is. Brahma points to Bharatvarsha as the land of karma, where sinful deeds lead to hell, virtuous actions lead to heaven, and selfless actions in devotion lead to liberation (Moksha). After this, he explains the geography of the islands of Bharatvarsha, and finally, he glorifies Lord Surya as the Parabrahman (Supreme Being) while explaining the greatness of Konaditya (the Sun God of the Konark Temple in Odisha), located on the eastern edge of India.

Brahma says that Lord Surya is the original Parabrahman, from whose light all creation and dissolution take place. He describes the twelve forms of Surya that manifest during the twelve months of the year (the twelve Adityas), with Indra as the first and Vishnu as the twelfth Aditya, who incarnates as a human to establish Dharma on Earth. Lord Surya is shown as the progenitor of all the gods, and as the one who sustains both the gods and humanity, as well as the entire universe. Brahma lists twenty-one names of Surya, the recitation of which can grant humans both worldly success and Moksha. One of these names is Brahma, signifying that Brahma, the Purusha emerging from Vishnu, is also a part of Surya, or in other words, they are one and the same. Thus, the Brahma Purana portrays Lord Surya as the Aditya Vishnu, the original Parabrahman, and shows that Brahma, as a portion of Vishnu, is unified with Surya. This is why the Brahma Purana is also referred to as the Saur Purana, where the Parabrahman in the form of Surya performs the functions of Vishnu, Brahma, and Rudra.

Ganesha Purana:

After compiling the four Vedas, Sage Vedavyasa decided to make the knowledge of the Vedas accessible to the masses by writing the Puranas. However, before beginning the task, he forgot to invoke Lord Ganesha. As a result, he kept forgetting the events and knowledge contained in the Puranas, and the task of writing the Puranas was halted. Seeking a solution, Vedavyasa went to Brahma, who told him, "Dvaipayana Vyasa, in your pride over your knowledge, you have forgotten to remember Adideva Ganesha, and that is why this is happening. Ganesha is the Adideva." Vedavyasa, unaware of Ganesha's supremacy, asked Brahma for enlightenment.

Brahma explained, "During the time of cosmic dissolution, when I, Vishnu, and Shiva were paralyzed in the darkness, uncertain of what to do, Parabrahman appeared before us, shining like a thousand suns in the form of Lord Ganesha, and told us to ask for a boon." The Trimurti (Brahma, Vishnu, and Shiva) requested the knowledge necessary for fulfilling their respective cosmic duties during the dissolution. In response, Lord Ganesha assigned Brahma the task of creation, Vishnu the role of preservation, and Shiva the task of dissolution. When Brahma asked how to carry out this responsibility, Lord Ganesha showed him the palm of his foot where Tridev saw countless universes, where millions of Brahmas, Vishnus, and Shivas were already performing their duties. After understanding their roles, Brahma praised Lord Ganesha and began the work of creation.

At one point, two demons named Madhu and Kaitabha attacked Brahma while he was creating the universe. Terrified, Brahma fled to Vishnu, who was resting on the cosmic waters in yogic sleep. Upon waking, Vishnu fought the demons for five thousand years but was unable to defeat them. Finally, Shiva told Vishnu, "Nothing happens in creation without the grace of Lord Ganesha." Vishnu then invoked Ganesha, who appeared and said, "O Vishnu, if you had invoked me on the first day, these demons would have already been defeated." Vishnu apologized and asked for Ganesha's devotion. Ganesha assured Vishnu, saying, "O Vishnu, the demons will soon be vanquished by your hands, Brahma's fear will be dispelled, and your great fame will spread. Now there will be no obstacles in your work." With these words, Lord Ganesha disappeared, and Vishnu soon defeated Madhu and Kaitabha, resuming his role as the preserver of the universe.

Thus, in the Ganesha Purana, Lord Ganesha is portrayed as the supreme embodied form of the formless Parabrahman. Only with his grace are the Trimurti able to perform their respective cosmic duties. Recognizing Ganesha as the Adideva, one of the supreme embodied forms of Parabrahman, Vedavyasa praised Lord Ganesha. In response, Ganesha appeared before him, bestowed his grace upon him, and removed all obstacles in the writing of the Puranas. Therefore, Ganesha, the remover of obstacles, is also one of the five supreme embodied forms of the original formless Parabrahman in Sanatan Dharma. He must be worshiped first of all before beginning any important work.

XX

Who is the Swami (Lord) of the Cosmos?

We have now learned about the forms of the Panchdev of Sanatan Dharma as described in the Vedas and Puranas. The formless, unmanifest, and eternal Brahman mentioned in the Vedas is the Swami of this entire Srishti (cosmos). This unmanifest Brahman manifests itself in multiple forms at various levels of the material and conscious in the cosmos. Thus, the sum of all these forms, both external and internal, is referred to as Parabrahman. In the Vedas, this Parabrahman first appears as the sound of OM. The vibration produced by the sound of OM is the original pulse of Parabrahman. OM is the first subtly manifest form of the formless God that we encounter, which is why OM is referred to as the eternal Brahman, or Aksharbrahman. Therefore, the one and only true God of Sanatan Dharma is OM. This supreme God in the form of OM is invoked in the Vedas as various forms of thirty-three saguna (manifest) deities. Among these thirty-three deities, the omnipresent Lord Vishnu is the highest, while Agni (the fire god) is the first and basic. All other gods exist between these two.

How should Panchdev be worshiped?

· Date: 06-05-2024 / Loksatta Jansatta

From the thirty-three deities of the Vedas, five have been developed in the Puranas as the embodied, personified forms of Parabrahman. Their characters have been further popularized through various stories, yet even in the Puranas, their essential nature is depicted as formless and unmanifest Parabrahman. Vishnu is the supreme, all-pervading deity. Rudra (Shiva) is the wise, heroic god, destroyer of sin, who meditates in his unmanifest form as peaceful Shiva. Goddess Bhagavati is the power (Shakti) that moves every particle, awakening human kundalini and transforming individuals into enlightened beings. Surya, in the form of Brahma, sustains all life on Earth and creates the universe. Ganesha, the embodiment of wisdom and intelligence, connects with the universal consciousness to remove obstacles and guide humans in their endeavors. In this way, Ganesha is the form that the supreme God takes to assist humans in fulfilling their righteous tasks.

So, which of the Panchdev should be worshiped? And which should not? Which type of person should consider one of these deities as their primary God, and how should they regard the remaining four?

The scriptures of Sanatan Dharma give individuals the freedom to choose any one of the Panchdev as their primary deity, considering the other four as extensions of that deity. In reality, one's chosen deity may change depending on their age and evolution of consciousness or intelligence in life. A young child is first taught to worship the sun by offering water to Suryanarayana, recognizing the sun as the primary source that sustains all life on Earth. As the child grows older, and if not forced to follow any other deity, he begins to worship Lord Ganesha, the first tangible form of God who blesses and removes obstacles. As they enter youth and their reasoning develops, they become inspired by the incarnations of Lord Vishnu, such as Rama and Krishna, whose stories and teachings provide guidance and direction in life. Further, as the individual seeks to know and experience cosmic truth, attaining self-realization and oneness with the divine, they progress on the path of Yoga, with Shiva becoming their chosen deity. As they advance on the Yogic path, they realize the need to awaken their kundalini energy, which leads them to the worship of Shakti (the Goddess), and during this phase, they begin to worship Maa Durga or Maa Kali. In this way, as a practitioner progresses from one stage to another, they evolve in worshiping deities from Suryadev to Shakti.

Thus, a follower of Sanatan Dharma should establish all five deities in their personal temple, worshiping one as their primary deity based on their situation and purpose, and offering respect to all five. In the morning, after offering salutations to the sun with Surya Namaskar, one should bathe and sit in the temple for worship. Regardless of their chosen deity, the worship should begin by praying to Lord Ganesha with the mantra "Vakratunda Mahakaya..." and seek his blessing for success in their endeavors. After this, if Shiva is their primary deity, they should pray to Maa Durga, Amba, or Maa Kali with the mantra "Sarvamangala Mangalye..." which means: "O Goddess, who brings all blessings, O Gauri, who accomplishes all of Shiva's purposes, I bow to you in surrender, grant me the power to fulfill Shiva's work." After this, one should recite the mantra "Shantakaram Bhujagashayanam..." and offer prayers to Lord Vishnu. Then, the devotee should chant Hanuman Chalisa which connects Shiva and Vishnu through Lord Hanuman. And then, he/she should do Abhishek of water over the Shivalinga while chanting "Om Namah Shivaya."

If Vishnu is the primary deity, the arrangement between Shiva and Vishnu should be reversed. First, after praying to Ganesha, one should recite the Maha Mrityunjaya mantra and "Om Namah Shivaya" for Shiva's worship, followed by Hanuman Chalisa, and then offer prayers to Vishnu with the "Shantakaram Bhujagashayanam..." mantra and recite Vishnu Sahasranama. If Shakti (the Goddess) is the chosen deity, one should recite mantras for all the other deities, reflecting on their meanings, and finally, offer a Devi Suktam or another Goddess prayer before the established image of the Goddess. If Ganesha is the primary deity, the worship should start with the "Vakratunda Mahakaya..." mantra, followed by worship of all deities, and ends with a special aarti for Lord Ganesha.

After completing worship in the temple, one should go outside and offer water to the sun at sunrise. In this way, even if a family has only one temple, they can establish the Panchdev and each member of the family can worship their suitable deity among Panchdev according to their age, spiritual state, and purpose, following the Panchdev worship method. This represents the ideal form of worship (Upasana) for a follower of Sanatan Dharma.

In the earlier parts, we discussed which deities to worship based on one's stage of life and purpose. However, once all these purposes are fulfilled, one reaches the state of a Brahmagnani (one who has attained knowledge of Brahman). After attaining Brahmagnana, one may either abandon the worship of embodied deities and remain absorbed in meditation on the formless Brahman with subtle chanting of OM, or continue the worship of the Shivalinga as a symbol of the formless and unmanifest God by doing abhishekam of water over it. The Shivalinga is also considered a symbol of the formless and unmanifest nature of God. However, if the Brahmagnani decide to re-enter worldly life as Vishnu, they must first become a devotee of Vishnu and stabilize themselves in the Vishnu state. After stabilizing in the Vishnu state, they become a devotee of Shiva and Shakti to stay connected to the supreme consciousness of formless Parbrahman and receive the necessary spiritual power.

Finally, after understanding the knowledge of Srishti from all the Puranas, we should organize this understanding in the form of a chart. This is important because the sect of the fake Narayan has misled Hindus by creating their own perverted charts with Hindu scriptural terminology.

Chart of Samsara in Sanatan Dharma:

In the presented chart, the creation of atoms, particles, the sun, and the Earth from the Pancha Mahabhutas (five great elements) is shown. The primordial atoms and particles first emerged as flammable clouds of hydrogen gas, which represents the element of Agni (fire). These flames remained active in the form of the sun. As the Earth separated from the sun and cooled down, the elements of land, water, air, and space emerged.

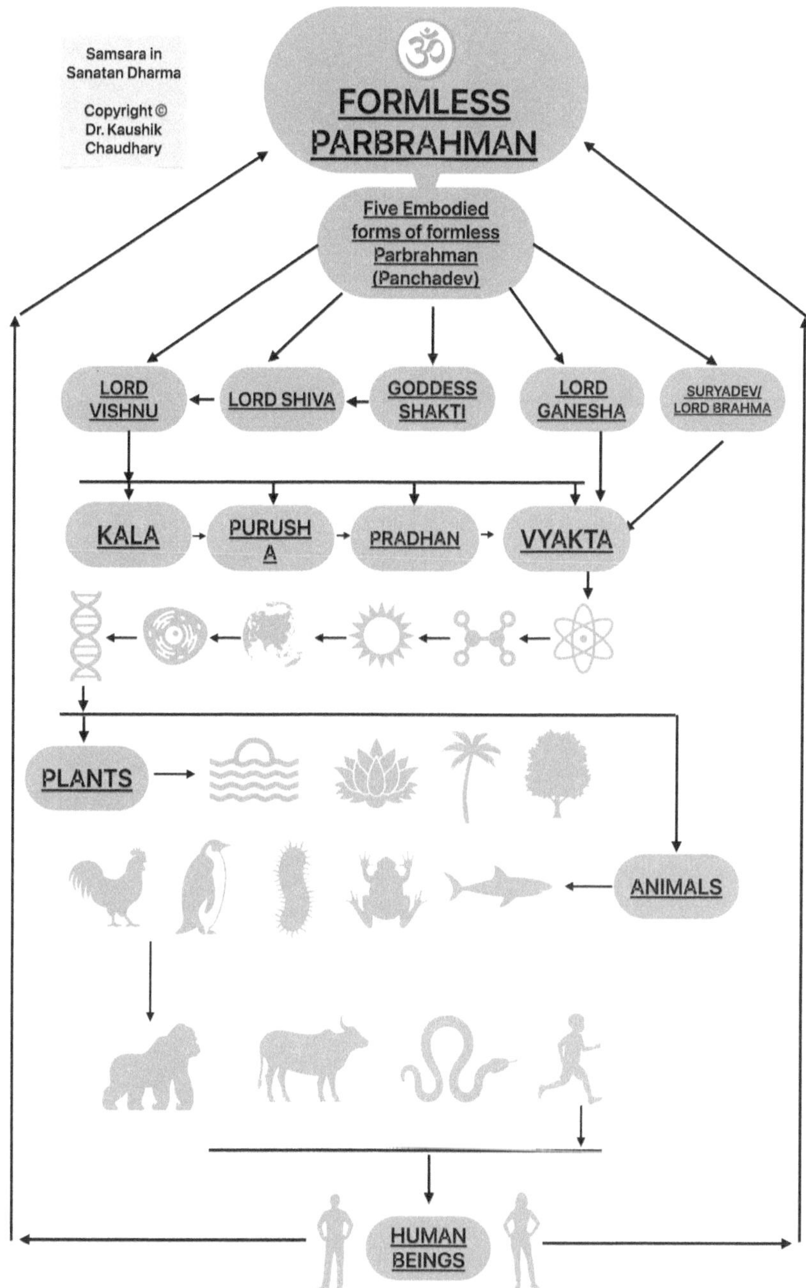

Srishti in Sanatan Dharma Scriptures